GEORGE ELIOT

George Eliot was born Mary Anne (known as Marian) Evans in 1819, near Nuneaton, Warwickshire. She was brought up as an Evangelist, and received a classical education at local boarding schools. After the death of her mother in 1836, she moved to Coventry with her father and became acquainted with free-thinkers Charles and Cara Bray, which led to her translating Strauss's *Life of Jesus* (1846). After her father's death in 1849, she moved to London, where she met George Henry Lewes, who was separated from, but crucially unable to divorce, his wife. Moving to Germany with him in 1854, she lived as his common-law wife for twenty-four years. Under his encouragement she began writing fiction under her nom de plume: the successful serial *Scenes of Clerical Life* (1858); the best-selling *Adam Bede* (1859); followed by a number of poems and further highly praised works such as *The Mill on the Floss* (1860), *Silas Marner* (1861), *Middlemarch* (1871–2) and *Daniel Deronda* (1876). Lewes's death in 1878 saw the effective end of her writing career. A few short months into her marriage to a man twenty years her junior, she died in December 1880.

GEOFFREY BEEVERS

After studying History at Oxford University, Geoffrey Beevers trained as an actor at LAMDA. In the theatre he has worked at the RSC, the National Theatre, Shakespeare's Globe and the West End, and has made over two hundred television appearances including *The Jewel in the Crown*, *A Very British Coup* and *Dr Who*; countless radio broadcasts including many book readings; and films from *Victor/Victoria* to *Miss Potter*.

He also writes and directs. At the Orange Tree Theatre he has directed many plays, including his own, and several by Václav Havel. He has also directed in repertory theatres and drama schools. His writing work includes about a dozen plays produced in the theatre and on radio. His latest publications include an audio CD *Unintelligent Design* (2011), and a novel *The Forgotten Fields* (2014).

He has long had a particular love for George Eliot's work. He has previously adapted *Adam Bede* for the stage (Time Out Award) and also *Silas Marner*. One of his plays for Radio 4 was *A Proper Woman*, a drama-documentary about George Eliot's marriage.

George Eliot

THE MIDDLEMARCH TRILOGY

adapted for the stage by
Geoffrey Beevers

NICK HERN BOOKS
London
www.nickhernbooks.co.uk

A Nick Hern Book

The Middlemarch Trilogy first published in Great Britain in 2014 as a paperback original by Nick Hern Books Limited, The Glasshouse, 49a Goldhawk Road, London W12 8QP

The Middlemarch Trilogy copyright © 2014 Geoffrey Beevers

Geoffrey Beevers has asserted his moral right to be identified as the author of this work

Cover image: cast of the Orange Tree Theatre production, 2013 © Stuart Burgess

Designed and typeset by Nick Hern Books, London
Printed in Great Britain by Mimeo Ltd, Cambridgeshire PE29 6XX

A CIP catalogue record for this book is available from the British Library

ISBN   978 1 84842 405 0

Contents

Adapting *Middlemarch*
Geoffrey Beevers

Drama involves the way characters react under the stress of action. When I adapted George Eliot's *Adam Bede* many years ago, it was an obviously 'dramatic' story – seduction, child murder and a trial scene. But I was always fascinated by the bigger challenge of adapting *Middlemarch*, a much more subtle drama of developing human lives, and to discover whether it could work on stage. The characters are so rich and their problems so close to our own, in spite of the difference in time – misguided relationships and money worries, future expectations raised and dashed – and it seemed to me to carry a detail of original observation not often portrayed in theatre.

I was also inspired by the thought of bringing Eliot's language alive for a live audience. On the page, one's eye can glide over the sentences, and sometimes miss her subtlety and, above all, her sense of humour. People sometimes confess to giving up on George Eliot because they find it 'heavy'. But, like Shakespeare, her dialogue reveals so much more when spoken aloud and shared; her language dense, but very speakable. And I wanted to include her own distinctive voice, shared by the cast, and her ironic comments on the action as it unfolds. I've tried to use only her words throughout.

I've always loved the challenge of huge themes in intimate spaces, where the principle must be, not: 'What can we do with this?' but: 'What can we do without? How can we tell this story, as simply as possible, so the story will shine through?' I wanted to use only her words, a few actors and a minimum of setting, and leave as much as possible to the audience's imagination.

I also believe audiences enjoy the versatility of actors. I relished doubling characters that have dramatic similarities but are, in fact, very different – the indulgent Vincy parents could double with the stricter Garths; the introverted Casaubon with the extrovert Featherstone; the vague Brooke with the focused Bulstrode; Will, who has so much pride, with Fred, who has so little.

The shape of the trilogy emerged as I worked on it. I took the three main strands from the book – Dorothea's story, the Doctor's story and Fred and Mary's story (county, town and country) – to make three self-contained plays, each in its own social sphere, with differing attitudes to status and money. I knew I would need certain scenes repeated from one play to the next, as the stories overlapped, but enjoyed the fact that these scenes could be angled differently to meet a different perspective. I also became interested in the structural similarities between the stories. It's obvious that each is based on a marriage, or a potential marriage, and at least the hint of an 'eternal triangle'; but each play also has, at its centre, an onstage death which has unexpected repercussions on everything that follows. And it became clear that the third play (a strand sometimes considered more of a lighter subplot in the novel) answers the first two plays, and provides solutions to the problems the protagonists face. Dorothea impulsively leaps into her first marriage, Lydgate drifts into his, both with disastrous results. Each expects something from their partners that they are unable to give, because they have opposite ways of thinking. But Mary waits for Fred until he has found his feet, and they both know each other well enough so they can truly share the same values.

Of course, a trilogy can be no substitute for a great novel. For a start, there is little place in drama for description or philosophical digression. But every examination of a classic should throw up something of interest, if attempted honestly. My aim has been to reach, as simply and directly as possible, the dramatic heart of the book, where the characters are tested by their actions; and above all to share with a live audience the compassion, the wit and the irony of George Eliot's incomparable mind.

My thanks to Sam Walters for the opportunity to present all three plays in one season, and to the wonderfully creative actors who brought them so vividly to life.

Production Notes

The three plays can be performed as a trilogy, or as separate stand-alone plays. If the latter, single editions of each play can be printed on demand for your requirements. Please contact info@nickhernbooks.co.uk.

These plays were written for a small theatre-in-the-round, where the actors could be seated with the audience, close to the acting area, able to stand to deliver a comment on the action, or move easily into the space to play a scene. There should always be enough actors present to give the impression of the whole company telling the story, though in practice, some actors may get breaks.

There are about fifty speaking parts. The smallest cast possible is eleven (ten for *Dorothea's Story*).

The cast all share the author's voice and take it in turns to 'narrate' the action. The actor should speak directly to the audience. Sometimes this narration is an aside from the character onstage; sometimes it is a comment on the action from the sidelines relating more, or less, to the character; sometimes it is pure comment or narrative and doesn't relate to the character at all. In the latter case, the character's name in the script is only there as a guide to which actor originally spoke it. It may be more convenient, in a different production, for a different actor to take the line.

The minimum amount of furniture is two chairs, a table and a chaise longue. The chaise can double as a bed or a sofa. A chair can become a horse. The table can be a carriage, a bar, a desk, a billiards table, or an early piano (there could, for example, be a lid in it which opens). The moving of even one piece of furniture by a narrator may denote a change of location. Lighting can help, creating windows, fireplaces and time of day... Each location needs to be very specifically placed and imagined by the actors; a view from a window, a portrait on the

wall, a glass jar on a shelf, a yew tree, an open field...
Sometimes unneeded furniture can be removed from the stage,
sometimes it can be ignored. Two extra chairs may be needed
occasionally, such as for a party or a board meeting.

Some props may be imagined, such as glasses at a party, a deck
of cards, or a jelly and spoon. Some may be felt to be significant
enough to be real, such as Casaubon's workbook, Raffles'
whiskey or Bulstrode's chequebook.

Each actor needs a basic costume and one distinguishing prop
or item of clothing for each character. It may be a wig, or a coat
(on or off), a scarf, glasses, or whatever. The change should not
take more than a few seconds, and should happen openly as the
actor comes onstage, rather than secretly or offstage.

In the first production, Ben and Letty were life-sized dolls, with
button eyes. They were manipulated and voiced by whoever in
the company was holding them, or nearest them. The baby, the
dog and the effigy of Brooke were made in the same style (the
cat was imaginary).

The intention is that the scenes should flow one to another
without any pause for the changing of costume or set. A scene
may end with a momentary stillness, and then should move on.
The less attention drawn to scene changes the better, so we find
ourselves in a new place almost without noticing, and the
momentum is not lost (I believe Shakespeare should be done
more often like this).

But in the end there are no rules, except to ask what tells the
story most clearly and simply, so we may apply our
imaginations to George Eliot's words.

The plays of *The Middlemarch Trilogy* were first performed at the Orange Tree Theatre, Richmond, in 2013. *Dorothea's Story* opened on 23 October, *The Doctor's Story* opened on 13 November, *Fred and Mary's Story* opened on 4 December. The complete trilogy was first performed on 27 December. The cast was as follows:

DOROTHEA	Georgina Strawson
CELIA/MRS PLYMDALE/MARY	Daisy Ashford
BROOKE/BULSTRODE/SOLOMON	Christopher Ettridge
SIR JAMES/TRUMBULL/ FAREBROTHER	Christopher Naylor
CASAUBON/SPRAGUE/ FEATHERSTONE	Jamie Newall
MRS CADWALLADER/ MRS BULSTRODE/MRS WAULE	Liz Crowther
WILL/WRENCH/FRED	Ben Lambert
VINCY/RAFFLES/GARTH	Michael Lumsden
ROSAMOND	Niamh Walsh
LYDGATE	David Ricardo-Pearce
MRS VINCY/MRS GARTH	Lucy Tregear

Other parts were played by members of the company

Director	Geoffrey Beevers
Designer	Sam Dowson
Lighting Designer	Stuart Burgess
Stage Management	Stuart Burgess, Sophie Acreman, Becky Flisher, Poppy Walker, Tim Bifield, Katy Mills
Assistant Director	Sophie Boyce

DOROTHEA'S STORY

Dorothea's Story can be performed as part of the full
Middlemarch Trilogy, or as a separate stand-alone play.

If the latter, a single edition of the play can be printed on
demand for your requirements. Please contact
info@nickhernbooks.co.uk

Characters

DOROTHEA BROOKE
CELIA BROOKE, *her sister*
MR BROOKE, *their uncle*
SIR JAMES CHETTAM, *Brooke's neighbour*
THE REV MR CASAUBON, *Rector of Lowick*
MRS CADWALLADER
WILL LADISLAW, *Casaubon's relative and dependent*
MR VINCY, *Mayor of Middlemarch*
ROSAMOND VINCY, *his daughter*
MR LYDGATE, *doctor*
MR BULSTRODE, *banker*
MR TRUMBULL, *auctioneer and agent*
MR RAFFLES, *blackmailer*
SIR JAMES'S DRIVER
MR BROOKE'S SERVANT
THE LYDGATES' SERVANT
JENNY
MAN AT AUCTION
WOMAN AT AUCTION

Plus: congregation at church, townspeople at Brooke's speech, people at auction

Suggested Doubling

DOROTHEA

CELIA

BROOKE / MR BROOKE'S DRIVER / BULSTRODE

SIR JAMES / TRUMBULL

CASAUBON / BROOKE'S SERVANT

MRS CADWALLADER / THE LYDGATES' SERVANT / WOMAN AT AUCTION

WILL

VINCY / RAFFLES

ROSAMOND /JENNY

LYDGATE / MAN AT AUCTION

ACT ONE

Prologue

The cast are gathered around the acting area.

DOROTHEA. Middlemarch.

CASAUBON. In 1829 –

BROOKE. – before Reform had done its part –

CELIA. – in their scattered country mansions –

SIR JAMES. – the local gentry lived –

MRS CADWALLADER. – in a rarified social air…

DOROTHEA. Dorothea's Story.

Scene One

Tipton Grange. The library. DOROTHEA *is working at some architectural drawings.* CELIA *watches from a distance.*

DOROTHEA. Celia, come and look…

CELIA. Dorothea, dear, if you're not very busy… we have guests tonight… suppose we look at Mother's jewels? I believe you've never thought of them since Uncle gave them to you…

DOROTHEA. My dear, we should never wear them.

CELIA. I think we're wanting in respect for Mamma's memory to put them by – and necklaces are quite usual now.

DOROTHEA. Oh, *you'd* like to wear them? Of course. (*Rises*.) But where are they?

CELIA. They are here.

CELIA *has been holding a jewellery box behind her back. They open the box and look.*

DOROTHEA. They're beautiful. Like fragments of Heaven. There, Celia, you can wear that with your Indian muslin. And this cross –

CELIA. You must keep the cross, Dodo...

DOROTHEA (*shudders*). No, no, it's the last thing I'd wear as a trinket.

CELIA. You might like to keep it for Mamma's sake.

DOROTHEA. Oh, I've other things of Mamma's, plenty of things. Take them away now... (*Goes back to work*.)

CELIA (*holding up the necklace and looking in a mirror*). Sir James will be here tonight. (*Glances at* DOROTHEA.)

Slight pause.

DOROTHEA. Come and look at my plans for some workers' cottages. I shall think I'm a great architect!

Dorothea was remarkably clever.

CELIA. But Celia was spoken of as having more common sense.

DOROTHEA. Dorothea was enamoured of intensity and greatness.

BROOKE. She was not yet twenty.

CELIA. It was scarcely a year since the sisters had come to live at Tipton Grange with their uncle –

BROOKE. Mr Brooke.

Scene Two

BROOKE, SIR JAMES, CASAUBON, DOROTHEA *and* CELIA *are coming into the library after dinner.*

BROOKE (*as he takes his place in front of the fire*). Well now, Sir James, I dined with Sir Humphry Davy years ago at Cartwright's, and Wordsworth was there too – the poet Wordsworth, you know. There's an oddity, Sir James. But Davy was there.

SIR JAMES. I'm reading his *Agricultural Chemistry* because I'm going to take one of my farms into my own hands and see if something cannot be done in setting a good pattern of farming among my tenants. (*To* DOROTHEA.) Do you approve of that, Miss Brooke?

DOROTHEA. Yes, I do, I –

BROOKE. A great mistake, Sir James, making a parlour of your cow-house, that kind of thing. It won't do. Your fancy-farming – expensive – better to keep a pack of hounds.

DOROTHEA. Surely it's better to make the most of the land, than to keep hounds and horses to gallop over it.

BROOKE. Young ladies don't understand political economy, you know. I remember when we were all reading Adam Smith. There's a book now. I took in all the new ideas at one time – human perfectibility, now. But some say history moves in circles. The fact is, human reason may carry you a little too far. It carried me a good way at one time, but I saw it wouldn't do. I pulled up, I pulled up in time. But not too hard. We must have Thought, else we shall be landed back in the Dark Ages. But talking of books, I'm reading Southey of a morning? You know Southey, Casaubon?

CASAUBON (*precisely*). No. I have little leisure for literature. I have been using up my eyesight on old characters lately. I feed too much on the inward sources, I live too much with the dead. My mind is something like the ghost of an ancient, wandering about the world, and trying to construct it as it used to be, in spite of ruin and confusing change. But I find it necessary to use the utmost caution about my eyesight.

Pause. DOROTHEA *is fascinated*.

SIR JAMES. But you're fond of riding, Miss Brooke. I wish you'd let me send over a chestnut for you to try. I saw you on Saturday, cantering over a hill on a nag not worthy of you.

DOROTHEA. Thank you, but I mean to give up riding.

Dorothea felt she enjoyed riding in a pagan, sensuous way, and always looked forward to renouncing it.

SIR JAMES. No, that's too bad. (*To* CELIA.) Your sister is given to self-mortification, is she not?

CELIA. I think she is. She likes giving up.

DOROTHEA. If that were true, Celia, my giving up would be self-indulgence, not self-mortification.

SIR JAMES. Exactly. I'm sure you give up from some high, generous motive.

DOROTHEA (*slightly irritated*). No, not exactly, I didn't say that.

Slight pause.

CASAUBON (*to* BROOKE). Documents are hard on the eyesight.

BROOKE. Yes, I have documents. I began a long while ago to collect documents. How do you arrange yours?

CASAUBON (*startled*). In pigeonholes, partly.

BROOKE. Ah, pigeonholes won't do – everything gets mixed.

DOROTHEA. I wish you'd let me sort your papers for you, Uncle.

CASAUBON (*to* DOROTHEA). I perceive you have an excellent secretary at hand –

BROOKE. No, no, young ladies are too flighty…

DOROTHEA *is hurt*.

Come and see my study and I'll show you what I mean. Come, Sir James.

The MEN *withdraw. The two* SISTERS *remain.*

CELIA. How very ugly Mr Casaubon is!

DOROTHEA. Celia! He's one of the most distinguished-looking men I ever saw.

CELIA. He has two white moles with hairs on them.

DOROTHEA *is shocked.*

And he's so sallow.

DOROTHEA. All the better. Oh, Celia –

CELIA. I wonder you show temper, Dorothea.

DOROTHEA. It's so painful in you, that you will look at human beings as if they were merely animals, and never see the great soul in a man's face.

CELIA. Has Casaubon a great soul?

DOROTHEA (*decisively*). Yes, I believe he has. Everything I see in him corresponds to his pamphlet on Biblical cosmology.

CELIA. He talks very little.

DOROTHEA. There's no one for him to talk to.

SIR JAMES *and* CASAUBON *return.* SIR JAMES *goes straight to* DOROTHEA.

SIR JAMES. Let me hope you will rescind that resolution about the horse, Miss Brooke. I assure you, riding is the most healthy of exercises.

DOROTHEA. I'm aware of it. (*Trying to include* CELIA.) I think it would do Celia good.

SIR JAMES. But you're such a perfect horsewoman. Every lady ought to be a perfect horsewoman that she may accompany her husband.

DOROTHEA. Then I should never correspond to your pattern of a lady.

CASAUBON *approaches.*

SIR JAMES. How may horsemanship be wrong?

DOROTHEA. I may think it wrong for me.

SIR JAMES. Oh, why?

CASAUBON. We must not enquire too curiously into motives. Miss Brooke knows they are apt to become feeble in the utterance – the aroma is mixed with the grosser air. We must keep the germinating grain away from the light...

DOROTHEA (*quietly*). Thank you, sir.

SIR JAMES. Exactly. I'm sure her reasons would do her honour.

He did not feel Dorothea's sharp mode of answering to him at all offensive. Why should he? A man's mind –

DOROTHEA. What there is of it –

SIR JAMES. – has always the advantage of being masculine.

Scene Three

SIR JAMES. Sir James visited Tipton Grange frequently –

CASAUBON. – and so did Casaubon.

DOROTHEA. Are not ecclesiastical forms of secondary importance, compared with the spiritual, the submergence of self in Divine Perfection? (*Tentatively*.) Is that not expressed in the best Christian books?

CASAUBON (*smiling*). Indeed. Such a view, duly tempered with wise conformity, is surely correct. I could mention many historical examples you may not know of... For example –

A bark. She turns, and across the stage SIR JAMES *is presenting a little dog*.

SIR JAMES. It's yours! (*Slight pause*.) You don't like little dogs?

DOROTHEA *shakes her head*.

Ladies are usually fond of little dogs.

DOROTHEA. It's painful to see creatures bred merely as helpless pets.

SIR JAMES. You have your opinion about everything, Miss Brooke, and it's always a good opinion. (*Puts the dog aside.*) I can form an opinion about persons. I know when I like people. But about other matters, you know – one hears sensible things said on opposite sides.

DOROTHEA. Or that seem sensible. Perhaps we don't always discriminate between sense and nonsense.

SIR JAMES. Exactly. I hear you have a plan for cottages. Do you know that's one of the things I wish to do – build cottages on my estate. Of course, it's sinking money. But after all, it's worth doing.

DOROTHEA. Yes indeed.

SIR JAMES. Will you show me your plans?

DOROTHEA (*warming to him*). Yes, certainly.

SIR JAMES. Sir James took away the sense that he was making great progress with Miss Brooke.

But now CASAUBON *is talking*. DOROTHEA *turns back to listen.*

CASAUBON. I am undertaking to show that all the mythical fragments in the world were corruptions of a tradition originally revealed. Having once mastered the true position, the vast field of mythological constructions becomes intelligible, nay luminous with the reflected light of correspondences. My notes already make a formidable array of volumes, but the crowning task, would be to condense these to fit a little shelf.

DOROTHEA. What would this work be called?

CASAUBON. *The Key to All Mythologies.*

Scene Four

BROOKE (*as he changes into* SIR JAMES'S DRIVER). One day, Dorothea and Celia had been to see the building site for the new cottages on Sir James's estate, and were being driven home.

The table has become an open carriage, a chair the driver's seat. A cold day. They bump along.

CELIA. Sir James seems determined to do everything you wish about the cottages.

DOROTHEA. But it's not the object of his life to please me.

CELIA. Now, Dodo – can you really believe that?

DOROTHEA. Certainly. He thinks of me as a future sister, that's all. It's you he –

CELIA. Pray don't make that mistake any longer, Dodo. I'm quite sure Sir James means to make you an offer, and he believes you will accept him, especially since you've been so pleased with him about the plans. And Uncle too – I know he expects it.

DOROTHEA. How could he expect it? I've never agreed with Sir James about anything but the cottages. I was barely polite to him before.

CELIA. He's begun to feel you're quite fond of him.

DOROTHEA. 'Fond of him', Celia. How could you make such odious expressions. Besides, it's not the right word for the feeling I must have towards the man I would accept as a husband.

CELIA. Well, I'm sorry for Sir James. I thought it right to tell you, because you went on treading in the wrong place. You always see what nobody else sees, and never see what's quite plain. That's your way, Dodo.

Slight pause.

DOROTHEA. It's very painful. I can have no more to do with the cottages. It's very painful.

CELIA. Poor Dodo. It's your favourite fad to draw plans.

DOROTHEA. 'Fad' to draw plans! How can one ever do anything nobly Christian, among people with such petty thoughts!

They arrive. BROOKE *is there to greet them. They dismount from the carriage.*

BROOKE. Well, my dears. (*Notices their mood.*) I hope nothing disagreeable has happened?

CELIA. No, Uncle.

DOROTHEA. We've been to Freshitt to look at the cottages.

BROOKE. I lunched at Lowick and saw Casaubon's library and that kind of thing. He gave me a couple of pamphlets for you, Dorothea.

She goes into the house at once.

(*Calling after her.*) In the library… On the table. (*Puts the pamphlet on the table.*)

Scene Five

She comes eagerly into the library and picks up the pamphlet.

BROOKE. There's a sharp air, driving. Won't you sit down by the fire, my dear? You look cold.

DOROTHEA. Oh yes, Uncle. (*Goes to warm her hands.*)

BROOKE. Casaubon is a little buried in books, you know.

DOROTHEA. When a man's writing a great work, he must give up seeing much of the world.

BROOKE. That's true. But a man mopes, you know. I've always been a bachelor too, but I never moped. He wants a companion, you know.

DOROTHEA. That would be a great honour to anyone.

BROOKE. You like him, eh? Well now, I've known Casaubon ten years. Never got anything out of him – any ideas, you know. However, he's a tip-top man, and may be a bishop, that kind of thing, you know. And he has a very high opinion of you, my dear...

DOROTHEA *is silent*.

Very high indeed. In short he asked my permission to make you an offer of marriage. I told him I thought there wasn't much chance. But I thought I'd better tell you, my dear.

DOROTHEA. Thank you, Uncle. I'm very grateful. If he makes me an offer I shall accept.

Shocked silence.

BROOKE (*at last*). Ah... well. I shall never interfere against your wishes, my dear. People should have their own way in marriage and that sort of thing – up to a certain point, you know. But I've good reason to believe that Sir James Chettam wishes to marry you. He's a good match. And our land ties together.

DOROTHEA. If Sir James Chettam thinks of marrying me he has made a great mistake.

BROOKE (*surprised again*). I should have thought he was just the sort of man a woman would like, now!

DOROTHEA. Pray don't mention him in that light again, Uncle. There's nothing I like in him – I mean in the light of a husband. He's kind and well meaning... (*Shrugs*.)

BROOKE. Well. But Casaubon now. He's over five and forty you know. A good seven and twenty years older than you. His income is good, a handsome property, independent of the Church, still, he's not young, and I mustn't conceal from you, I think his health is not strong.

DOROTHEA. I shouldn't wish to have a husband very near my own age. I should wish to have a husband above me in judgement and knowledge.

BROOKE. I thought you liked your own opinion – liked it, you know.

DOROTHEA. A wise man would help me see which opinions had the best foundations.

BROOKE. Very true. You couldn't put the thing better: beforehand, you know. But life isn't cast in a mould. I never married myself. Never loved anyone well enough to put myself in a noose for them. And it is a noose, you know. Temper now. And a husband likes to be master.

DOROTHEA. I know that I must expect trials, Uncle. Marriage is a state of high duties.

BROOKE. You've quite made up your mind, I see. Well, my dear, I have a letter for you.

Mr Brooke felt that women were an inexhaustible subject of scientific study. He felt they could hardly be less complicated than the revolutions of an irregular solid.

Scene Six

DOROTHEA, *alone, reading a letter.*

CASAUBON (*his voice from the shadows*). My dear Miss Brooke, our conversations have made sufficiently clear to you the tenor of my life and purposes – a tenor unsuited, I am aware, to the commoner order of minds. But I have discerned in you both elevation of thought and capability of devotedness. It was, I confess, beyond my hope to meet with this rare combination, adapted to supply aid in graver labour, and to cast a charm over vacant hours. To be accepted by you as your husband and the earthly guardian of your welfare I should regard as the highest of providential gifts. In return I can at least offer you an affection hitherto unwasted. I await the expression of your sentiments with anxiety. In any case, I shall remain yours, with sincere devotion, Edward Casaubon.

DOROTHEA *weeps with happiness.*

BROOKE. How could it occur to her to examine the letter critically? Her whole soul was possessed by the fact that a fuller life was opening before her.

CASAUBON, *alone, reading a letter.*

DOROTHEA (*her voice from the shadows*). My dear Mr Casaubon. I'm very grateful to you for loving me and thinking me worthy to be your wife. I cannot now dwell on any other thought than that I may be through life, yours devotedly, Dorothea Brooke.

Scene Six (A)

DOROTHEA *and* CELIA *in the library.*

DOROTHEA. Mr Casaubon is coming to dine tonight, Celia.

CELIA. I hope there's someone else. Then I shall not hear him eat his soup so.

DOROTHEA. What is there remarkable about his soup-eating?

CELIA. Really, Dodo, can't you hear how he scrapes his spoon? And he always blinks before he speaks.

DOROTHEA. Celia, pray don't make any more observations of that kind.

CELIA. Why not? They're quite true.

DOROTHEA. It's right to tell you, Celia, that I'm engaged to marry Mr Casaubon.

Shocked silence.

CELIA. Oh, Dodo. I hope you will be happy. Is it quite decided then?

DOROTHEA. Yes.

CELIA. I beg your pardon if I've said anything to hurt you, Dodo. (*Embraces her.*)

DOROTHEA. Never mind, Kitty, we should never admire the same people. I often offend in the same way.

CASAUBON *enters*. CELIA *withdraws, watches from a distance*.

CASAUBON. My dear young lady, Miss Brooke, Dorothea. This is a happiness greater than I had ever imagined to be in reserve for me. Hitherto I have known few pleasures save of the severer kind: I have been little disposed to gather flowers that would wither in my hand, but now I shall pluck them with eagerness to place them in your bosom.

DOROTHEA. I'm very ignorant. I've so many thoughts that may be quite mistaken, and now I shall be able to tell them all to you. But I will not trouble you too much. You must often be weary with the pursuit of subjects in your own track. I shall gain enough if you will take me with you there...

CASAUBON. How shall I now be able to persevere in my path without your companionship. (*Kisses her forehead*.)

BROOKE. It was decided the marriage should take place within weeks.

Scene Seven

MRS CADWALLADER. Mrs Cadwallader was a lady of immeasurably high birth, married to the Vicar of Tipton.

MRS CADWALLADER *and* BROOKE *in the library*.

Don't let the Whigs lure you to the hustings, my dear Mr Brooke. A man always makes a fool of himself speechifying. You'll be pelted by everybody.

BROOKE. That's what I expect, you know. As an Independent. I may go with the Whigs up to a certain point – up to a certain point, you know. But that's what you ladies never understand.

MRS CADWALLADER. Where that certain point is? No. Nobody knows where Brooke will be – there's no counting on Brooke. That's what people say of you, to be quite frank. Now, do turn respectable.

BROOKE. I don't pretend to argue with a lady on politics.

MRS CADWALLADER. You of all people! Who are going to marry your niece – as good as your daughter – to one of our best Tory men. Sir James would be cruelly annoyed if you hawk yourself about as –

BROOKE. I hope Sir James and I shall always be good friends, but I'm sorry to say there's no prospect of his marrying my niece.

MRS CADWALLADER. Why not? It's hardly a fortnight since you and I were talking about it.

BROOKE. My niece has chosen another suitor.

MRS CADWALLADER. Whom do you mean?...

BROOKE (*sees through the window*). Ah, here's Celia back from her walk. I must speak to Wright about the horses... (*Backs out.*)

MRS CADWALLADER (*to* CELIA *as she enters*). My dear child, what is this about your sister's engagement?

CELIA. She's engaged to marry Mr Casaubon.

Shocked silence.

MRS CADWALLADER. Frightful. How long has it been going on?

CELIA. I only knew of it yesterday.

MRS CADWALLADER. Well, my dear...

CELIA. I'm so sorry for Dorothea.

MRS CADWALLADER. It's her doing, I suppose.

CELIA. Yes, she says Mr Casaubon has a great soul. (*Slight pause.*) Oh, Mrs Cadwallader, I don't think it can be nice to marry a man with a great soul.

MRS CADWALLADER. Well, my dear, take warning. So. Your sister never cared about Sir James. Well, I must go straight to Sir James and break this to him. (*Starts to leave.*) We're all disappointed, you know. Young people should think of their families in marrying. I set a bad example, married a poor clergyman and made myself a pitiable object among the DeBracys. Obliged to get my coals by stratagem, and pray to Heaven for my salad oil. However, Casaubon has money enough, I must do him that justice. But I must go straight to Freshitt. (*Goes rapidly.*)

Scene Eight

SIR JAMES. At Freshitt Hall, Sir James was on the terrace.

The terrace at Freshitt Hall. Sunshine and birdsong.

(*Horsewhip in hand.*) Mrs Cadwallader?

MRS CADWALLADER (*approaches rapidly up the drive*). Sir James, Sir James. I've a great shock for you. I hope you're not so far gone in love as you pretended.

SIR JAMES (*alarmed*). What can you mean?

MRS CADWALLADER. Oh – er... I do believe Brooke is going to stand for Middlemarch after all. On the Liberal side. He looked silly and never denied it – talked about the Independent line and the usual nonsense.

SIR JAMES. Is that all?

MRS CADWALLADER. No, there's worse... I really feel a little responsible. I always told you Miss Brooke would be such a fine match.

SIR JAMES. What has happened to Miss Brooke?

MRS CADWALLADER. She is engaged to be married. Engaged to Casaubon.

Shocked silence.

SIR JAMES. Casaubon?

She nods.

Good God! It's horrible. He's no better than a mummy.

MRS CADWALLADER. A great bladder for dried peas to rattle in!

SIR JAMES. Brooke ought not to allow it. She's not of age. What's a guardian for?

MRS CADWALLADER. As if you could ever squeeze a resolution out of Brooke.

SIR JAMES. Your husband might talk to him?

MRS CADWALLADER. Not he! Humphrey finds everybody charming. I never can get him to abuse Casaubon. He'll even speak well of the Bishop, though I tell him it's unnatural in a beneficed clergyman. Come come, cheer up, you're well rid of Miss Brooke. Between ourselves, little Celia is worth two of her and likely after all to be the better match. This marriage to Casaubon is as good as going to a nunnery.

SIR JAMES. For Miss Brooke's sake, I think her family should try to use their influence.

MRS CADWALLADER. If I were a man, I should prefer Celia. The truth is, you've been courting one and have won the other. I can see that she admires you.

SIR JAMES. Giving up Dorothea was very painful to Sir James, but when he next went to see Brooke at Tipton Grange, there was present in him the sense that Celia would be there, and he should pay her more attention than he had done before.

Scene Nine

BROOKE. Meanwhile, the betrothed must see her future home, the Manor House at Lowick, and dictate any changes she would like.

MRS CADWALLADER. A woman dictates before marriage –

CASAUBON. – in order that she may have an appetite for submission afterwards.

The Manor House at Lowick. The library. Three tall windows on one side. BROOKE, CASAUBON, CELIA *and* DOROTHEA.

BROOKE. I've always thought your library rather dark, Casaubon, rather dark, you know.

CELIA (*at window*). Look at those clumps of yew trees, not ten yards from the windows! Oh dear.

DOROTHEA (*going to* CASAUBON). It's all I could wish. All those books and maps. I see nothing to alter.

CELIA (*in a low voice*). I'm sure Freshitt Hall would have been pleasanter than this.

And Sir James so much more agreeable.

CASAUBON. Let me show you your room upstairs.

He leads off. They follow, and then…

Scene Nine (A)

…turn and re-enter into an upstairs room. The same arrangement, with windows on one side, but slightly lighter.

CASAUBON. Would you like this room as your boudoir?

BROOKE. It might be a pretty room with some new hangings, and sofas, that sort of thing.

DOROTHEA. Uncle, don't speak of altering anything. Perhaps it was your mother's room.

CASAUBON. It was.

DOROTHEA. Whose portrait is this? (*Studies a small picture on the wall*.)

CASAUBON. My mother's sister.

DOROTHEA (*fascinated*). It's a peculiar face. Such deep grey eyes.

CASAUBON. My aunt made an unfortunate marriage. I never saw her.

DOROTHEA *looks at him questioningly, but he doesn't answer.*

DOROTHEA. Shall we not walk in the garden now?

BROOKE. And you'd like to see the church there – (*Points.*) And Lowick village.

DOROTHEA. Yes please.

BROOKE. A grand vantage point here, you know.

CASAUBON. I'll fetch the key to the church gate. (*Goes.*) Follow me.

CELIA (*still looking from the window*). Look, there's someone quite young, coming up the walk there.

DOROTHEA. Is that so astonishing, Celia?

BROOKE. There may be a young gardener, you know – why not?…

They go, and turn…

Scene Ten

WILL. And on their way back from the village –

The yew-tree walk – sun-dappled. Cawing of rooks. WILL sits sketching under a tree. The party approach from a distance.

DOROTHEA. I'm almost wishing the people wanted more to be done for them here.

CASAUBON. Your duties, as mistress of Lowick, will not, I trust, leave any yearning unfulfilled. Now this fine yew tree is the chief hereditary glory of the grounds.

BROOKE. Who's that youngster, Casaubon?

CASAUBON. That is a young relative of mine, a second cousin. The grandson, in fact, of the lady whose portrait you've been noting, my Aunt Julia.

As they approach, WILL *rises.*

Dorothea, let me introduce you to my cousin, Mr Ladislaw. Will, this is Miss Brooke.

BROOKE (*looking at sketchbook*). You're an artist, I see.

WILL. No, I only sketch a little. There's nothing fit to be seen there.

BROOKE. Oh, come. This is what I call a nice thing. I did a little in this way myself at one time, you know. Look here now. (*Shows* DOROTHEA.) Done with what we used to call 'brio'.

DOROTHEA (*looking*). I'm no judge. It's a language I don't understand. I suppose there's some relation between pictures and nature, which I'm too ignorant to feel – (*To* CASAUBON.) just as you see what a Greek sentence stands for, which means nothing to me.

CASAUBON *bows his head to her.*

BROOKE. You don't understand this sort of thing, sketching, and so on – else this is just the thing for girls. (*To* WILL.) You'll come to my house, I hope, and I'll show you what I did in this way.

WILL. Thank you.

BROOKE. I have no end of these things. One gets rusty, you know – not you, Casaubon, you stick to your studies, but my best ideas get out of use, you know. You clever young men must guard against indolence –

CASAUBON. – that is a seasonable admonition –

BROOKE. I was too indolent, you know, else I might have been *anywhere* at one time.

CASAUBON. Let us go back to the house now...

They start to leave. WILL bows, and goes off laughing to himself. They pause and look after him.

BROOKE. What's your cousin going to do with himself, Casaubon? In the way of a career, you know.

CASAUBON. The answer to that question is painfully doubtful. On leaving Rugby, he declined to go to an English university, and chose Heidelberg. And now he wants to go abroad again. He declines to choose a profession.

BROOKE. He has no means but what you furnish, I suppose.

CASAUBON. I have always given him reason to understand that I would furnish in moderation what was necessary for launching him respectably.

DOROTHEA. Perhaps he has scruples founded on his own unfitness. Because law and medicine should be very serious professions to undertake, should they not?

CASAUBON. Doubtless, but I fear that my young relative has a dislike of steady application. I have pointed to my own manuscript volumes which represent the toil of years preparatory to a work not yet accomplished. He replies by calling himself Pegasus and every form of prescribed work 'harness'.

CELIA *laughs*.

BROOKE. Well, you know, he may turn out a Byron, a Marlborough, that sort of thing – there's no telling. Shall you let him go to Italy or wherever?

CASAUBON. Yes, I shall let him be tried by the test of freedom.

DOROTHEA (*delighted*). That's very kind of you. It's noble. After all, people may seem idle and weak because they are growing. We should be very patient with each other, I think…

They go.

WILL. A few days later, Will Ladislaw set off for the Continent.

CASAUBON. He declined to fix any more precise destination than the entire area of Europe.

WILL. Genius, he held, is necessarily intolerant of fetters.

DOROTHEA. Though genius consists in a power to do, not anything in general – (*Turning to* CASAUBON.) but something in particular.

MRS CADWALLADER. The world is full of handsome dubious eggs called possibilities.

Scene Eleven

DOROTHEA. As the day fixed for her marriage came nearer, Dorothea looked forward to higher initiation in ideas, as she was looking forward to marriage, and blending her dim conceptions of both.

The library at Lowick Manor. CASAUBON *at work.* DOROTHEA *at a distance.*

BROOKE. Mr Casaubon too was determined to abandon himself to the stream of feeling –

SIR JAMES. – but perhaps was surprised to find what a shallow rill it was.

CELIA. Perhaps there was some deficiency in Dorothea to account for the moderation of his abandonment –

SIR JAMES. – but he was unable to discern the deficiency.

MRS CADWALLADER. He concluded that the poets had much exaggerated the force of masculine passion.

SIR JAMES. And he sometimes found himself as utterly condemned to loneliness, as to the despair which sometimes threatened him while toiling in the morass of authorship.

BROOKE. And his was that worst loneliness which would shrink from any sympathy.

CASAUBON. I regret your sister is not to accompany us on our wedding journey. You'll have many lonely hours for I shall be constrained to make the utmost use of my time during our stay in Rome, and I should feel more at liberty if you had a companion.

DOROTHEA (*annoyed*). Do you think I should not willingly give up whatever interfered with your using your time to the best purpose?

CASAUBON. That's very amiable in you, my dear.

DOROTHEA (*relenting*). Don't be anxious about me. I shall have so much to think about when I'm alone, I couldn't bear Celia – she would be so miserable.

Scene Twelve

BROOKE. It was the last of the parties at Tipton Grange before the wedding.

SIR JAMES. In that part of the country, before Reform had done its part, there was a clearer distinction of ranks –

MRS CADWALLADER. – but Brooke's miscellaneous invitations seemed to belong to his general laxity.

Tipton Grange library. The GUESTS *arrive*.

SIR JAMES. Of course there was Sir James, and Lady Chettam, his mother –

MRS CADWALLADER. And the Cadwalladers –

MR VINCY (*entering with his daughter*). But there was also Mr Vincy, the Mayor of Middlemarch –

ROSAMOND (*coming forward*). – though not, of course, the Vincy's daughter, Rosamond, for Mr Brooke would not have chosen that his nieces should meet the daughter of a Middlemarch manufacturer. (*Turns and leaves.*)

BROOKE. That would be going too far, you know –

BROOKE *becomes* BULSTRODE *as he comes forward.*

BULSTRODE. And there was also Mr Bulstrode, the rich banker and religious philanthropist who predominated so much in the town –

CELIA. Some called him a Methodist –

VINCY. – others a hypocrite –

BULSTRODE. – according to the resources of their vocabulary.

LYDGATE (*entering*). And then there was the new arrival in Middlemarch, the young surgeon, Mr Lydgate.

He talks to DOROTHEA, *while others assess him from a distance.*

MRS CADWALLADER. I'm told he's wonderfully clever.

SIR JAMES. He is a gentleman.

CELIA. Yes, Uncle says he's one of the Lydgates of Northumberland –

MRS CADWALLADER. Oh, *really* well connected. One doesn't expect it in a practitioner of that kind.

SIR JAMES. I like a medical man more on a footing with the servants. Look at them –

MRS CADWALLADER. I expect she's talking cottages.

BULSTRODE (*approaching*). I, for my part, hail the advent of Mr Lydgate. He's likely to be first-rate. He's studied in Paris – wants to raise the profession. He's brought a new instrument called a stethoscope.

SIR JAMES. What's that?

No one has any idea.

BULSTRODE. I hope to confide my new hospital to his management.

MRS CADWALLADER. If you'd like him to kill a few people for charity, Mr Bulstrode, I've no objection. But I'm not going to have experiments tried on me. I like treatment that's been tested.

VINCY approaches.

BULSTRODE. Ah, here's our new Mayor. We were talking of modern medical treatments, Mr Vincy.

VINCY. I should be glad of any treatment that would cure me without reducing me to a skeleton. It's an uncommonly dangerous thing to be left without any padding against the shafts of disease. Ah –

BULSTRODE. Excuse me –

The party is in full swing. BULSTRODE returns to being BROOKE. LYDGATE leaves DOROTHEA to join the main group. DOROTHEA and CASAUBON apart.

BROOKE. Ladies and gentlemen. To the bride-to-be – may their marriage be long and happy!

All raise their glasses.

ALL. To the bride-to-be!

Scene Thirteen

SIR JAMES. Not long after that party, Dorothea had become Mrs Casaubon, and was in Rome on her wedding journey.

Rome. A gallery. Dark, violent Renaissance paintings appear. Scenes of nudity or rape. They remain during the Rome sequence. DOROTHEA stares at them, confused.

LYDGATE. Some discouragement at the new real future which replaces the imaginary is not unusual.

CASAUBON (*entering, hovers*). Does this interest you, Dorothea? I'm ready to stay if you wish it? Or should you like to go to the Farnese, Dorothea? It contains celebrated frescos by Raphael which most persons think it worthwhile to visit?

DOROTHEA (*passionately.*) But do *you* care about them?

CASAUBON (*drily*). They are, I believe, highly esteemed. Some of them represent the fable of Cupid and Psyche which is probably a romantic invention, and cannot, I think, be reckoned as a genuine mythical product. But you will then, I think, have seen the chief work of Raphael. The opinion of the cognoscenti –

DOROTHEA. No, never mind. I'll stay here a little longer. I wouldn't keep you from your studies.

CASAUBON (*relieved*). Ah.

She kisses his sleeve. He is slightly startled.

You are of a most affectionate and truly feminine nature.

He politely draws up a chair for her and then goes...

She sits and stares at a painting, depressed. She is in a shaft of light.

BROOKE. The huge vistas and fresh air which she had dreamed of finding in her husband's mind, had been replaced by anterooms and winding passages which seemed to lead nowhere.

LYDGATE. Once embarked on her marital voyage, it was impossible not to be aware that the open sea was not within sight, that, in fact, she was exploring an enclosed basin.

WILL *enters, and watches her from afar, fascinated.*

Scene Fourteen

The Casaubons' lodgings in Rome.

CASAUBON. I trust that the time has not been passed unpleasantly to you.

They look out of the window.

I think this is one among several cities to which an extreme hyperbole has been applied – 'See Rome and die' – but in your case I would propose an emendation and say: 'See Rome as a bride and live henceforth as a happy wife.'

He had not found marriage a rapturous state, but he had no idea of being anything but an irreproachable husband.

DOROTHEA. I hope you're satisfied with our stay – I mean, with the results so far as your studies are concerned.

CASAUBON (*half a negative*). Yes, I have been led farther than I had foreseen, and various subjects for annotation have presented themselves. But your society has prevented me from that too continuous prosecution of thought beyond the hour of study which has been the snare of my solitary life.

DOROTHEA. I'm glad my presence has made any difference to you. I hope when we get back to Lowick I shall be more useful to you, and be able to enter a little more into what interests you.

CASAUBON. Doubtless, my dear. The notes I have made here will want sifting –

DOROTHEA (*with increasing passion*). And all your notes – all those rows of volumes – will you not now do what you used to speak of? Will you not make up your mind and begin to write the book which will make your vast knowledge useful to the world? I will write to your dictations.

CASAUBON. My love. You may rely on me for knowing the different stages of a work which is not to be measured by the facile conjectures of ignorant onlookers. It had been easy for me to gain a temporary effect, but it is ever the trial of the scrupulous to be saluted with the impatient scorn of chatterers who attempt only the smallest achievements, being equipped for no other. The true subject matter lies entirely beyond the reach of their superficial judgements.

DOROTHEA (*indignantly*). My judgement *was* a superficial one. But you have often said that your notebooks wanted digesting. I only begged you to let me be of some good to you.

They are standing, staring at each other, both in a state of shock.

CASAUBON. This bride had turned out to be capable of agitating him just where he needed soothing. She was a personification of that shallow world which surrounds the ill-appreciated author.

Instead of getting a soft defence against the cold, shadowy audience of his life, had he only given it a more substantial presence?

Scene Fifteen

WILL. Later that day a relation of Mr Casaubon's was announced.

DOROTHEA. This would be the cousin to whom her husband had been so generous.

WILL (*approaches shyly*). I had not been aware that you and Mr Casaubon were in Rome. But by chance I saw you in the Vatican Museum. I knew you at once – I mean, I was anxious to pay my respects to Mr Casaubon as early as possible.

DOROTHEA. Pray sit down. He's not here. He goes to read in the library of the Vatican every day. He's usually away almost from breakfast to dinner. But I'm sure he'll wish you to dine with us.

WILL (*between disgust and laughter*). But surely –

Pause. Suddenly WILL smiles broadly. She wonders at him and then smiles too.

DOROTHEA. Something amuses you?

WILL. Yes. I'm thinking of the figure I cut the first time I met you, when you annihilated my poor sketch with your criticism.

DOROTHEA. Criticism? Surely not. I always feel particularly ignorant about painting.

WILL. I suspected you of knowing so much. You said – I dare say you don't remember – that the relation of my sketch to nature was quite hidden from you. (*Laughs*.)

DOROTHEA. That was really my ignorance. I've gone about with just the same ignorance in Rome. I feel a kind of awe, like a child present at great ceremonies where there are grand robes and processions. But when I begin to examine them, the life goes out of them, or else is something violent and strange.

WILL. Oh, there's a great deal in the feeling for art which must be acquired. Sometimes the chief pleasure is the mere sense of knowing.

DOROTHEA. You mean perhaps to make painting your profession? Mr Casaubon will like to hear that you've chosen a profession.

WILL. Oh no. I've been seeing a great deal of the German artists here – some are brilliant fellows but I shouldn't like to get into their way of looking at the world.

DOROTHEA. That I can understand. There are so many things more wanted in the world than pictures.

WILL. And if things don't come easily to me I never get them.

DOROTHEA (*a little shocked*). I've heard Mr Casaubon say he regrets your want of patience.

WILL. He and I differ.

DOROTHEA. Such power of devoted labour as Mr Casaubon's is not common.

WILL. No indeed. And therefore it's a pity it should be thrown away for want of knowing what's being done by the rest of the world. If only he read German –

DOROTHEA (*alarmed*). I don't understand you.

WILL. I merely mean that the Germans have taken the lead in historical inquiries and they laugh at results which are got by groping about in the woods with a pocket compass when they have built good roads.

Silence. She looks at her hands. He relents.

It wouldn't signify so much in a man whose talents were less distinguished.

DOROTHEA. How I wish I'd learnt German. But now I can be of no use.

Silence.

CASAUBON (*entering suddenly*). Oh. Will Ladislaw.

WILL. I was in Rome and –

CASAUBON. I thought your intention was to remain in Germany. I hope you are passing your time here profitably as well as pleasantly.

WILL. Indeed.

CASAUBON. At present I'm somewhat weary. I beg you to come tomorrow when we can converse more at large.

WILL. Of course, that would be a pleasure. Till tomorrow then...

CASAUBON. Indeed.

WILL goes. There is a silence, then –

DOROTHEA. Forgive me for speaking so hastily to you this morning. I was wrong. I fear I hurt you and made the day more burdensome.

CASAUBON. I'm glad you feel that, my dear.

DOROTHEA. But do you forgive me?

CASAUBON. My dear Dorothea: 'Who with repentance is not satisfied is not of Heaven nor Earth.'

DOROTHEA cries.

You're excited, my dear. And I also am feeling some unpleasant consequences of too much mental disturbance. I think it is time to dress for dinner.

He starts to leave.

He did not like to remind her that she ought not to have received young Ladislaw in his absence...

Scene Sixteen

WILL. Next day, Will was encouraged to urge the Casaubons to visit the studio where he worked.

(*To* CASAUBON.) My friend Naumann thinks that a sketch of your head would be invaluable for the St Thomas Aquinas in his painting – is it too much to ask?

CASAUBON. You astonish me greatly. (*Slight pause.*) But if my poor physiognomy can be of any use in furnishing some traits for the angelical doctor I shall feel honoured. That is to say, if the operation will not be a lengthy one. Perhaps I could arrange for the purchase of the picture afterwards...

So their return to England was delayed by a few days...

Scene Seventeen

WILL. One day Will called again when Mr Casaubon was not at home.

DOROTHEA *at the table, looking at some cameos.*

DOROTHEA. I'm so glad you've come. Perhaps you understand about cameos and can tell if these are good.

WILL (*looking*). They are exquisite – and the colour is fine. This one will just suit you. (*Holding it up against her.*)

DOROTHEA (*taking it*). Oh no – they're for my sister. She has a different complexion and is very pretty – at least *I* think so. We were never so long away from each other in our lives. I should be sorry for them not to be good after their kind.

WILL. You seem not to care. I should have expected you to be very sensitive to the beautiful.

DOROTHEA. I should like everyone's life to be beautiful. But all this immense expense of art. It spoils my enjoyment of anything when I think that most people are shut out from it.

WILL. I suspect you have some false belief in the virtue of misery, and want to make your life a martyrdom.

DOROTHEA. You mistake me. I'm not a melancholic creature. I'm angry and naughty – not like Celia. I've great outbursts and then all seems glorious again.

WILL. And yet now you will go and be shut up in that stone prison at Lowick – you'd be buried alive – it makes me savage to think of it. (*Fears he has gone too far*.)

DOROTHEA (*smiles*). It's very good of you to be anxious about me – it's because you didn't like Lowick yourself. But Lowick is my Chosen Home.

Slight pause.

WILL. Will saw it would not be useful for him to embrace her slippers and tell her that he would die for her. It was clear that she required nothing of the sort.

DOROTHEA. I wanted to ask you about something you said the other day.

WILL. What was it?

DOROTHEA. I mean what you said about the necessity of Mr Casaubon knowing German. But he must have before him the same materials as German scholars, has he not?

WILL. No. New discoveries are constantly making new points of view. It's of no use now to be crawling after the men of the last century and correcting their mistakes, furnishing up broken-legged theories about Chus and Mizraim!

DOROTHEA. How can you bear to speak so lightly! I wonder it doesn't affect you more painfully if you really think that a man like Mr Casaubon, of so much goodness, power and learning, should in any way fail in what has been the labour of his best years...

WILL. I submit. I'm not in a position to express my feeling towards Mr Casaubon. It would at best be a dependant's eulogy.

DOROTHEA. Pray excuse me. I'm at fault for having introduced the subject. But failure after long perseverance is much grander than never to have a striving.

WILL. I agree. So much so that I've made up my mind not to run that risk. Mr Casaubon's generosity has perhaps been dangerous to me, and I mean to renounce the liberty he has given me. I mean to go back to England shortly and work my own way.

DOROTHEA. That is fine – I respect that feeling.

WILL. I shall not see you again.

DOROTHEA. Oh, stay till Mr Casaubon comes. I'm so glad we met in Rome. I wanted to know you.

WILL. And I've made you angry. I've made you think ill of me.

DOROTHEA. Oh no! My sister tells me I'm always angry with people who don't say just what I like.

WILL. Still, I've made myself an unpleasant thought to you.

DOROTHEA. Not at all. I like you very much. And I'm quite interested to see what you will do. Perhaps you will be a poet?

WILL. That depends. To be a poet is to have a soul so quick to discern that no shade of quality escapes it, and in which knowledge passes instantaneously into feeling, and feeling flashes back as new knowledge. One may have that condition by fits only.

DOROTHEA. You leave out the poems. I think they are wanted to complete the poet.

WILL. You are a poem.

DOROTHEA (*laughing*). I'm very glad to hear it. What very kind things you say to me.

WILL. I wish that I could ever be of the slightest service to you. I fear I shall never have the opportunity.

DOROTHEA. Oh yes! It will come. And I shall remember how well you wish me. I quite hoped we should be friends when I first saw you, because of your relationship to Mr Casaubon. There is one thing you can do. Promise me that you'll not again speak about Mr Casaubon's writing – I mean in that kind of way.

WILL. Certainly.

DOROTHEA (*gives her hand*). Goodbye.

WILL. Goodbye. (*Goes.*)

If he never said a cutting word about Mr Casaubon again, and left off receiving favours from him, it would clearly be possible to hate him the more.

Goethe says the poet must know how to hate.

Scene Eighteen

Later that day.

DOROTHEA. I have something to tell you about our cousin Mr Ladislaw which I think will heighten your opinion of him.

CASAUBON (*coldly*). What is that, my love?

DOROTHEA. He has made up his mind to give up his dependence on your generosity. He means soon to go back to England, and work his own way.

CASAUBON. Did he mention the precise order of occupation?

DOROTHEA. No. But do you not think better of him for his resolve?

CASAUBON. I shall await his communication on the subject.

DOROTHEA. I'm sure he knows that all you did for him was for his own welfare. I remembered your goodness in what you said about him when I first saw him at Lowick. (*Puts her hand on his.*)

CASAUBON (*laying his other hand on hers*). I had a duty towards him. The young man, I confess, is not otherwise an object of interest to me, nor need we discuss his future course, which will not be ours to determine.

LYDGATE. There is a sort of jealousy, which needs very little fire.

BROOKE. It is hardly a passion, but a blight.

Scene Nineteen

BROOKE. Mr and Mrs Casaubon returned to Lowick Manor from their wedding journey.

CELIA. Mr Brooke and Celia were there to greet them.

The library at Lowick Manor.

Dodo!

They kiss.

BROOKE. Rome has agreed with you, I see – happiness, the antique – that sort of thing. But Casaubon's a little pale – studying hard in his holidays is carrying it too far. I overdid it at one time. You may go to any length in that sort of thing and nothing may come of it, you know. (*To* DOROTHEA.) Yes, you must talk with Celia, she has great news, you know.

A look from CELIA.

I leave it to her. Mr Casaubon and I will be in the next room.

They go.

CELIA (*shyly*). Do you think it nice to go to Rome on a wedding journey?

DOROTHEA. It would not suit all. Not you, dear, for example…

CELIA. Mrs Cadwallader says it's all nonsense, people going on a long journey when they are married. She says they get tired to death of each other, and can't quarrel comfortably…

DOROTHEA. Celia, have you really any great news?

CELIA. It was because you went away, Dodo. There was nobody but me for Sir James to talk to.

DOROTHEA. I understand. It is as I used to hope and believe. (*Takes* CELIA*'s face between her hands.*)

CELIA. It was only three days ago. And his mother is very kind.

DOROTHEA. And you are very happy?

CELIA. Yes.

DOROTHEA (*embraces her*). I do believe you could not marry better, Kitty. Sir James is a good, honourable man.

CELIA. He has gone on with the cottages, Dodo. Shall you be glad to see him?

DOROTHEA. Of course I shall.

CELIA. Only I was afraid you'd be getting so learned…

She regarded Mr Casaubon's learning as a kind of damp, which might, in time, saturate a neighbouring body.

Scene Twenty

DOROTHEA. Dorothea soon succeeded in making it a matter of course that she should take her place at an early hour in the library and have work of reading aloud or copying assigned to her.

CASAUBON. At present a monograph on some indications concerning the Egyptian mysteries whereby certain assertions of Warburton's may be corrected…

They are working on either side of the table.

Dorothea, here is a letter for you, enclosed in one addressed to me.

DOROTHEA (*puzzled*). Mr Ladislaw. What can he have to say to me?

CASAUBON. But I may as well say beforehand, that I must decline the proposal it contains to pay a visit here. I trust I may be excused for desiring an interval of complete freedom from such distractions as have been hitherto inevitable, and especially from guests whose desultory vivacity makes their presence a fatigue.

DOROTHEA. You speak as if you had to contend against me, as if I had some wish to annoy you!

CASAUBON. Dorothea –

DOROTHEA (*rises*). Wait at least till I appear to consult my own pleasure apart from yours –

CASAUBON (*rises*). You are hasty –

DOROTHEA. I think it was you who were first hasty.

She awaits an apology.

CASAUBON. I have neither leisure, nor energy for this kind of debate.

After a moment she sits and they try to get on with their work. DOROTHEA *leaves the letter unread. Then* CASAUBON *rises to find a book – from the bookshelves, using a small stepladder. He stretches up, then convulses in pain, gasping for breath.* DOROTHEA *rises and crosses to him, alarmed.*

DOROTHEA. Can you lean on me, dear?

She helps him to sit.

Shall I send for a doctor?

He nods and gestures, feebly.

(*Calling.*) Help me, someone!

Scene Twenty (A)

SIR JAMES. The new doctor was called in.

LYDGATE (*entering*). He gave the case a great deal of attention, using his new stethoscope, and sitting quietly by his patient.

CASAUBON. After a few days, Mr Casaubon began to recover his usual condition. (*Leaves*.)

LYDGATE. But Mr Lydgate was determined to speak to Dorothea.

Scene Twenty-One

DOROTHEA (*alarmed*). Is he not making progress?

LYDGATE. Such cases are peculiarly difficult…

DOROTHEA. I beseech you to speak plainly. Sit down.

They both sit.

LYDGATE. He may possibly live for fifteen years, or more…

DOROTHEA. You mean if we are very careful.

LYDGATE. Yes, careful against mental agitation of all kinds. But it is one of those cases in which death is sometimes sudden.

DOROTHEA (*low voice*). Help me. Tell me what I can do?

LYDGATE. What do you think of foreign travel? You've been lately in Rome, I think?

DOROTHEA. Oh, that would be worse than anything. (*Tearful*.) Nothing will be of any use that he does not enjoy…

LYDGATE. Lydgate was deeply touched, wondering about her marriage. It was something of which he had, as yet, no personal experience.

I think it desirable for him to know nothing more than that he must not overwork himself. Anxiety of any kind would be precisely the most unfavourable condition for him. (*Rises to go.*)

DOROTHEA. You're a wise man. You know about life and death. What can I do? He's been labouring all his life. He minds about nothing else. And I mind about nothing else...

Pause.

LYDGATE. I'll see him again tomorrow. (*Bows and goes.*)

DOROTHEA (*notices Ladislaw's letter, still on the desk*). Oh.

BROOKE *enters*.

Uncle.

BROOKE. My dear?

DOROTHEA. Will you do something for me?

BROOKE. Of course, my dear.

DOROTHEA. Will you reply to Mr Ladislaw for me? He wants to visit – here's the letter – but can you let him know that Mr Casaubon's health will not allow the reception of any visitors.

BROOKE. To be sure I'll write. He's a clever young fellow, this Ladislaw. A rising young man. I'll tell him...

But when he came to write, Mr Brooke's pen found it such a pity that young Ladislaw should not come into the neighbourhood at that time, in order that Mr Brooke might make his acquaintance more fully, that by the end of the second page it had persuaded Mr Brooke to invite young Ladislaw – since he couldn't be received at Lowick – to come to him at Tipton Grange. Why not?

Scene Twenty-Two

MRS CADWALLADER. Now the country gentry of old time lived in a rarefied social air.

SIR JAMES. Dotted apart on their station up the mountain –

BROOKE. – they looked down with imperfect discrimination on the belts of thicker life below.

SIR JAMES. In May, it was a certain old Mr Featherstone's funeral.

MRS CADWALLADER. The gentry watched from the upstairs rooms at Lowick Manor.

The upstairs room at Lowick Manor. MRS CADWALLADER, DOROTHEA, CELIA, SIR JAMES *all looking out of the windows. A bell tolling.*

SIR JAMES. A big burial…

DOROTHEA. Why isn't Mr Casaubon burying him?

MRS CADWALLADER (*shrugs*). Mr Featherstone specified my Humphrey. And it gives us a good excuse to visit you.

CELIA. I don't like funerals.

MRS CADWALLADER. My dear, when you have a clergyman in your family you must accommodate your tastes.

CELIA. I shan't look any more. (*Goes and sits apart.*) I dare say Dodo likes it – she's fond of melancholy things and ugly people.

DOROTHEA. I'm fond of knowing something about the people I live with. One is constantly wondering what sort of lives other people lead. I'm quite obliged to Mrs Cadwallader for calling me out of the library.

MRS CADWALLADER. Quite right. Your Lowick farmers are as curious as any buffaloes.

SIR JAMES. I'm told the old fellow left a good deal of money as well as land.

BROOKE *enters.*

MRS CADWALLADER. Ah, Mr Brooke, I felt we were incomplete. You've come to see this odd funeral?

BROOKE. No, I came to see how Casaubon goes on, you know. And to bring a little news. I looked into the library downstairs and I saw Casaubon over his books. I didn't tell him my news – I said he must come up.

MRS CADWALLADER. Ah, now they're all coming out of church. Dear me, what a wonderfully mixed set. Mr Lydgate, as doctor, I suppose. But there's a good-looking family. Who are they, Sir James, do you know?

SIR JAMES. I see Vincy, the Mayor of Middlemarch, they're probably his wife and children.

BROOKE. A good fellow is Vincy, a credit to the manufacturing interest.

MRS CADWALLADER. Ah yes, one of your reforming committee. And one of those who suck the life out of the local hand-loom weavers. That's how his family look so fair and sleek... Those purple-faced people are an excellent foil, like a set of jugs. Oh, do look at my husband – oh, Humphrey! (*Giggles*.)

BROOKE. It's a solemn thing, though, a funeral. If you take it in that light, you know.

MRS CADWALLADER. But I'm not taking it in that light. I can't wear my solemnity too often, else it will go to rags. It was time that mean old man died and none of these people are sorry.

DOROTHEA. How piteous. I can't bear to think that anyone should die and leave no love behind –

CASAUBON *enters and she stops. He sits in the background.*

MRS CADWALLADER (*pointing*). There's a new face in the neighbourhood – queerer than any of them. A sort of frog-face.

CELIA. Let me see! (*Goes to take* SIR JAMES*'s hand.*) Oh yes. And who's that? Why, Dodo, you never told me that Mr Ladislaw was come again.

DOROTHEA *is shocked. Everyone looks at her, she looks to her uncle.*

BROOKE. He came with me, you know – he's my guest, puts up with me at Tipton Grange. And we've brought the picture with us on top of the carriage. I knew you'd be pleased with the surprise, Casaubon. There you are to the very life – as Aquinas, you know. And you'll hear Ladislaw talk about it – he talks uncommonly well –

CASAUBON *bows with cold politeness.*

MRS CADWALLADER. Who is Mr Ladislaw?

SIR JAMES. A young relative of Mr Casaubon's.

BROOKE. I hope he'll stay with me a long time and we shall make something of my documents. I've plenty of ideas, you know, and he's just the man to put them into shape. I invited him when you were ill, Casaubon. Dorothea said you couldn't have anybody here and she asked me to write.

CASAUBON. I see.

DOROTHEA. But I – (*Stops herself.*)

CASAUBON. You are exceedingly hospitable, my dear sir.

CELIA. Now you can see him, Mrs Cadwallader. He's just like the portrait of Mr Casaubon's aunt – quite nice looking.

MRS CADWALLADER. A very pretty sprig.

BROOKE. He's trying his wings. He'd make a good secretary now, like Hobbes, Milton, Swift – that sort of man.

MRS CADWALLADER. I understand. One who can write your speeches for you.

BROOKE. I'll fetch him in now, eh, Casaubon?

Scene Twenty-Three

CASAUBON. So now Casaubon was forced to countenance occasional meetings with Ladislaw.

WILL. But Will was impatient to talk with Dorothea alone.

MRS CADWALLADER. However slight the terrestrial intercourse between Dante and Beatrice, in later days it is preferable to have fewer sonnets and more conversation.

BROOKE. One morning when Mr Brooke had to drive along the Lowick road, Will asked to be set down with his sketchbook and camp stool...

WILL. But rain obliged Will to take shelter at the Manor. He was shown into the library.

The library at Lowick Manor.

DOROTHEA. Mr Casaubon has gone to the Archdeacon's. I don't know if he'll be home before dinner. Did you want to say anything particular to him?

WILL. No, I came to sketch, but the rain drove me in. Else I would not have disturbed you. I know he dislikes interruptions at this hour.

DOROTHEA. I'm indebted to the rain then. I'm so glad to see you.

WILL. I really came for the chance of seeing you alone. I wanted to talk about things, as we did in Rome. It always makes a difference when other people are present.

DOROTHEA. Yes. Sit down.

They sit.

I've often thought I'd like to talk to you again. It seems strange how many things I said to you.

WILL. I remember them all.

DOROTHEA. I've tried to learn a great deal since we were in Rome. I can read Latin a little and understand just a little Greek, and I can help Mr Casaubon better now – and save his eyes. Even as a little girl, it seemed that I should like to help someone who did great works, that his burden might be lighter.

WILL. But you already look paler. It would be better for Mr Casaubon to have a secretary.

DOROTHEA. How can you think that? I should have no happiness if I didn't help him in his work. Please not to mention that again.

WILL. Certainly not. But I've heard both Mr Brooke and Sir James Chettam express the same wish.

DOROTHEA. Yes, but they don't understand – they want me to be a great deal on horseback, and have the garden altered, and new conservatories to fill up my days. I thought you could understand that one's mind has other wants. Besides, Mr Casaubon cannot bear to hear of a secretary.

WILL. In the old days he held out that prospect to me. But I turned out to be – not good enough.

DOROTHEA (*playfully*). You were not a steady worker enough.

WILL. No, and Mr Casaubon doesn't like anyone to look over his work. He's too doubtful of himself. And he dislikes me because I disagree with him.

Slight pause.

DOROTHEA. But he has supported you.

WILL. Yes, he has shown a sense of justice in family matters. It was an abominable thing that my grandmother should have been disinherited because she made a misalliance. Though there was nothing against her husband except that he was a Polish refugee.

DOROTHEA. Do you know much about them?

WILL. No. They both died early. And I never knew much of my father. I remember his long thin hands. One day remains with me when he was lying ill, and I was very hungry. He died soon after, but my mother and I were well taken care of after that. Mr Casaubon recognised it was his duty to take care of us because of the harsh injustice shown to the family.

DOROTHEA. Is your mother still living?

WILL. No, she died four years ago. It's curious that she too ran away from her family, but she would never tell me anything about them, except that she forsook them to get her own living – went on the stage, in fact. You see I come of rebellious blood on both sides. (*Smiles brightly*.)

After a moment, DOROTHEA *smiles too*.

DOROTHEA. That's your apology for having been rather rebellious to Mr Casaubon. But if he's shown any painful feelings towards you, you must consider how sensitive he's become from the wearing effects of study. (*Pleads*.) Perhaps my uncle hasn't told you how serious Mr Casaubon's illness was. It would be petty of us who are well and can bear things to think much of small offences from those who carry a weight of trial.

WILL. I'll never grumble on that subject again. I'll never again do or say what you would disapprove.

DOROTHEA (*smiles*). That's very good of you. I shall have a little kingdom then, where I shall give laws. But you'll soon go away, out of my rule, I imagine. You'll soon be tired of staying at the Grange.

WILL. That's one of the reasons I wished to speak to you alone. Mr Brooke proposes I should stay in this neighbourhood. He's bought one of the Middlemarch newspapers – *The Pioneer* – and he wishes me to conduct that.

DOROTHEA. Wouldn't that be a sacrifice of higher prospects for you?

WILL. Perhaps – but I've always been blamed for not settling to anything. And here is something. If you'd not like me to accept it, I'll give it up. Otherwise I'd rather stay in this part of the country. I belong to nobody anywhere else.

DOROTHEA. I should like you to stay very much.

WILL. Then I will stay. (*Goes to the window*.)

DOROTHEA (*reflecting*). But I spoke without thinking. I think you should be guided by Mr Casaubon. Can you not wait and mention it to him?

WILL. I can't wait today. The rain is quite over now. I shall strike back across Halsell Common. It's only five miles.

DOROTHEA. I wish you could have stayed.

She rises and they shake hands.

She wanted to say: 'You ought to consult Mr Casaubon.'

WILL. He longed to say: 'Don't mention the subject to Mr Casaubon.' And yet –

DOROTHEA *and* WILL. Goodbye.

Scene Twenty-Four

DOROTHEA. That day, Mr Casaubon's carriage did not appear till four o'clock.

Have you had a fatiguing day?

CASAUBON. I've had the gratification of meeting a former acquaintance who spoke very handsomely on my late tractate on the Egyptian mysteries, using, in fact, terms which it would not become me to repeat. (*Nods.*)

DOROTHEA. I'm glad. Before you came, I'd been regretting you happened to be out today.

CASAUBON. Why so, my dear?

DOROTHEA. Because Mr Ladislaw has been here, and he's mentioned a proposal of my uncle's. It appears dear Uncle has bought one of the Middlemarch newspapers – *The Pioneer* – and has asked Mr Ladislaw to conduct the paper for him. What's your opinion?

CASAUBON. Did Mr Ladislaw come on purpose to ask my opinion?

DOROTHEA. No. But he, of course, expected me to tell you of the proposal.

Silence.

I feared you might feel some objection. But a young man with so much talent might be very useful to my uncle. He's been blamed for not seeking a fixed occupation, and he would like to stay in the neighbourhood because no one cares for him elsewhere.

Silence.

CASAUBON. The next morning, without Dorothea's knowledge, Mr Casaubon dispatched a letter.

WILL *reading the letter.*

Dear Mr Ladislaw, Mrs Casaubon informs me that a proposal has been made to you which involves your residence in this neighbourhood in a capacity which touches my own position. Your acceptance would be highly offensive to me. There are certain social proprieties which should hinder a somewhat near relative of mine from becoming conspicuous in the vicinity in a status not only much beneath my own, but associated with political adventurers. The contrary issue must exclude you from further reception at my house. Yours faithfully, Edward Casaubon.

Scene Twenty-Five

Slow fade to night.

DOROTHEA. That night, in her room upstairs, Dorothea's mind was at work. Many fresh images gathered around the portrait of that Aunt Julia who was Will's grandmother. (*Studies the portrait.*) What a wrong to cut off the girl from the family protection and inheritance...

CELIA. She was blind to many things obvious to others – likely to tread in the wrong places, as Celia had warned her.

WILL. Her blindness carried her by the side of precipices, where vision would have been perilous with fear.

The upstairs room at Lowick Manor. CASAUBON *is asleep in a chair.* DOROTHEA *sits watching him.*

CASAUBON. Dorothea, since you are up, will you light a candle?

DOROTHEA (*obeying him*). Do you feel ill, dear?

CASAUBON. No, not at all. But I shall be obliged, since you are up, if you will read me a few pages of Lowth's theology?

DOROTHEA. May I talk to you a little instead?

CASAUBON. Certainly.

DOROTHEA. I've been thinking about money all day – that I've always had too much, and especially the prospect of too much.

CASAUBON. These, my dear, are providential arrangements.

DOROTHEA. But if one has too much in consequence of others being wronged...

CASAUBON. What, my love, is the bearing of your remark?

DOROTHEA. That you've been too liberal in arrangements for me, and that makes me unhappy.

CASAUBON. How so? I've none but comparatively distant connections.

DOROTHEA. I've been led to think about your Aunt Julia – and how she was left in poverty only because she married a poor man. It was on that ground, I know, that you educated Mr Ladislaw and provided for his mother.

Silence.

But surely we should regard his claim as a much greater one, even to the half of that property which I know you've destined for me. I think he ought at once to be provided for on that understanding. I think it's not right that he should be in the dependence of poverty while we are rich.

CASAUBON. Mr Ladislaw has been speaking to you on this subject?

DOROTHEA. Indeed no! How can you imagine it! He only told me a little about his parents and grandparents. (*Goes to kneel beside him.*) You're so good, so just, you've done everything you thought to be right. But it seems to me clear that more than that is right, and I must speak about it…

Pause.

CASAUBON. Dorothea, my love, this is not the first occasion, but it were well it should be the last, on which you have assumed a judgement on subjects beyond your scope. You are not qualified to discriminate. What I wish you to understand is that I accept no revision, still less dictation, within that range of affairs which are distinctly and properly mine. It is not for you to interfere between me and Mr Ladislaw, and still less to encourage communications from him to you which constitute a criticism of my procedure.

Silence. She stands.

DOROTHEA. Dorothea felt a dumb inward cry for help to bear this nightmare of a life in which every energy was arrested by dread.

Scene Twenty-Five (A)

CASAUBON. The next day, Casaubon received an answer from Will Ladislaw.

CASAUBON *reading the letter.*

WILL. Dear Mr Casaubon, I have given all due consideration to your letter of yesterday, but I'm unable to take your view. Pardon me for not seeing that my past obligations should restrain me from using the ordinary freedom of living where I choose and maintaining myself by any lawful occupation I may choose. I remain yours – Will Ladislaw.

CASAUBON. To this, Mr Casaubon remained proudly, bitterly silent. But he had forbidden Will to come to Lowick Manor, and he was mentally preparing other means of frustration.

Scene Twenty-Six

SIR JAMES. That summer, on the Terrace at Freshitt Hall…

The terrace at Freshitt Hall. Sunshine and birdsong. SIR JAMES *sitting with* MRS CADWALLADER, *reading his newspaper,* The Trumpet.

MRS CADWALLADER. *The Pioneer* at Tipton Grange! It's frightful.

SIR JAMES (*from his newspaper*). They're beginning to attack Brooke in *The Trumpet*.

MRS CADWALLADER. Is he really going to be put into nomination? Humphrey says he's getting up a pretty strong party. There's Bulstrode, the banker –

SIR JAMES. What I care for most, Mrs Cadwallader, is his own dignity. He's getting on in life now. And this Ladislaw – we've had him two or three times to dine here as Brooke's guest, thinking he was only on a flying visit. And now I find – (*Tapping the paper.*) he's the editor of *The Pioneer*. There are stories about him in Middlemarch as a foreign spy and whatnot…

MRS CADWALLADER. He's a dangerous sprig – with his opera songs and his ready tongue.

SIR JAMES. And a newspaper fellow! What a position for anybody with decent connections.

MRS CADWALLADER. An amorous conspirator it seems to me –

SIR JAMES. I hope he won't go into extreme opinions and carry Brooke on.

MRS CADWALLADER. It's Thomas Aquinas' fault. Why didn't he get Ladislaw sent to India. That's how families get rid of troublesome sprigs.

SIR JAMES. But if Casaubon says nothing, what can I do?

MRS CADWALLADER. Well, my Humphrey says don't make too much of it. Brooke and Ladislaw will get tired of each other. And Brooke won't like his money oozing away on election expenses.

SIR JAMES. And he won't like having things raked up against him. There's the management of his estate, they've begun upon that already. I do think one's bound to do the best for one's tenants. I want him to take on Garth again. Garth's made such a capital plan for my buildings.

MRS CADWALLADER. But look, here comes our Independent politician. You ply him with *The Trumpet*, Sir James.

SIR JAMES. The fact is I don't like to begin it with Brooke, the whole thing is so unpleasant. I do wish people would behave like gentlemen.

BROOKE (*entering*). Here you are, eh? This is pleasant. Thought I'd come by, Chettam. Good to see you here, Mrs Cadwallader. Very pleasant. Well, what do you think of things? – Going on a little fast?

MRS CADWALLADER. Here's *The Trumpet* accusing you of lagging behind – do you see? (*Takes paper from* SIR JAMES.)

BROOKE. Eh? No. (*Looking for his eyeglass.*)

MRS CADWALLADER (*keeps the paper*). It's about a landlord not a hundred miles from Middlemarch – (*Reads out.*) 'who cannot bear corruption but doesn't mind honest tenants being half-starved, who roars himself red at rotten boroughs and doesn't mind if every field on his farms has a rotten gate.'

BROOKE. Come, that's rather good, you know. (*Takes the paper and looks.*) But I never made a speech about rotten boroughs in my life. Good satire should be true up to a certain point.

SIR JAMES (*carefully*). Well, that really is a hit about the gates. Garth has invented a new pattern of gate – I wish you'd try it.

BROOKE. You go in for fancy-farming, you know, Chettam. That's your hobby and you don't mind the expense.

MRS CADAWALLADER. I thought the most expensive hobby in the world was standing for Parliament.

BROOKE. Nothing of the kind.

SIR JAMES. The fact is, if a man goes into public life he must make himself proof against calumny. I would choke *The Trumpet* at once by giving Garth carte blanche to make repairs.

BROOKE. That's a showy sort of thing to do, you know. I'd like you to tell me of another landlord who has distressed his tenants for arrears as little as I have. I let the old tenants stay on. I'm uncommonly easy, let me tell you, uncommonly easy – oh! (*Puts paper down.*) I must go back to the Grange. There's a packet I forgot to send. You must excuse me. Goodbye. Goodbye. (*Goes quickly.*)

Pause.

SIR JAMES. I see he's nettled.

MRS CADWALLADER. It was all very well for him to ride hobby horses at home and call them ideas – but if you put him a-horseback on politics, I warn you of the consequences.

SIR JAMES (*thoughtfully*). On the management of his estate, I wonder if Dorothea might bring her influence to bear with him. Casaubon's illness can't take her up entirely...

Scene Twenty-Seven

BROOKE. It was a few days later, and politics were going on apace at Tipton Grange.

Tipton Grange library. Papers on the table.

WILL. Things will ripen quickly now the question of Reform has set in. What we have to work at now is *The Pioneer*, and political meetings.

BROOKE. Quite right. Only I want to keep myself Independent about Reform you know. I don't want to go too far.

WILL. If you go in for the principle of Reform, you must be prepared to take what the situation offers.

BROOKE. Yes, yes, I agree – I should support the Bill, you know. But I don't want to change the balance of the constitution.

WILL. But that's what the country wants. And as for Reform short of that, it's like… asking for a bit of an avalanche which has already begun to thunder.

BROOKE. That is fine, Ladislaw, that's the way to put it. Write that down now. You have a way of putting things. I can't help wishing someone had a pocket-borough to give you. That avalanche and the thunder, now. I want that sort of thing – not ideas, you know, but a way of putting them.

WILL. Pocket-boroughs would be a fine thing if they were always in the right pocket.

Will found Brooke occasionally irritating but he was beginning thoroughly to like the work, and he studied the political situation with as ardent a practical interest as he had ever given to poetic meters or medieval painting.

DOROTHEA. But suddenly Mrs Casaubon was announced.

WILL *starts up*.

BROOKE. Well, my dear, this is pleasant now. You've left Casaubon with his books, I suppose… that's right, we mustn't have you getting too learned for a woman, you know.

DOROTHEA. There's no fear of that, Uncle – (*Shakes hands with* WILL *as she continues*.) I'm very slow. I find it not so easy to be learned as to plan cottages.

BROOKE. Why yes, my dear. But hobbies are apt to run away with us. I always pulled up. That's what I tell Ladislaw. He and I are alike, you know, he likes to go into everything. We shall do a great deal together.

DOROTHEA. Yes. Sir James tells me he's in hope of seeing a great change in the management of your estates. You're thinking of having repairs made and the cottages improved. Oh, how happy! (*Childlike again*.) If I were at home still I should take to riding again – go about with you and see all that! And you're going to engage Mr Garth, who praised my cottages, James says.

BROOKE. Chettam's a little hasty, my dear. I never said –

DOROTHEA. He only feels confident you'll do it because you mean to enter Parliament as a member who cares about the improvement of the people. Think of the Downes, Uncle, with seven children and two rooms, and those poor Dagleys where they live in the back kitchen and leave the other room for the rats. I used to come from the village, with all that coarse ugliness like a pain within me, and the simpering pictures on the walls here seemed like a wicked attempt to find delight in what is false, while we don't mind how hard the truth is for our neighbours outside. I think we have no right to urge wider changes for the good till we've tried to alter the evils which lie in our own hands.

Dorothea had forgotten everything except the relief of pouring forth her feelings, unchecked by her husband.

BROOKE. There's something in what you say, my dear, but not everything, eh, Ladislaw. Young ladies are a little ardent, you know – a little one-sided, my dear. But – eh – what?

SERVANT. Just then it was announced that one of Dagley's boys had been caught with a leveret in his hand – just killed.

BROOKE. I'll come, I'll come. I shall let him off easily, you know. Wait for me here…

WILL *and* DOROTHEA *left alone*.

DOROTHEA. I hope you feel how right this change is that I –
that Sir James wishes for.

WILL. I do, now that I've heard you speak. But can you –
(*Impatiently*.) I may not have another opportunity of
speaking to you about what's occurred.

DOROTHEA. Tell me.

WILL. I presume you know Casaubon has forbidden me to go
to his house.

DOROTHEA. No, I didn't. (*Moved*.) I'm very, very sorry.

WILL. He considers my position here – (*Indicates papers*.)
unsuited to my rank as his cousin. I've told him I can't give
way. It's a little hard to expect my course in life is to be
hampered by his prejudices. I would not have accepted the
position if I'd not meant to make it useful and honourable.

DOROTHEA (*wretched*). It's better not to speak on the subject,
since you and Mr Casaubon disagree. You intend to remain?

WILL. Yes, but I shall hardly ever see you now.

DOROTHEA. No, but I shall hear of you – what you're doing
for my uncle.

WILL. But no one will tell me anything about you.

DOROTHEA. Oh, my life is very simple. I'm always at
Lowick.

WILL. That's a dreadful imprisonment.

DOROTHEA. No, don't think that. I've no longings for myself.
But I've a belief that comforts me.

WILL. What's that?

DOROTHEA. That by desiring what's perfectly good, even
when we don't quite know what it is, and can't do what we
would, we're widening light and making darkness narrower.

WILL. That's a beautiful mysticism – it's –

DOROTHEA. Please, not to call it by any name. You'll say it's Persian, or something else geographical. It's my life. I've found it out and I can't part with it. I only told you, that you might know quite well how my days go at Lowick.

WILL. God bless you for telling me.

DOROTHEA. What's the belief that helps you most?

WILL. To love what is good and beautiful when I see it. But I'm a rebel. I don't feel bound, as you do, to submit to what I don't like.

DOROTHEA. But if you like what's good, that comes to the same thing – but how long my uncle is – I must go and look for him. I must really go on to Freshitt Hall. Celia's expecting a baby – did you know?

BROOKE. Mr Brooke offered to go with Dorothea as far as Dagley's to speak about the boy caught with the leveret. There he was shouted at by a resentful Mr Dagley whose idea of Reform was to send Mr Brooke and all his like a-scuttling.

DOROTHEA. And Dorothea, on returning to Lowick, was for the first time silent about having seen Will.

Scene Twenty-Eight

CASAUBON. There was no denying that Dorothea was as virtuous and lovely a lady as Mr Casaubon could have obtained for a wife.

DOROTHEA. She nurtured him, she read to him, she anticipated his wants.

CASAUBON. But there entered into the husband's mind that she judged him.

Suspicion and jealousy of Dorothea's impressions, suspicion and jealousy of Will Ladislaw's intentions were constantly at their weaving work.

The yew-tree walk. Sun-dappled. Rooks.

(*To himself, pacing up and down.*) He has a personal
animosity towards me – I'm sure of it – and he has
fascinated Dorothea's attention. He has evidently tried to
impress her mind with the notion that he has claims beyond
anything I have done for him. Even if I live I shall not be
without uneasiness as to what he may attempt. If I die – and
he's on the watch for that – he will persuade her to marry
him. He thinks of an easy conquest and of entering into my
nest. That, it is my duty to hinder.

Ruminating on the probabilities of his own life, he determined
to ask Lydgate's opinion, though he shrank from it.

LYDGATE *enters*.

LYDGATE. I hope your wish to see me is not due to the return
of unpleasant symptoms?

CASAUBON. Not immediately, no. But I must mention that my
life derives an importance from the incompleteness of certain
labours. I have long had on hand a work – *The Key to All
Mythologies* – which I would fain leave behind in such a
state that it might be committed to the press by – er... You
have not implied to me that the symptoms were those of a
fatal disease. But were it so, I should desire to know, so that
it may be a guide in the determination of my course.

LYDGATE. I must impress on you diseases of the heart are
difficult to found predictors on. Your condition may be
consistent with a tolerably comfortable life for another
fifteen years or more. At the same time no such result can be
predicted. It's my duty to tell you that death is often sudden.

Slight pause.

CASAUBON. I thank you. Did you communicate this to Mrs
Casaubon?

LYDGATE. As to the possible issues, yes.

CASAUBON. I thank you. The day has a rare beauty has it not.

Slight pause.

LYDGATE. I'll leave you. (*Goes*.)

CASAUBON. On the dark river-brink of death, Casaubon heard the plash of the oncoming oar, not discerning the forms, but expecting the summons.

DOROTHEA (*entering*). Dearest?

She dreads to approach. He walks past her. She tries to link her arm with his. He breaks away and leaves.

CASAUBON. Casaubon shrank from pity. And he felt the suspicion that his grief might even be a source of contentment to her.

Scene Twenty-Eight (A)

DOROTHEA *alone*.

DOROTHEA (*violently*). What have I done? He never knows what is in my mind. Never cares. What's the use of anything I do? He wishes he had never married me... Is it my fault that I believed in him? I shut my best soul in prison just to please him.

CASAUBON (*entering*). I am much occupied, and wish to be quite alone this evening. (*Goes*.)

DOROTHEA. In such a crisis as this some women begin to hate.

Pause. She is motionless.

LYDGATE. The struggle within her changed continually, as that of a man who begins with a movement towards striking, and works to conquer that desire.

WILL. The evening deepened into night.

She moves a chair to suggest a corridor. She sits in the dim light.

DOROTHEA. She waited outside her room for his coming upstairs.

CASAUBON (*approaching*). Dorothea. Were you waiting for me?

DOROTHEA. Yes, I didn't want to disturb you.

CASAUBON. Come, my dear, come. You are young, and need not to extend your life by watching.

They take hands.

They went along the broad corridor together.

DOROTHEA. She felt something like the thankfulness that might well up in us if we had narrowly escaped hurting a lamed creature.

Scene Twenty-Nine

DOROTHEA. Two days later, she determined to see the doctor, and learn whether her husband had felt any depressing change of symptoms which he was concealing from her.

LYDGATE. She drove to the town, to Mr Lydgate's house.

A hallway at the Lydgates'.

SERVANT. Dorothea remembered that the doctor had recently married the Mayor's daughter, Miss Vincy.

DOROTHEA. Is Mrs Lydgate at home?

SERVANT. I believe so.

DOROTHEA. Will you ask her if she can see me – Mrs Casaubon – for a few minutes?

The SERVANT goes in. From within, there is the sound of a piano, a man's voice, and opera singing – 'Lungi dal caro bene'. It stops.

ROSAMOND (*entering*). Mrs Casaubon?

DOROTHEA. Thank you for allowing me to interrupt you. I'm anxious to see Mr Lydgate if possible.

ROSAMOND. I'm afraid he's not at home.

DOROTHEA. Can you tell me where I could find him?

ROSAMOND. He's at the new hospital, but I can send for him.

WILL (*comes forward*). Will you let me go and fetch him?

DOROTHEA (*surprised*). Oh – I had no thought of seeing you here.

WILL. May I go to the hospital for you?

DOROTHEA. I'll go myself, thank you. Pray excuse me, Mrs Lydgate. I'm very much obliged to you. (*Goes.*)

In driving to the hospital, Dorothea found herself wondering that Will Ladislaw was passing his time with pretty Mrs Lydgate in her husband's absence.

And then she couldn't help remembering that he had passed time with her under like circumstances.

ROSAMOND. Why should there be any unfitness in the fact?

DOROTHEA. But she felt confusedly unhappy.

Slight pause.

WILL. But Ladislaw felt mortified.

It's always fatal to have music or poetry interrupted. May I come another day about the rendering of 'Lungi dal caro bene'?

ROSAMOND. I shall be happy to be taught. But I'm sure you admit the interruption was a very beautiful one. I quite envy your acquaintance with Mrs Casaubon. Is she very clever? She looks it.

WILL. Really I never thought about it.

ROSAMOND. That's just the answer my husband gave me. What is it you gentlemen are thinking of when you're with Mrs Casaubon?

WILL. Herself. When one sees a perfect woman, one never thinks of her attributes – one is conscious of her presence.

ROSAMOND. I shall be jealous when my husband goes to Lowick Manor. He'll come back and think nothing of me.

WILL. That doesn't seem to have been the effect on him hitherto. Mrs Casaubon is too unlike other women for them to be compared with her.

ROSAMOND. You're a devout worshipper, I perceive. You often see her, I suppose.

WILL. No. Worship is usually a matter of theory rather than of practice. But I'm practising it to excess just at this moment – I must really tear myself away.

ROSAMOND. Pray come again some evening. Mr Lydgate will like to hear the music, and I cannot enjoy it so well without him…

Scene Thirty

LYDGATE. Meanwhile, Dorothea had been talking to Mr Lydgate at the new hospital.

The new hospital.

DOROTHEA. So there are no signs of change in my husband's condition?

LYDGATE. No, only this new anxiety to know the truth about his illness. Perhaps there has been some crisis in his mind?

Pause while she considers.

If I might urge another subject? I remember at Tipton Grange you were asking me some questions about the health of the poor. I don't know whether you or Mr Casaubon's attention has been drawn to the needs of our new hospital here.

DOROTHEA. I shall be grateful if you'll tell me how I can help.

LYDGATE. This hospital is a capital piece of work, due entirely to Mr Bulstrode's exertions and in a great degree to the banker's money. But now there's a petty feud against the thing in the town.

DOROTHEA. What can be the reason?

LYDGATE. Mr Bulstrode's unpopularity to begin with. People don't like his religious tone, he's masterful, and since he has put the medical direction into my hands, the medical profession in Middlemarch here have set themselves tooth and nail against the hospital, and hinder subscriptions.

DOROTHEA. How very petty!

LYDGATE. There's no stifling the offence of being young, and a newcomer and happening to know more than the old doctors. Still, I believe I can pursue certain observations which may be a lasting benefit to medical practice. I should be a base truckler if I allowed any consideration of personal comfort to hinder me. And the course is all the clearer from there being no salary to put my persistence in an equivocal light.

DOROTHEA. I'm glad you've told me this, Mr Lydgate. I feel sure I can help. I have some money and I'm sure I can spare two hundred a year for a grand purpose like this. How happy you must be to know things that you feel sure will do great good. (*Slight pause.*) Come to Lowick and tell us more. I'll mention the subject to Mr Casaubon.

CASAUBON. Mr Casaubon made no objection to the money – but he felt sure she wished to know what had passed between him and Lydgate on the matter of his health, and he distrusted her.

LYDGATE. What loneliness is more lonely than distrust?

Scene Thirty-One

WILL. Will Ladislaw had now moved out of Tipton Grange and into lodgings in Middlemarch.

LYDGATE. He was really a sort of gypsy.

MRS CADWALLADER. One oddity was that in houses where he got friendly –

WILL (*lies on the floor*). – he was given to stretch himself at full length on the rug while he talked –

SIR JAMES. – and was apt to be discovered in this attitude by occasional callers –

MRS CADWALLADER. – for whom such an irregularity was likely to confirm the notions of his dangerously mixed blood and general laxity.

LYDGATE. The house where he visited oftenest and lay most on the rug was Lydgates'.

The Lydgates' drawing room. ROSAMOND *on the sofa with embroidery,* LYDGATE *reads* The Pioneer. WILL *lies by the fire.*

It's no good your puffing Brooke as a reforming landlord in *The Pioneer*, Ladislaw, they only pick more holes in his coat in *The Trumpet*.

WILL. No matter. Those who read *The Pioneer* don't read *The Trumpet*. Do you suppose the public reads with a view to its own conversion?

LYDGATE. Brooke's not fitted to be a public man. He would disappoint everybody.

WILL. He's good enough for the occasion.

LYDGATE. That's the way with you political writers – crying up the men who are part of the very disease that wants curing.

WILL. Are we to try for nothing till we find immaculate men to work with?

LYDGATE. Oh. I see – of course. Suppose the worst opinion about Bulstrode were true, that wouldn't make it less true that he has the resolution to do what ought to be done in respect to the hospital. But I wouldn't cry him up on any personal ground.

WILL (*nettled*). Do you mean that I cry up Brooke on any personal ground? (*Starts to get up.*)

LYDGATE. Not at all. I was simply explaining my own actions. I meant that a man may work with others whose motives are equivocal if he's quite sure he's not working for his private interest – either place or money.

WILL. You've no more reason to imagine that I have personal expectations from Brooke than I have to imagine that you have personal expectations from Bulstrode!

LYDGATE. You quite mistake me, Ladislaw. I beg your pardon. In fact, I should rather attribute to you a romantic disregard of your own interests. I referred simply to intellectual bias in general.

ROSAMOND. How very unpleasant you both are this evening. I can't conceive why money should have been referred to. Politics and medicine are sufficiently disagreeable.

LYDGATE. Poor Rosy. Disputation is not amusing to cherubs. Have some music. Ask Ladislaw to sing with you.

He places a chair for her. ROSAMOND *opens the piano lid and starts to sing – 'Lungi dal caro bene'.* WILL *joins in.*

Scene Thirty-Two

WILL. It was irritating to Will that he had harnessed himself to Brooke, and his exertions did not seem as heroic as he would like.

But far more irritating that he couldn't see Dorothea.

DOROTHEA. He suddenly determined to go to Lowick Church to see her.

WILL. It will annoy Casaubon, but is he to have everything to himself? Let him smart, as others are obliged to do.

He walked to Lowick, crossing Halsell Common, as if he had been on the way to Paradise.

Lowick church. As WILL *enters, the* CONGREGATION *is gathering, singing 'All people that on earth do dwell…'* DOROTHEA *enters. She bows briefly to* WILL *as she takes her place on the other side of the aisle.* CASAUBON *enters and faces the* CONGREGATION.

To his surprise, he felt suddenly uncomfortable. The service was immeasurably long. He dared not look at her.

CASAUBON. The grace of our Lord Jesus Christ, and the love of God, and the fellowship of the Holy Ghost, be with us all evermore. Amen.

CASAUBON *goes out with* DOROTHEA. WILL *is left looking after them, as the* CONGREGATION *disperses.*

WILL. He walked back sadly to his lodgings. He had made a wretched blunder.

This was what a man got by worshipping the sight of a woman.

DOROTHEA. Dorothea felt Will's presence at church was quite excusable – a movement towards a reconciliation with her husband. But now she felt she could never again introduce the subject.

Scene Thirty-Three

WILL. Will was receding into the distant world of warm activity and fellowship –

DOROTHEA. – while she was to live more and more in a virtual tomb.

The library at Lowick Manor. The light is slowly fading.

CASAUBON (*at the table with a notebook*). You will oblige
me, my dear, if, instead of other reading this evening, you
will go through this aloud, pencil in hand, and where I say
'mark' will make a cross with your pencil. This is a first step
in a sifting process, which I have long had in view, and as we
go on I shall be able to indicate to you certain principles of
selection.

MRS CADWALLADER. After she had read and marked for
two hours, he said:

CASAUBON. We will take the volume upstairs – and the pencil
if you please – and in case of reading in the night, we can
pursue this task. It's not wearisome to you, I trust, Dorothea?

DOROTHEA. I prefer always reading what you like best to hear.

Scene Thirty-Three (A)

CELIA. The reading in the night did come.

The upstairs room. Firelight. CASAUBON *sitting by the fire.*
DOROTHEA *approaches with a candle.*

DOROTHEA. Are you ill, Edward?

CASAUBON. I felt some uneasiness in a reclining posture. I'll
sit here for a time.

DOROTHEA. You'd like me to read to you?

CASAUBON. You would oblige me greatly by doing so. I'm
wakeful – my mind is remarkably lucid.

DOROTHEA. I fear the excitement may be too great for you.

CASAUBON. No, I'm not conscious of undue excitement.
Thought is easy. Where were we? Ah yes. You marked that.

She goes to kneel the other side of the fireplace.

Pass on to the next head. I omit the second excursus on Crete…

DOROTHEA (*starts reading*). 'Notwithstanding the unfounded assertions of those who – '

CASAUBON. Omit that.

DOROTHEA. 'It can hardly be denied that the persistent influence of the – '

CASAUBON. Yes, mark that.

DOROTHEA. Dorothea was amazed at the bird-like speed with which his mind was surveying the ground where it had been creeping for years. Some hours passed.

CASAUBON. Close the book now, my dear, we will resume our work tomorrow. I have deferred it too long, and would gladly see it completed. But you observe the principle on which my selection is made? It is to give adequate and not disproportionate illustration to each of the theses enumerated in my introduction, as at present sketched. You have perceived that distinctly, Dorothea?

DOROTHEA. Yes.

CASAUBON. And now, I think I can take some repose.

She lays a blanket over him. Takes the candle and starts to leave.

Before I sleep, I have a request to make, Dorothea.

DOROTHEA (*dread*). What is it?

CASAUBON. It is that you will make me a deliberate promise – that in the case of my death, you will carry out my wishes. You will avoid doing anything that I deprecate, and apply yourself to what I should desire.

Silence.

You refuse?

DOROTHEA. No, I do not yet refuse. But it's too solemn – I think it's not right – to make a promise when I'm ignorant what it will bind me to. Whatever affection prompted, I would do without promising.

CASAUBON. But you'd use your own judgement. I ask you to obey mine. You refuse.

DOROTHEA. No, dear, no! But may I wait and reflect a little? I desire with my whole soul to do what will comfort you – but I cannot give any pledge suddenly, still less a pledge to do I know not what.

CASAUBON. You cannot then trust the nature of my wishes?

DOROTHEA (*pleads*). Grant me till tomorrow.

Silence.

CASAUBON. Till tomorrow then.

Pause. He starts to breathe more heavily.

DOROTHEA. He slept, but there was no more sleep for her.

LYDGATE. It was clear that he would expect her to devote herself to sifting those heaps of material, days, and months and years – sorting fragments wrought from crushed ruins –

WILL. Sorting them as food for a theory which was already withered in the birth like an elfin child.

DOROTHEA. But had she not married him that she might help him in his life's labour?

BROOKE. But had she not thought the work was to be something greater?

CELIA. Was it right, even to soothe his grief, to promise to work as in a treadmill, fruitlessly. Would it be possible?

DOROTHEA. But if he lived for fifteen years or more, her life would certainly be spent helping and obeying him.

SIR JAMES. Still, there was a deep difference between devotion to the living and an indefinite promise of devotion to the dead.

MRS CADWALLADER. Might he mean to demand more from her than she had been able to imagine?

DOROTHEA. No, his heart was bound up in his work only.

ROSAMOND. Suppose she were to say: 'If you die, I will put no finger to your work…'

DOROTHEA. She would crush that bruised heart.

Pause.

LYDGATE. At last the morning came.

CASAUBON (*rising unsteadily*). I had hoped to set to work at once this morning but I find myself under some indisposition. I'm going to take a turn in the shrubbery, since the air is milder.

DOROTHEA. I'm glad. Your mind was too active last night.

CASAUBON. I'd fain have it set at rest on the point I last spoke of, Dorothea. You can now, I hope, give me an answer.

DOROTHEA. May I come out to you in the garden presently?

CASAUBON. I shall be in the yew-tree walk for the next half-hour.

DOROTHEA. Dorothea felt too weak, too full of dread. She felt she was going to say 'yes' to her own doom.

CASAUBON. Nothing compelled her, only –

DOROTHEA. – she must not delay longer.

Scene Thirty-Four

The yew-tree walk. CASAUBON *is bent over in a chair, a book in his hand.*

DOROTHEA. I've come, Edward. I'm ready. I'm ready. Wake, dear. Listen. I'm come to answer.

She touches him. The book drops.

LYDGATE. But she never gave her answer.

As LYDGATE *steps forward,* DOROTHEA *turns to him, half-delirious.*

DOROTHEA. Tell him I'm ready to promise. Only thinking about it was so dreadful it has made me ill. But I shall soon be better. Go and tell him I'm ready to promise…

LYDGATE. But the silence in her husband's ear was never more to be broken.

Fade on CASAUBON.

End of Act One.

ACT TWO

Scene Thirty-Five

The library at Lowick Manor. Papers on the table. SIR JAMES *and* BROOKE.

SIR JAMES. I say there never was a meaner – a more ungentlemanly action than this – this codicil to the will – a positive insult to Dorothea! I wish to God we could hinder Dorothea from knowing.

BROOKE. That would be difficult, you know, Chettam, she's an executrix and likes to go into these things. She's twenty-one now, you know.

SIR JAMES. I'll tell you what – until Dorothea is well, all business must be kept from her, and as soon as she is able to be moved from upstairs – (*Indicates above.*) she must come to us at Freshitt. Being with Celia and the baby will be the best thing. And meanwhile you must get rid of Ladislaw.

BROOKE. That's easily said, Chettam, easily said. And sending him away won't hinder gossip. I might get rid of Ladislaw up to a certain point – take away *The Pioneer* and that sort of thing, but I couldn't send him out of the country if he didn't choose to go.

SIR JAMES. Good God! Let's get him a post. Let's spend money on him. Some colonial governor – Grampus might take him –

BROOKE. He won't be shipped off like a head of cattle, my dear fellow. Things may come round. Don't let us be firing off our guns in a hurry, you know.

SIR JAMES. Then am I to conclude that you decline to do anything!

BROOKE. I really don't see what I could do. Ladislaw is a gentleman.

SIR JAMES. I'm glad to hear it. I'm sure Casaubon was not!

BROOKE *shrugs*.

I can only say, Dorothea was sacrificed once because her family were too careless. I shall do what I can, as her brother, to protect her now.

BROOKE. You can't do better than to get her to Freshitt as soon as you can. I approve of that plan altogether!

Scene Thirty-Six

CELIA. Dorothea had been safe at Freshitt Hall nearly a week –

SIR JAMES. – before she asked dangerous questions.

The terrace at Freshitt Hall. CELIA *and her baby and baby basket;* DOROTHEA *in a mourning black cap.*

CELIA. Look, Dodo. Look at him. Did you ever see anything like that?

DOROTHEA. What, Kitty?

CELIA. What? Why, his upper lip. See how he's drawing it down as if he meant to make a face. Isn't it wonderful. He may have his little thoughts. Do look at him. Don't be sad, Dodo, kiss baby.

It seemed clear to Celia that where there was a baby, things were right enough, and where they were wrong, it was a mere lack of that central poising force.

What are you brooding over so? I'm sure you did everything and a great deal too much. You should be happy now.

DOROTHEA. I wonder if Sir James would drive me back to Lowick. I want to look over everything, see if there were any words written for me.

CELIA. Not till Mr Lydgate says you may go. Besides, you've got a wrong notion in your head as usual, Dodo, I can see that. (*To the baby.*) Isn't she wrong?

DOROTHEA (*meekly*). Where am I wrong, Kitty?

CELIA. You want to find out if there's anything uncomfortable to do now because Mr Casaubon wished it. But he's behaved very badly. James is as angry as he can be. (*Slight pause.*) I'd better tell you, to prepare you.

DOROTHEA (*alarmed*). Celia. Tell me what you mean.

CELIA. He's made a codicil to his will, to say that the property was all to go away from you, if you married.

DOROTHEA. That's of no consequence –

CELIA. But only if you married Mr Ladislaw – not anybody else. Of course that's of no consequence in one way – you never *would* marry Mr Ladislaw – but that only makes it worse of Mr Casaubon.

Silence.

James says it's abominable and not like a gentleman. And there never was a better judge than James. It's as if Mr Casaubon wanted to make people believe you would wish to marry Mr Ladislaw, which is ridiculous. Only James says it was to hinder Mr Ladislaw from wanting to marry you for your money – as if he ever would think of making you an offer. Oh, look, baby's almost asleep. (*Sets him in his basket.*)

DOROTHEA. Dorothea felt a violent shock of repulsion from her departed husband. It had never before entered her mind, that Will Ladislaw could, under any circumstances, be her lover.

CELIA. I never did like Mr Casaubon, and James never did. The corners of his mouth were dreadfully spiteful. And now he's behaved in this way, I'm sure religion doesn't require you to make yourself uncomfortable about him. If he's been taken away, that's a mercy, we shouldn't grieve, should we, baby?

The unconscious centre and poise of the world was really a Buddha in Western form.

CELIA (*as* LYDGATE *enters from the drive*). Ah, the doctor.

LYDGATE (*going to* DOROTHEA). I fear you're not so well as you were, Mrs Casaubon. Allow me to feel your pulse.

CELIA. She wants to go back to Lowick to look over papers. She ought not, ought she?

LYDGATE. I hardly know. She should do what would give her the most repose of mind. That will not always come from being forbidden to act.

DOROTHEA. Thank you. There are so many things I ought to attend to. Why should I sit here idle? For example, the church, I have a living to give away. You know everyone in Middlemarch, I think, Mr Lydgate. I shall ask you. You know Mr Tyke, the apostolic man, and there's Mr Farebrother, who must certainly be considered and… (*Bursts into sobs.*)

LYDGATE (*to* CELIA). I think she wants perfect freedom.

Mr Lydgate felt sure she had been suffering from the conflict of self-repression.

DOROTHEA (*going to the table*). At Lowick the desks and drawers were empty of personal words for her. She found only papers that confirmed he meant her to toil on at his researches.

MRS CADWALLADER. But now his cold grasp on her life had slipped away.

DOROTHEA (*to herself*). I can't work without hope at what I have no belief in.

Scene Thirty-Seven

WILL. No gossip about Mr Casaubon's codicil had yet reached Ladislaw. He busied himself entirely with the coming election.

MRS CADWALLADER. To keep Mr Brooke steadily to the idea of voting for the Reform Bill was not an easy task.

SIR JAMES. Before the day of nomination, Mr Brooke was to explain himself to the worthy electors of Middlemarch – (*Becomes one.*) from the balcony of The White Hart.

The Town Square. BROOKE *above. The* TOWNSPEOPLE *gather below.* WILL *distributes leaflets to them.*

BROOKE. This looks well, eh, Ladislaw? I shall have a good audience at any rate. I like this now… Gentlemen – electors of Middlemarch! (*Slight pause.*) I'm uncommonly glad to be here – I was never so proud and happy in my life – never so happy, you know.

A little applause.

I'm a close neighbour of yours – my good friends – I've always gone a good deal into public questions – machinery now, and machine-breaking – you're many of you concerned with machinery –

Reactions.

– and I've been going into that lately. It won't do, you know, breaking machines – everything must go on – trade, manufactures – that kind of thing – since Adam Smith that must go on.

An effigy of BROOKE *is raised on a pole.*

We must look all over the globe.

A parrot-like Punch-voiced echo: 'Globe.'

We must look everywhere 'From China to Peru' as somebody says – Johnson, I think, 'The Rambler', you know. That's what I've done up to a certain point – not as far as Peru –

'Peru' mockingly.

– but I've not always stayed at home, I saw it wouldn't do. I've been in the Levant, where some of your Middlemarch goods go – and then again in the Baltic. The Baltic now –

'The Baltic' mockingly; laughter.

SHOUTS. What about Middlemarch?

BROOKE. That reminds me… We want ideas, you know…

SHOUTS. We want the Bill!

BROOKE. There is something in what you say. Freedom to speak our minds. The Reform Bill now...

Crumpled leaflets thrown at BROOKE*'s effigy.*

You shall have the Bill.

Echo: 'You shall have the Bill.'

All that is very well...

A fiercer tone in the crowd; missiles thrown at BROOKE. *Chaos and* BROOKE *steps down. The* TOWNSPEOPLE *move away, chanting 'We want the Bill!'...*

As the tumult fades, BROOKE *comes down into the Square.* WILL *is clearing up crumpled leaflets.*

It's rather coarse work, this electioneering, eh, Ladislaw. I dare say I should withdraw. It won't do to carry it too far. (*Feeling his heart.*) Poor Casaubon was a warning, you know; I must pull up... However, we've dug a channel with *The Pioneer.* A more ordinary man than you might carry it on now – more ordinary, you know.

WILL. Do you wish me to give it up? I'm ready to do so.

Mr BROOKE. You might – might find a better field. But I'll write you any letters, you know.

WILL. I'm exceedingly obliged, but I need not trouble you. (*Goes.*)

If the impassable gulf between himself and Dorothea was ever to be filled up, it must be by his going away and getting into a thoroughly different position.

Scene Thirty-Eight

DOROTHEA. The deep longing which had really determined
Dorothea to return to Lowick, was the longing to see Will
Ladislaw. She was helpless, her hands had been tied from
making up any unfairness in his lot, but her soul thirsted to
see him.

LYDGATE. When the meeting finally happened, it was in a
formal way, quite unexpected by her.

The library at Lowick Manor. DOROTHEA *and* WILL
shake hands. They sit.

WILL. I hope I've not presumed too much in calling. I couldn't
bear to leave the neighbourhood without saying goodbye.

DOROTHEA. I should have thought it unkind if you'd not
wished to see me. Are you going away immediately?

WILL. Very soon. I intend to go to town and become a barrister,
since they say that's the preparation for all public business.
There will be a great deal of political work to be done and I
mean to do some of it. Other men have managed to win a
position without family, or money.

DOROTHEA. Besides, you have so many talents. I've heard
from my uncle how clearly you can explain things. And you
care that justice should be done to everyone. I'm so glad.
When we were in Rome, I thought you only cared for poetry
and art, but now I know you think about the rest of the
world.

WILL. You approve of my going away, for years then, and
never coming back till I have made some mark in the world?

Pause. She looks out of the window.

DOROTHEA. The rose bushes outside the window seemed to
have in them the summers of all the years Will would be away.

Yes, it must be right. I shall be very happy when I hear
you've made your value felt. But you must have patience.
(*Her voice trembles.*) It will perhaps be a long while.

WILL. You'll forget all about me.

DOROTHEA. I shall never forget you. I've never forgotten anyone. My life has never been crowded. And I've a great deal of space for memory at Lowick, haven't I? (*Smiles*.)

WILL. Good God! (*Stands and moves away, almost angry*.)

DOROTHEA (*after a moment*). I wonder if you'd like to have that portrait which hangs upstairs – of your grandmother. I think it's not right for me to keep it. It's wonderfully like you.

WILL. No, it's not consoling to have one's own likeness. It would be more consoling if others wanted it.

DOROTHEA. I thought... as a family memorial.

WILL. Why should I have that when I've nothing else?

DOROTHEA (*stung*). You're much the happier of us two, Mr Ladislaw, to have nothing.

WILL *is startled. They look at each other: 'A strange, questioning gravity'.*

WILL. I never felt it a misfortune to have nothing till now. But it may divide us from what we most care for.

DOROTHEA (*relenting*). Sorrow comes in so many ways. Two years ago I had no notion of the unexpected way in which trouble comes and ties our hands and makes us silent when we long to speak. I used to despise women a little for not shaping their lives more and doing better things. I was very fond of doing as I liked, but I've almost given it up.

WILL. I've not given up doing as I like but I can very seldom do it. The thing one most longs for may be surrounded by conditions that would be intolerable.

SIR JAMES. At that moment, Sir James was announced.

DOROTHEA *and* WILL *turn away from each other.*

(*Entering*.) Dorothea.

He shakes hands with DOROTHEA, *bows very slightly to* WILL, *who repays the bow.*

WILL. I must say goodbye, Mrs Casaubon. And probably for a long while.

DOROTHEA. Goodbye, Mr Ladislaw.

He goes. She turns to SIR JAMES.

How is Celia?

SIR JAMES. And Sir James was obliged to behave as if nothing had annoyed him.

WILL. Will had a proud resolve not to seem the needy adventurer seeking a rich widow. He knew nothing of the codicil.

DOROTHEA. But she had supposed that Mr Casaubon's codicil seemed to Will, as it did to her, a cruel bar to any friendship between them.

WILL. Their young delight in speaking to each other was forever ended.

DOROTHEA. She did not know then that it was love. She only felt there was something irrevocably amiss.

Scene Thirty-Nine

The terrace at Freshitt Hall. CELIA *with the baby in the basket,* DOROTHEA, SIR JAMES *and* MRS CADWALLADER.

CELIA. I wish you'd come to Freshitt more often, Dodo. You never see baby washed, and that's quite the best part of the day.

DOROTHEA. But to an aunt who does not recognise her infant nephew as Buddha, and has nothing to do for him but to admire, the interest of watching him is apt to be exhaustible.

I prefer to be alone now and in my own home. Now Mr Farebrother is to be the new Rector at Lowick, I wish to get to know the Farebrothers better and talk about what's to be done in Middlemarch. And then –

CELIA. Do throw off that widow's cap, Dodo. I'm sure it must make you feel ill.

DOROTHEA. I'm so used to it – it's become a sort of shell. I feel rather exposed when it's off.

CELIA. I must see you without it. (*Takes it off.*)

SIR JAMES. Ah!

CELIA. Dodo needn't make such a slavery of her mourning. She needn't wear it any more among her friends.

SIR JAMES. A widow must wear her mourning for at least a year.

MRS CADWALLADER. Not if she marries again before the end of it.

SIR JAMES. That's very rare, I hope.

MRS CADWALLADER. But if she can marry blood, beauty and bravery, the sooner the better. I can think of several... There's Lord –

SIR JAMES. I think the subject of our conversation is very ill-chosen. Suppose we change it.

DOROTHEA. Not on my account, Sir James. If you're speaking on my behalf I can assure you that no question can be more indifferent than second marriage.

SIR JAMES *bows and leaves. After a moment,* MRS CADWALLADER *follows.*

No, Kitty, I shall never marry again.

CELIA. Really? Not anybody at all – if he were very wonderful indeed?

DOROTHEA. Not anybody at all. I have delightful plans. I should like to take a deal of land, and make a little colony, where everyone should work, and all the work should be done well. I'm going to have great consultations with Mr Garth.

CELIA. Then you *will* be happy if you have a plan, Dodo. (*To the baby.*) Perhaps little Arthur will like plans when he grows up and then he can help you.

Scene Forty

WILL. Will still lingered in Middlemarch.

MRS CADWALLADER. We all know the difficulty of carrying out a resolve when we secretly long for it to be unnecessary.

LYDGATE. One day he was at the Lydgates' when the doctor was away.

The Lydgates' drawing room. WILL *lying by the fire, and* ROSAMOND *on the sofa with embroidery.*

ROSAMOND. I know why you haven't gone to London yet. I know all about it. There's a powerful magnet in the neighbourhood.

WILL (*light gallantry*). Nobody knows better than you!

ROSAMOND. It really is the most charming romance. Mr Casaubon jealous, and foreseeing that there was no one else who would so much like to marry her as a certain gentleman and then laying a plan to spoil all by making her forfeit her property if she did marry that gentleman – and then – and then – oh, I've no doubt the end will be thoroughly romantic.

WILL. Great God! What do you mean? Don't joke. Tell me what you mean.

ROSAMOND (*no longer playful*). You really don't know?

WILL. No!

ROSAMOND. You don't know that Mr Casaubon has left it in his will that if Mrs Casaubon marries you she is to forfeit all her property?

WILL. How do you know that it's true?

ROSAMOND. My brother Fred heard it from the Farebrothers.

WILL *starts up from the floor.*

I dare say she likes you more than the property.

WILL. Pray don't say any more about it. It's a foul insult to her and to me. (*Sits, staring absently.*)

ROSAMOND. Now you're angry with *me*. It's too bad. You ought to be obliged to me for telling you.

WILL (*abruptly*). So I am.

ROSAMOND (*playful again*). I expect to hear of the marriage…

WILL. Never! You will never hear of the marriage!

He goes. ROSAMOND *sighs, bored*.

Scene Forty-One

WILL. But Will was about to hear more of his family background which would make any relation with Dorothea still more impossible.

BULSTRODE (*at his desk*). Mr Bulstrode, the rich town banker, had asked Will to secure a painting at auction on behalf of his wife.

If it won't interfere with the arrangements for your departure – which I know is imminent…

MRS CADWALLADER. At Middlemarch a large auction was regarded as a kind of festival.

Town Square. Fairground music. A CROWD *gathers around the auctioneer,* TRUMBULL, *and his assistant,* JENNY.

TRUMBULL. Now, ladies, I shall appeal to you – here is a fender – for quality of steel and quaintness of design – half a crown you said – thank you – going at half a crown – yes, Mr Ladislaw, by and by – hold it up well, Jenny, three shillings – four shillings…

WOMAN. The edge is like a knife, Mr Trumbull – if a child's head fell against it – (*Winces.*)

TRUMBULL. Uncommonly useful to have a fender that will cut – if you have a shoetie that wants cutting, gentlemen, here's a fender that if you had the misfortune to hang yourselves would cut you down in no time – four and sixpence – with astonishing celerity – six shillings – thank you, sir – going at six shillings – going – gone! Be handy, Jenny.

A conspicuous stranger, RAFFLES, *has come in and is staring at* WILL.

Now, ladies. Lot 235. Here's an engraving of the Duke of Wellington on the field of Waterloo, and notwithstanding recent events which have, as it were, enveloped our great hero in a cloud, I will be bold to say that a finer subject the understanding of man could hardly conceive. Angels perhaps, not men.

MAN. I'll bid a pound.

TRUMBULL (*quickly*). It's yours, sir. Now, *The Supper at Emmaus.* Yes, Mr Ladislaw, yes, this interests you as a connoisseur, I think. A painting of the Italian school, by the celebrated Guydo, the greatest of the Old Masters. I've seen a great many of the Old Masters, some of them are darker than you might like and not family subjects. But here is a Guydo which any lady might be proud to hang up. Mr Ladislaw, having been abroad, understands the merit of these things.

WILL. Five pounds.

TRUMBULL. The frame alone is worth that! Five guineas. Six pounds – six guineas. Such a low figure – it's an insult to religion. Seven… eight… guineas.

WILL. Ten guineas.

Pause.

TRUMBULL. Going – going – gone. It's yours, Mr Ladislaw. And that's it, ladies and gentlemen, for the present. Thank you, thank you.

CROWD *disperses, leaving* WILL *with* RAFFLES.

RAFFLES. Excuse me, Mr Ladislaw – was your mother's name Sarah Dunkirk?

WILL. Yes, sir, it was. What's that to you?

RAFFLES. No offence, sir, no offence. I knew her when she
   was a girl. Still alive?

WILL. No!

RAFFLES. Should be glad to do you a service, Mr Ladislaw.
   I've been abroad myself, seen the world, used to *parlez-vous*
   a little... I've often wondered what became of your mother.
   She ran away when she was a young lass – proud, spirited
   lass and pretty, by Jove. *I* knew the reason why. (*Slow wink*.)

WILL. You know nothing dishonourable of her, sir.

RAFFLES. Not a bit. She was a little too honourable to like her
   family – that was it. (*Slow wink again*.) I knew all about
   them – a little in what you might call the respectable
   thieving line. High style of receiving house in the West End
   of London – first-rate – those stolen goods brought high
   profits and no mistake. But Lord, Sarah would have known
   nothing about it – a dashing young lady she was – fine
   boarding school – fit for a lord's wife – only when she
   found out, she ran away from the whole concern. They
   didn't mind at first – godly folk, sir, very 'religious', they
   were, and she was for the stage. Your mother... What do
   you say, Mr Ladislaw – (*Pointing*.) shall we turn in to The
   Blue Bull and have a glass?

WILL. No, I must collect the picture and say good evening. (*As*
   RAFFLES *walks away*.) What's your name, sir?

RAFFLES. Raffles...

Scene Forty-Two

WILL. Will delivered the picture to Mr Bulstrode the banker at
   his mansion.

BULSTRODE. Now, Bulstrode was a solidly religious man,
   and a public benefactor.

WILL. So that the interview was of an unexpected nature.

BULSTRODE*'s house*. BULSTRODE *and* WILL.

Will Mrs Bulstrode be satisfied?

BULSTRODE. Thank you, quite satisfied.

WILL *is about to go*.

– and – I have a communication of a sacredly confidential nature to make to you. Nothing I dare say has been further from your thoughts, than that there had been important ties in the past, which connect your history with mine.

WILL. No indeed.

BULSTRODE. You see before you, Mr Ladislaw, a man who is deeply stricken. But for the knowledge that I am before the bar of One who seeth not as man seeth, I should be under no compulsion to make any disclosure. So far as human laws go, you have no claim on me. (*Motions* WILL *to sit*.) I am told that your mother's name was Sarah Dunkirk and that she ran away from her family to go on the stage. Can you confirm this?

WILL. Yes, it's true.

BULSTRODE. Did she never mention *her* mother to you?

WILL. I heard her say she thought her mother never knew the reason of her running away. She said 'poor Mother'…

BULSTRODE. That mother was my first wife. You have a claim on me, Mr Ladislaw. I was enriched by that marriage, which I probably would not have been, if my wife could have discovered her daughter. That daughter, I gather, is no longer living?

WILL (*rising*). No.

BULSTRODE. Pray be seated, Mr Ladislaw. I entreat your patience with one who is already bowed down by inward trial. It is my wish, Mr Ladislaw, to make amends for the deprivation which befell your mother.

WILL *sits again*.

I know you are without fortune and I wish to supply you adequately from a store which would have been yours had my wife been able to find her daughter.

Pause.

WILL. I suppose you knew of my mother's existence, and where she might have been found.

BULSTRODE (*faltering*). I will not deny it. I wish to make atonement. I'm ready to allow you five hundred pounds yearly during my life, and the capital at my death.

Silence.

WILL. Before I reply, Mr Bulstrode, answer this. Were you connected with the business by which that fortune was made?

BULSTRODE (*after a moment*). Yes.

WILL. And was that business a thoroughly dishonourable one? One that might have ranked those concerned with it with thieves and convicts?

BULSTRODE (*angrily*). The business was established before I became acquainted with it, sir; nor is it for you to institute an enquiry of that kind.

WILL (*stands*). Yes it is. It is eminently mine, when I have to decide whether I will accept your money. My unblemished honour is important to me. It is important to me to have no stain on my birth and connections. And now I find there is a stain which I can't help. My mother felt it and tried to keep clear of it, and so will I. You shall keep your ill-gotten money. If I had a fortune of my own, I would willingly pay it to anyone who could disprove what you have told me. Goodnight, sir. (*Goes quickly*.)

In the rush of impulses by which he flung back that offer, there was mingled the sense that it would have been impossible for him ever to tell Dorothea that he'd accepted it.

Scene Forty-Three

DOROTHEA. Meanwhile, Dorothea had been visiting Freshitt Hall to talk to Mr Garth about the management of her land.

The terrace at Freshitt Hall. SIR JAMES, CELIA, *involved with the baby, and* MRS CADWALLADER.

SIR JAMES (*quietly to* MRS CADWALLADER). Mrs Cadwallader, I wonder if you could talk to Dorothea – (*Indicates* DOROTHEA *approaching up the drive.*) Only Dorothea should know there are reasons why she should not receive Ladislaw again, and I really can't say it to her.

MRS CADWALLADER. Enough – I understand. You shall be innocent.

SIR JAMES. It will come lightly from you.

MRS CADWALLADER. Dorothea! Do sit down.

DOROTHEA. Mrs Cadwallader. (*Sits.*)

MRS CADWALLADER. I hear Mr Brooke is quite cured of his Parliamentary fever and 'Pioneering'.

DOROTHEA. Yes –

MRS CADWALLADER. I'm told *The Pioneer* will be dying, because Mr Brooke's protégé, the brilliant young Ladislaw, was gone, or going. Have you heard that, Sir James?

SIR JAMES. Something of that sort.

MRS CADWALLADER. All false! He's not gone. He's making a scandal by warbling continually with Mr Lydgate's wife, who they tell me is as pretty as can be. It seems nobody goes into the house without finding this young gentleman lying on the rug, or warbling at the piano. But people in manufacturing towns are always disreputable.

DOROTHEA. I don't believe it. I'll not hear any evil spoken of Mr Ladislaw – he's already suffered too much injustice.

She rises. SIR JAMES *repentant.*

MRS CADWALLADER. Heaven grant it may not be true. But it's a pity young Lydgate should have married one of those

Middlemarch girls. He might have got a woman with good blood, and not too young, who'd have put up with his profession. I can think of several... However, it's no use being wise for other people.

DOROTHEA. I must go on to Tipton. (*Goes*.) It's not true, it's not true! He said he'd never do anything that I disapproved!

Scene Forty-Four

WILL. By chance, Will was at Tipton Grange fetching some of his own sketches which he had missed in the act of packing to leave.

Tipton Grange library. WILL *smiling ruefully at that sketch of the yew tree in a portfolio.* DOROTHEA *enters. A moment of silence.*

DOROTHEA. I'm very glad you were here.

WILL. I'm going away immediately.

DOROTHEA. I thought we'd parted weeks ago.

WILL. I was dreaming then that I might come back some day. Now I don't think I ever shall.

DOROTHEA (*timidly*). You wish me to know the reasons?

WILL. Of course. (*Motions her to sit.*) I've been grossly insulted in your eyes and in the eyes of others. There has been a mean implication against my character. I wish you to know that in no circumstances would I have lowered myself by – would I have given men the chance of saying that I sought money under the pretext of – something else. (*Goes to the window.*) There was no need of other safeguard against me. The safeguard of wealth was enough.

DOROTHEA (*rising*). I'm sure no safeguard was ever needed against you.

He goes to the table and fastens up his portfolio.

WILL. I must go.

DOROTHEA. What shall you do?

WILL. I shall work away at the first thing that offers. I suppose one gets a habit of doing things without hope.

DOROTHEA. Oh, what sad words.

WILL. There are certain things which a man can only go through once in his life and then he must know that the best is over. This has happened to me when I'm very young, that's all. What I care for more than I can ever care for anything else – is absolutely forbidden me, by my own pride and honour. Of course, I shall go on living as a man might do who had seen Heaven in a trance.

Pause.

Will felt it would be impossible for Dorothea to misunderstand this.

DOROTHEA. But Dorothea felt the sickening certainty that Will was referring to Mrs Lydgate.

Pause.

WILL. I must go. The day after tomorrow I leave Middlemarch.

DOROTHEA. You've acted in every way rightly.

She holds out her hand. They shake hands. He takes his portfolio and starts to go.

Please remember me.

WILL (*irritated*). Why say that? As if I were not in danger of forgetting everything else but you! (*Goes quickly.*)

DOROTHEA (*to herself*). But me. So it is really me he loves!

WILL. Later that day, Dorothea's carriage happened to overtake Will on the road.

DOROTHEA. I only wish I had known before – I wish he knew. Then we could be quite happy thinking of each other, though we're forever parted.

WILL. But Will was bitter. He had no assurance that she loved him.

LYDGATE. That evening he spent with the Lydgates.

WILL. The next evening he was gone.

Scene Forty-Five

BROOKE. Many months passed…

DOROTHEA. In the following spring, Dorothea was returned from a trip to Yorkshire, to be met at Lowick Manor by Mr Brooke.

The library at Lowick Manor.

BROOKE. Well, my dear, I've just come from a meeting – about the cholera case, you know.

DOROTHEA. Was Mr Lydgate there? I want to see him and increase my contribution to the hospital. I promised Mr Bulstrode –

BROOKE. Oh, my dear, we've been hearing bad news about Bulstrode, bad news, you know. And Mr Lydgate is implicated too.

DOROTHEA. What do you mean?

BROOKE. It seems that Mr Bulstrode has been disgraced. He'd been involved in some disreputable dealings.

DOROTHEA. Oh, Uncle.

BROOKE. I won't go into it, but someone died in Bulstrode's house in mysterious circumstances, and they say that money was paid to Lydgate to keep silent about it.

DOROTHEA (*shocked*). You don't believe that Mr Lydgate is guilty of anything base? I will not believe it!

BROOKE. Who knows, my dear –

DOROTHEA. Let's find out the truth and clear him! People are almost always better than their neighbours think they are. I'll invite him to Lowick. I cannot be indifferent to the troubles of a man who advised me in my trouble.

BROOKE. He must act for himself. You must not let your ideas run away with you. It won't do, you know…

Scene Forty-Six

The library at Lowick Manor. LYDGATE *shakes hands with* DOROTHEA.

DOROTHEA. I've wished very much to see you about the new hospital. I know so much there depends on you.

LYDGATE. I cannot advise you to increase your support. I may be obliged to leave the town.

DOROTHEA. Not because there is no one to believe in you? I know the unhappy mistakes about you. You would not do anything dishonourable.

LYDGATE (*deep breath*). Thank you.

DOROTHEA. I beseech you to tell me how everything was. I'm sure the truth would clear you. Then we can consult together.

He sits. Pause.

Do trust me. At the very least I could say you've made all the circumstances clear and I know you're not in any way guilty. My uncle would believe me and Sir James Chettam, and Mr Farebrother.

Slight pause.

LYDGATE. Well… I was called to a patient at Mr Bulstrode's house, a man named Raffles. At that time Bulstrode offered to help me with my finances. I was in desperate need, and accepted. My orders as to the man's treatment were later disobeyed and he died. How my orders came to be disobeyed is a question to which I don't know the answer. It is still possible that Bulstrode was innocent of any criminal intention. But all that has nothing to do with the public belief. That is grounded on the knowledge that I took money, that Bulstrode was being blackmailed by Raffles and had strong motives for wishing the man to die, and that he gave me the money as a bribe to hold my tongue. They are just the suspicions that can never be disproved. I'm simply blighted.

DOROTHEA. Oh, it is hard. And that all this should have come to you who had meant to lead a higher life than the common. I remember what you said when you first spoke to me about the hospital. There is no sorrow I've thought more about than that – to love what is great and good, and try to reach it, and yet to fail.

LYDGATE. Yes. I had some ambition. I meant everything to be different with me. But the most terrible obstacles are such that nobody can see except oneself.

DOROTHEA. Suppose we kept on the hospital, and you stayed, the evil feeling towards you would gradually die out. I have seven hundred of my own fortune and nineteen hundred Mr Casaubon left me. I wanted to buy land and found a village, but Sir James and my uncle have convinced me the risk would be too great. So you see I should rejoice to have something good to do with my money. (*Slight pause.*) The hospital would be one good and making your life whole and well again another.

LYDGATE. If only it could be done. (*Looks away. Suddenly.*) Why should I not tell you? – You know what sort of bond marriage is. It's impossible for me now to do anything without considering my wife's happiness. I can't see her miserable. She married me without knowing what she was going into, and it might have been better for her if she'd not married me.

DOROTHEA (*thinking of her own life*). I know, I know. You couldn't give her pain.

LYDGATE. And she wishes to go. The troubles she has had here have wearied her.

DOROTHEA. But when she saw the good that might come of staying? –

LYDGATE. She wouldn't see it. (*Slight pause*.) The fact is – we've not been able to speak to each other about it – she may fear I've really done something base. It's my fault. I ought to be more open.

DOROTHEA. May I go and see her? I would tell her you shall be cleared in every fair mind. I would cheer her heart. Will you ask her if I may see her?

LYDGATE. I'm sure you may. She would feel honoured – cheered by the proof that you have some respect for me. I'll not speak to her about your coming, that she may not connect it with my wishes at all. I know I ought to – but...

Pause.

DOROTHEA. How well Dorothea knew the invisible barriers to speech there might be between husband and wife.

I remember how pretty she is. I hope she will like me.

Scene Forty-Seven

MRS CADWALLADER. It was a clear spring morning, when Dorothea called next day to see Mrs Lydgate. (*Carries a letter*.)

LYDGATE. She had a plan to relieve Lydgate from his obligation to Bulstrode.

DOROTHEA. The scent of the moist earth, the fresh leaves just showing, seemed part of the cheerfulness she was feeling.

I shall bring her good news about her husband. Perhaps she will like to talk to me and make a friend of me.

SERVANT. The servant stood at the open street door.

DOROTHEA. Is Mrs Lydgate in?

SERVANT. I'm not sure, my lady. I've been out. If you'll please walk in…

DOROTHEA. The drawing-room door was unlatched.

Advancing unconsciously, she stopped in the terrible illumination of a certainty.

The Lydgates' drawing room. WILL *on the sofa with* ROSAMOND, *she flushed and tearful, he holding her upraised hands between his, speaking fervently to her.*

WILL. – my love is deeply committed –

DOROTHEA. Oh, I –

ROSAMOND *and* WILL *stand in shock.*

Excuse me, Mrs Lydgate, the servant didn't know you were here. I had a letter for Mr Lydgate, which I wished to put into your own hands.

She puts down the letter, and leaves. ROSAMOND *and* WILL *stand motionless. Eventually,* ROSAMOND *touches* WILL*'s sleeve.*

WILL. Don't touch me!

ROSAMOND. You can easily go after Mrs Casaubon and explain your preference.

WILL. Go after her! Do you think she would value any word I ever uttered to her again? Explain? How can a man explain at the expense of a woman?

ROSAMOND. You can tell her what you please.

WILL. Do you suppose she would like me better for sacrificing you? (*Moves about restlessly.*) I had no hope before – not much – of anything better to come. But I had one certainty – that she believed in me. That's gone. (*New fury.*) Explain? Tell a man to explain how he dropped into Hell. Explain my preference! I never had a *preference* for her, any more than I have a preference for breathing. No other woman exists by the side of her. I would rather touch her hand if it were dead, than I would touch any other woman's living.

He moves to go, then stops. His mute fury. She sits.

(*At length.*) Shall I come and see Lydgate this evening?

ROSAMOND. If you like.

He goes.

WILL. That evening it seemed to Will that he was sliding into that pleasureless yielding to small solicitations of circumstance, which is a commoner history of perdition than any single momentous bargaining.

LYDGATE. He dreaded Lydgate's unsuspecting goodwill –

WILL. He dreaded his own distaste for his spoiled life.

A foreboding was on him that his life might come to be enslaved by this helpless woman –

ROSAMOND. – who had thrown herself upon him in the dreary sadness of her heart.

Scene Forty-Eight

DOROTHEA. Dorothea had driven on to Freshitt Hall. She had drunk a great draught of scorn and took it as a sign of strength.

The terrace at Freshitt Hall. CELIA *and baby.* DOROTHEA *pacing.*

CELIA. Dodo, how very bright your eyes are. And you don't see anything you look at, Arthur or anything. You're going to do something uncomfortable, I know. Is it all about Mr Lydgate, or has something else happened?

DOROTHEA. Yes, dear, a great many things have happened.

CELIA. I wonder what…

DOROTHEA. Oh, all the troubles of all people on the face of the earth.

CELIA. Dear me, Dodo, are you going to have a scheme for them?

Celia was a little uneasy at this Hamlet-like raving.

SIR JAMES. Dorothea went from Freshitt to see the Reverend Farebrother, the new Rector of Lowick –

She may shake hands with FAREBROTHER.

DOROTHEA (*moving on*). – and from there to the schoolhouse to see about a new bell, giving eager attention to small details and getting up a dramatic sense that her life was very busy.

SIR JAMES. That evening she returned to the Farebrothers' to dine, where the talk turned –

WILL. – to Will Ladislaw.

DOROTHEA (*as she turns to see him*). I must go – I've overtired myself.

When she got home, and in her room, she locked the door.

The upstairs room at Lowick Manor. The light is fading into night.

(*Moans out.*) Oh, I did love him! (*Waves of suffering shake her. She sinks to the floor.*) I did love him.

MRS CADWALLADER. Her belief which she had planted and kept from a very little seed in Rome, was lost.

BROOKE. Her hope that along some pathway they should meet with unchanged recognition, was lost.

SIR JAMES. She sought hardness and weariness to bring relief from the mysterious might of her anguish.

ROSAMOND. She lay on the bare floor and let the night grow cold around her.

DOROTHEA (*angrily*). Why did he intrude his life into mine? His cheap regard, his deluding words? Why? (*Sobs.*)

Eventually she rises.

How shall I act now?

She opens the curtains at the three windows, one by one. The light comes in.

Far off in the bending sky was the pearly light; and she felt the largeness of the world, and the manifold waking of men to labour and endurance.

CELIA. She had not the less an active life before her, because she had buried a private joy.

Scene Forty-Nine

LYDGATE. By eleven o'clock she was walking to Middlemarch, having made up her mind she would make a second attempt to see Rosamond.

ROSAMOND. Rosamond dared not say no.

The Lydgates' drawing room. ROSAMOND, in dread of 'jealous hatred', coldly motions to DOROTHEA, and they both sit.

DOROTHEA (*at length*). I had an errand yesterday I didn't finish.

ROSAMOND *is silent.*

I came to talk to you about the injustice which has been shown to Mr Lydgate. You'll let me speak of this?

ROSAMOND (*relieved*). I know you've been very good. I shall like to hear anything about my husband.

DOROTHEA. I'd asked him to come to Lowick about the hospital, he told me everything about the sad event which has made ignorant people cast suspicions on him. He told me because I was very bold and asked. The truth is, he knew nothing of this man Raffles – and thought Mr Bulstrode offered him money in good faith. All his anxiety about the patient was to treat him rightly. And I've told Mr Farebrother and Mr Brooke and Sir James Chettam – they all believe in your husband. That will cheer you, will it not?

ROSAMOND. Thank you, you are very kind.

DOROTHEA. He felt he'd been wrong not to pour out everything to you. It was because he feels his life bound into one with yours and it hurts him more than anything that his misfortunes must hurt you. That's why I came yesterday. Trouble is so hard to bear, is it not? (*Taking* ROSAMOND*'s hand, 'speaking from the heart of her own trial to Rosamond's'.*) How can we live and think that anyone has trouble – piercing trouble – and we could help them, and never try...

ROSAMOND *bursts into violent tears. After a while she calms; they look at each other, without barriers.*

(*Timidly.*) We were talking about your husband. He said he'd been feeling very lonely in his trial, but I think he would have borne it better if he'd been able to be quite open with you.

ROSAMOND. He is so angry and impatient if I say anything. He ought not to wonder that I object to speak to him on painful subjects.

DOROTHEA. It was himself he blamed. He said he could not be happy doing anything which made you unhappy. He could say that to me because he knows I had much trial in my marriage, from my husband's illness, which hindered his plans and saddened him. He knows that I have felt how hard it is to walk always in fear of hurting another who is tied to us. (*Pause.*) Marriage is so unlike everything else. There is something even awe-ful in the nearness it brings. Even if we loved someone else better than – than those we were married to it would be no use – (*Low voice.*) I mean marriage drinks up all our power of giving or getting any blessedness in that sort of love. I know it may be very dear – but it murders our marriage – and then the marriage stays with us like a murder – and everything else is gone. And then our husband – if he loved and trusted us, and we've not helped him, but made a

curse in his life… (*Dreads going too far, then more rapidly.*)
I know, I know that the feeling may be very dear – it has
taken hold of us unawares – it's so hard, it may seem like
death to part with it – and we are weak – I am weak –

Waves of her own sorrow stop her. ROSAMOND *kisses her
forehead. They clasp each other 'as if in a shipwreck'.*

ROSAMOND (*half-whisper*). You're thinking what is not true.
(*Moves away, then turns.*) When you came in yesterday – it
was not as you thought. He was telling me how he loved
another woman that I might know he could never love me.
And now I think he hates me because you mistook him
yesterday. He says that you will think he is a false person. But
he's never had any love for me – I know he has not. He said
yesterday that no other woman existed for him besides you…
But now I've told you and he can't reproach me any more.

DOROTHEA. The tumult in Dorothea was too strong to be
called joy. She could only perceive this would be joy when
she had recovered her power of feeling it.

No, he can't reproach you any more.

Scene Fifty

ROSAMOND. Rosamond wrote to Will.

WILL *reading the letter.*

(*Her voice from the shadows.*) I have told Mrs Casaubon.
She is not under any mistake about you. I told her because
she came to see me and was very kind. You will have
nothing to reproach me with now. I shall not have made any
difference to you.

WILL. But Will was still in a state of doubt.

He was little more easy than a man who has escaped from
wreck by night, and stands on unknown ground in the
darkness.

DOROTHEA. On the second morning after the visit to
Rosamond, Dorothea felt rather angry with herself for her
childish restlessness.

The library at Lowick Manor.

There is nothing to be done in the village, everybody is well
and has flannel, nobody's pig has died. (*Muses*.) Political
economy… (*Looks at her books*.) No this is hopeless.
(*Paces*.) Should I go to Tipton? No, I prefer to stay here at
Lowick, for some reason. The geography of Asia Minor? My
husband used to rebuke me about my slackness on the
geography… (*Examines a wall map*.)

WILL. Will Ladislaw was announced.

WILL *appears. They face each other. She stands quite still,
doesn't offer her hand.*

I'm so grateful to you for seeing me.

DOROTHEA. I wanted to see you.

WILL. I fear you'll think me foolish for coming back to
Middlemarch so soon. I've been punished for my
impatience. I returned partly in the hope of getting Bulstrode
to apply some money to a public purpose – he'd offered me
compensation for an old injury – but I suppose you know the
disagreeable story about my parentage. (*Slight pause*.) You
know it must be altogether painful to me.

DOROTHEA. Yes, yes, I know.

WILL. I did not choose to accept an income from such a source.
I was sure you would not think well of me if I did so…

DOROTHEA (*brightening*). You acted as I should have
expected you to act.

WILL. I didn't believe you'd let any circumstances of my birth
create a prejudice in you against me. Though it was sure to
do in others.

DOROTHEA. Nothing could have changed me, but – (*Low
voice*.) thinking you were not as good as I had believed you
to be.

WILL. You are sure to believe me better than I am, in everything but my truth to you. When I thought you doubted that, I didn't care about anything. I thought there was nothing to try for – only things to endure.

DOROTHEA. I don't doubt you any longer.

She puts out her hand, he kisses it. She withdraws it in confusion, and moves away to the window.

See how dark the clouds have become, and how the trees are tossed.

They both look out of the window. Distant rumble of thunder. Then a closer flash of lightning and thunder. They start; then look at each other and smile.

That was wrong to say you'd nothing to try for. If we'd lost our own chief good, other people's good would remain, and that's worth trying for. I seemed to see that more clearly than ever when I was the most wretched. I can hardly think how I could have borne the trouble, if that feeling had not come to make strength.

WILL. You've never felt the misery of knowing you must despise me.

DOROTHEA. But I have felt worse – it was worse to think ill of –

She breaks off. Silence.

WILL. We may at least have the comfort of speaking to each other without disguise. Since I must go away – since we must always be divided – you may think of me as –

Flash of lightning. They step back from the window. Crack and roar. The rain pours. Watching, they are holding hands, then turn to each other.

Even if you loved me as well as I love you, I shall most likely always be poor. It's impossible for us ever to belong to each other. It's perhaps base of me to have asked for a word from you. I meant to go away into silence, but I've not been able to do what I meant.

DOROTHEA. Don't be sorry. I would rather share all the pain of our parting.

Neither taking the lead, their lips meet. Rain dashes against the window, a swoop of wind. DOROTHEA *starts to move away, he takes her hand again to stop her. A long moment.*

WILL (*suddenly breaks away*). It's intolerable. As fatal as a murder, or any other horror that divides people. To have our life maimed by petty accidents.

DOROTHEA. Don't say that – your life need not be maimed.

WILL. Yes it must. It's cruel of you to speak as if there's any comfort. You may see beyond the misery of it, but I don't. We shall never be married.

DOROTHEA. Some time – we might.

WILL. When? What's the use of counting on any success of mine? It's a toss-up whether I shall ever do more than keep myself – unless I choose to sell myself as a mere pen and mouthpiece.

Silence. DOROTHEA *can't speak.*

(*Exasperated.*) Goodbye. (*Starts to go.*)

DOROTHEA. Oh, I can't bear it – my heart will break. (*Tears.*) I don't mind about poverty. I hate my wealth...

Suddenly they run to each other, and hold each other close.

I want so little – no new clothes – and I will learn what everything costs...

Scene Fifty-One

The terrace at Freshitt Hall. SIR JAMES, CELIA *with baby,* MRS CADWALLADER *and* BROOKE. *Motionless.*

SIR JAMES. What!!

MRS CADWALLADER. Merciful Heaven! Not to young Ladislaw!

BROOKE. Yes. She's quite determined to marry him. It's no use opposing. I put it strongly to her. I did my duty, Chettam. But she can act as she likes, you know.

SIR JAMES. It would have been better if I'd called him out a year ago, and shot him!

CELIA. Really, James, that would have been very disagreeable.

SIR JAMES. However, I'm not surprised. The day after Casaubon's funeral I said what ought to be done. But I was not listened to.

BROOKE. You wanted the impossible, you know, Chettam, you wanted him shipped off. I told you Ladislaw was not to be done as we liked with. He had ideas – he was a remarkable fellow.

SIR JAMES. Yes, it's rather a pity you formed that high opinion of him. We're indebted to that for him being lodged in the neighbourhood. A man who takes Dorothea out of her proper rank, into poverty! – has the meanness to accept such a sacrifice!

BROOKE. I pointed everything out to her. I said: 'My dear, you don't know what it is to live on seven hundred a year and have no carriage and that kind of thing, and go amongst people who don't know who you are.' But the fact is she has a dislike to Casaubon's property. You'll hear what she says, you know.

SIR JAMES. No, excuse me, I shall not. I can't bear to see her again. It hurts me too much that a woman like Dorothea should have done what is wrong.

CELIA. It is very dreadful of Dodo. She said she would never marry again – not anybody at all.

MRS CADWALLADER. Of course, if she likes to be poor that's her affair. Humphrey had hardly a thousand a year when I married him, but he was a Cadwallader. It must be admitted that Ladislaw's blood is a frightful mixture.

SIR JAMES. He's simply not a man we can take into the family!

BROOKE. Well, you know, *I* can't turn my back on Dorothea. I must be a father to her. Up to a certain point, you know...

Scene Fifty-Two

The library at Lowick Manor. CELIA *and* DOROTHEA.

CELIA. It's very serious, Dodo, how will you live? And I shall never see you – and you won't mind about little Arthur.

DOROTHEA. Dear Celia – if you don't ever see me it won't be my fault.

CELIA. Yes it will. How can I come to you when James can't bear it? He thinks you're so wrong, Dodo. But you always were wrong – (*Embracing her.*) only I can't help loving you. Where can you go?

DOROTHEA. I'm going to London.

CELIA. How can you always live in a street?! And you'll be so poor.

DOROTHEA. Bless you, Kitty. Take comfort. James will forgive me some time.

CELIA. But it would be much better if you'd not be married. You know what mistakes you've always been making, Dodo.

DOROTHEA. It's true. I might be a wiser person, Celia. But I'm going to marry him.

CELIA. Is he very fond of you, Dodo?

DOROTHEA. I hope so. I'm very fond of him.

CELIA. That's nice… Only I'd rather you had such a sort of husband as James is, with a place very near, that I could drive to…

Epilogue

DOROTHEA. Dorothea never repented that she had given up position and fortune to marry Will Ladislaw.

WILL. They were bound to each other by a love stronger than any impulses that could have marred it.

BROOKE. Will became an ardent public man, getting at last returned to Parliament.

CELIA. In time they had two children.

ROSAMOND. Many who knew Dorothea thought it a pity that so rare a creature should have been absorbed into the life of another.

MRS CADWALLADER. But no one stated exactly what else was in her power.

SIR JAMES. For there is no creature whose inward being is so strong that it is not greatly determined by what lies outside it.

LYDGATE. But the effect of her being on those around her was incalculable.

CELIA. For the good of the world is partly dependent on unhistoric acts –

WILL. – and that things are not so ill with you and me as they might have been –

DOROTHEA. – is half-owing to the number who lived faithfully a hidden life, and rest in unvisited tombs.

The End.

THE DOCTOR'S STORY

The Doctor's Story can be performed as part of the full
Middlemarch Trilogy, or as a separate stand-alone play.

If the latter, a single edition of the play can be printed on
demand for your requirements. Please contact
info@nickhernbooks.co.uk

Characters

MR BROOKE , *landowner*
DOROTHEA BROOKE, *his niece*
THE REV MR CASAUBON, *Rector of Lowick*
MR VINCY, *Mayor of Middlemarch*
MRS VINCY, *the Mayor's wife*
ROSAMOND VINCY, *their daughter*
FRED VINCY, *their son*
MR LYDGATE, *doctor*
MR BULSTRODE, *banker*
MRS BULSTRODE, *his wife*
DR SPRAGUE, *doctor*
MR WRENCH, *doctor*
DR MINCHIN, *doctor*
MR FEATHERSTONE, *rich landowner*
THE REV MR FAREBROTHER, *vicar*
MRS FAREBROTHER, *the vicar's mother*
FAREBROTHER'S AUNT AND SISTER
MR PLYMDALE SNR, *member of the Infirmary Board*
MRS PLYMDALE, *townswoman*
NED PLYMDALE, *her son*
MRS SPRAGUE, *Mrs Plymdale's friend*
WILL LADISLAW, *Casaubon's relative and friend of Lydgate*
MR TRUMBULL, *auctioneer and agent*
MR RAFFLES, *blackmailer*
MR GARTH, *land agent and builder*
MRS ABEL, *housekeeper of Stone Court*
SIR GODWIN, *Lydgate's uncle*
MRS DOLLOP, *innkeeper*
FIRST MAN
SECOND MAN
FIRST WOMAN
SECOND WOMAN

Plus: bailiffs, billiards players

Suggested Doubling

DOROTHEA

BROOKE / BULSTRODE

CASAUBON / SPRAGUE / FEATHERSTONE / SIR
GODWIN / BAILIFF / SECOND MAN

FRED / WRENCH / WILL / FIRST MAN

VINCY / RAFFLES / GARTH

ROSAMOND

LYDGATE

FAREBROTHER / PLYMDALE SNR / NED PLYMDALE /
TRUMBULL

MRS VINCY / MRS SPRAGUE / SECOND WOMAN

MRS BULSTRODE / MRS FAREBROTHER /
FAREBROTHER'S AUNT AND SISTER / MINCHIN /
MRS DOLLOP

MRS PLYMDALE / MRS ABEL / FIRST WOMAN

ACT ONE

Prologue

The cast are gathered around the acting area.

LYDGATE. Middlemarch.

MRS BULSTRODE. In 1829 –

BROOKE. – before Reform had done its part –

VINCY. – in the growing manufacturing town –

MRS VINCY. – the busy people lived –

ROSAMOND. – in a ferment of aspiration…

LYDGATE. The Doctor's Story.

Scene One

Tipton Library.

BROOKE. Mr Brooke's dinner party at Tipton Grange, was held as a proper preliminary to the wedding –

DOROTHEA. Of his niece Dorothea –

CASAUBON. To the Reverend Mr Casaubon.

MRS BULSTRODE. But Brooke's miscellaneous invitations seemed to belong to his general laxity.

VINCY (*entering with his daughter*). There was Mr Vincy, the newly elected Mayor of Middlemarch –

ROSAMOND (*comes forward*). – though not, of course, the Vincy's daughter Rosamond, for even Mr Brooke would not have chosen that his nieces should meet the daughter of a Middlemarch manufacturer. (*Turns and leaves*.)

BROOKE. That would be going too far, you know.

BROOKE *becomes* BULSTRODE *as he comes forward*.

BULSTRODE. And there was Bulstrode, the rich banker and religious philanthropist who predominated so much in the town.

MRS PLYMDALE. Some called him a Methodist –

VINCY. – others a hypocrite –

BULSTRODE. – according to the resources of their vocabulary.

VINCY. And there were various other townspeople, and professional men.

LYDGATE. Among them, the new arrival in Middlemarch, the young surgeon Mr Lydgate.

He goes to talk to DOROTHEA, *while others assess him from a distance. First a group of* WOMEN.

MRS VINCY. I'm told he's wonderfully clever. He certainly looks it.

MRS BULSTRODE. And he's a gentleman. Mr Brooke says he's one of the Lydgates of Northumberland.

MRS VINCY. Oh, really? Such high birth is unusual in a medical man… Look at him now. Miss Brooke seems to be having quite a conversation with him.

MRS BULSTRODE. I expect he's talking hospitals.

Then a group of MEN.

WRENCH. What do you think of our new colleague, Dr Sprague?

SPRAGUE. Mr Lydgate? He's studied abroad, Mr Wrench, but says he wants to raise the profession. Has ideas. About ventilation… and diet…

WRENCH. Do you think that's quite sound, upsetting the old treatments? The lowering system…

SPRAGUE. The strengthening system… I'm told he's brought a new instrument called a stethoscope.

WRENCH. What's that?

They have no idea.

BULSTRODE (*approaches*). I for my part hail the advent of Mr Lydgate. Medical knowledge is at a low ebb among us. I hope to find good reason for confiding my new hospital to his management.

SPRAGUE. Well, I'm not going to try any experiments. I like to carry out treatments that have been tested. The strengthening system –

WRENCH. The lowering system – I agree.

BULSTRODE. Ah, here's our new Mayor.

VINCY approaches.

We were talking of modern medical treatments, Mr Vincy.

VINCY. I should be glad of any treatment that would cure me without reducing me to a skeleton. It's an uncommonly dangerous thing to be left without any padding against the shafts of disease… Ah –

BULSTRODE. Excuse me…

The party is in full swing. BULSTRODE *returns to being* BROOKE. SPRAGUE *has returned to being* CASAUBON. LYDGATE *leaves* DOROTHEA *to join the main group.* DOROTHEA *and* CASAUBON *apart.*

BROOKE. Ladies and gentlemen. To the bride-to-be…

All raise their glasses.

May their marriage be long and happy.

ALL. To the bride-to-be!

Scene One (A)

LYDGATE *alone*.

FAREBROTHER. Mr Lydgate quitted the party early, and
would have thought it tedious, but for certain introductions.

LYDGATE. Miss Brooke's a fine girl, but a little too earnest.

DOROTHEA. Evidently she was not his 'style' of woman.

LYDGATE. I'd prefer to go from my work, to recline in a
paradise with blue eyes for a heaven.

ROSAMOND *is crossing the stage. She is blue-eyed and
fair-haired. He turns to watch her pass by.*

FAREBROTHER. But Mr Lydgate might have experience
before him which would modify his opinion as to the most
excellent things in women.

CASAUBON (*looking from* ROSAMOND *to* LYDGATE).
Destiny stands by sarcastic with our cast of characters folded
in her hand…

Scene Two

ROSAMOND. Rosamond Vincy was the reverse of Miss
Brooke.

MRS VINCY. She was the flower of the chief school in the
country, where the teaching included all that was demanded
of the accomplished female.

VINCY. Even to extras, such as the getting in and out of a
carriage.

MRS VINCY. Her musical execution was quite exceptional…

The Vincys' drawing room. After breakfast. MRS VINCY *sits
on the sofa with some mending,* ROSAMOND *with
embroidery.*

ROSAMOND. Mamma, when Fred comes down I wish you'd not let him have herrings. I can't bear the smell of them all over the house at this hour of the morning.

MRS VINCY. Oh, my dear, you're so hard on your brother. It's your only fault. You've the sweetest temper in the world but –

ROSAMOND. Brothers are so unpleasant.

MRS VINCY. Be thankful if they have good hearts. A woman must learn to put up with little things. You'll be married some day.

ROSAMOND. Not to anyone like Fred.

MRS VINCY. I wonder you're not glad to have such a gentlemanly young man for a brother, although he couldn't take his degree. And you'll not find any Middlemarch young man who's not got something against him.

ROSAMOND. But I shall not marry any Middlemarch young man.

MRS VINCY. So it seems, my love, for you've as good as refused the pick of them.

ROSAMOND. I wish you wouldn't say 'the pick of them'. It is rather a vulgar expression.

MRS VINCY. What should I say?

ROSAMOND. 'The best of them.'

MRS VINCY. Well, with your education you must know.

FRED (*entering*). Have you nothing else for breakfast? (*Calling back.*) Bring me a grilled bone.

ROSAMOND. Really, Fred. If you must have hot things for breakfast, I wish you'd come down earlier. You can get up at six o'clock to go hunting.

FRED. That's because I like it.

ROSAMOND. What would you think of me if I came down two hours after everyone else and ordered grilled bone?

FRED. I should think you were uncommonly fast.

ROSAMOND. I can't see why brothers are to make themselves disagreeable.

FRED. Disagreeable is a word that describes your feelings and not my actions.

ROSAMOND. I think it describes the smell of grilled bone.

FRED. Not at all. It describes a sensation in your little nose associated with certain finicking notions. Look at Mother – you don't see her objecting. She's my notion of a pleasant woman.

MRS VINCY. Bless you, my dears, don't quarrel. Come, Fred, tell us all about the new doctor. How is your Uncle Featherstone pleased with him.

FRED. Pretty well I think.

MRS VINCY. And what do you think of him? They say he's of excellent family.

ROSAMOND. It always makes a difference to be of good family.

Rosamond felt she might have been happier if she had not been the daughter of a Middlemarch manufacturer. And she disliked anything which reminded her that her mother's family had been innkeepers.

MRS VINCY. I thought it was odd that his name was Tertius. But, of course, it's a family name. But tell us what sort of a man he is.

FRED. Oh, clever – rather a prig I think.

ROSAMOND. I can never make out what you mean by a 'prig'.

FRED. A fellow who wants to show he has opinions.

MRS VINCY. Why, my dear, doctors must have opinions. What are they there for else? (*Slight pause.*) Are you going to Stone Court today to see your Uncle Featherstone?

FRED. Yes, after breakfast. Where is breakfast? (*Throws himself onto the sofa with a novel.*)

MRS VINCY. It's a thousand pities *you* haven't patience to see your Uncle Featherstone more, Rosamond. There's no

knowing what he might have done for you, as well as for
Fred when he dies. He can't be long for this world now and
he's rich beyond anything.

ROSAMOND (*shrugs indifferently*). I'd rather not have
anything left to me, if I must earn it by enduring my uncle's
cough. But I could ride with Fred. Papa says I may have the
chestnut to ride now. I can see cousin Mary.

In truth she was curious to see this new doctor.

MRS BULSTRODE. Strangers have always had a fascination
for the virgin mind.

Scene Three

ROSAMOND. After she'd seen Mary Garth –

FRED. – whom she and Fred had known since childhood –

FEATHERSTONE. – her Uncle Featherstone asked her to sing
for him.

Stone Court upstairs. FEATHERSTONE *lying ill.* FRED *in
attendance.* ROSAMOND *sings unaccompanied a verse of
'Flow On, Thou Shining River', while keeping an eye on the
window.* FEATHERSTONE *is coughing.*

ROSAMOND. At last Mr Lydgate's horse passed the window.

ROSAMOND *breaks off singing as* LYDGATE *enters.*

FEATHERSTONE. Ah, doctor, you're late. You've met my
nephew, Fred. This is my niece, Rosamond Vincy.

He greets her briefly, then examines FEATHERSTONE.

Miss Rosy has been singing me a song – you've nothing to
say against that, eh, doctor? I like it better than your physic.

ROSAMOND. How the time is going on. Fred, we must really
go.

FRED. Very good.

LYDGATE (*his mind still on the patient*). Miss Vincy is a musician then?

FEATHERSTONE. The best in Middlemarch, I'll be bound, eh, Fred? (*Slight pause.*) Speak up for your sister!

FRED. My evidence would be good for nothing, sir.

ROSAMOND. Middlemarch has not a very high standard, Uncle.

FRED. Goodbye, sir.

ROSAMOND. Goodbye, Uncle. Oh –

She has forgotten her whip. LYDGATE *passes it to her.*

LYDGATE. Your whip.

ROSAMOND. Thank you.

Their eyes meet.

Here was Mr Lydgate suddenly corresponding to her ideal –

MRS BULSTRODE. Being altogether foreign to Middlemarch –

MRS VINCY. Carrying a certain air of distinction –

MRS PLYMDALE. Possessing connections which offered vistas of that middle-class heaven, rank –

MRS BULSTRODE. A man of talent, whom it would be especially delightful to enslave.

ROSAMOND *takes the whip and goes.*

ROSAMOND. Riding home, she was far on in the costume and introductions of her wedded life.

Scene Four

LYDGATE. But nothing at present could seem less important to Lydgate than marriage.

Lydgate's study. LYDGATE *sets up an experiment, with microscope and notebook. The light concentrates around him.*

SPRAGUE. In the multitude of middle-aged men, there is always a good number who once meant to alter the world a little.

FAREBROTHER. The story of their coming to be shapen after the average, and fit to be packed by the gross, is hardly ever told, even in their consciousness.

LYDGATE. I do not mean to be one of those failures.

BULSTRODE. He had carried to his studies in London, Edinburgh and Paris, the conviction that the medical profession might be the finest in the world.

VINCY. But it wanted reform, and he studied with the determination that he would keep away from London intrigues and social truckling, would settle in some provincial town and win celebrity, however slowly, by the independent value of his work.

BULSTRODE. He would fight quackery, take no percentage from druggists, and was also fired by the possibility that he might work out the proof of an anatomical discovery, and so enlarge the scientific rational basis of his profession.

LYDGATE. As to women, he had once been drawn headlong by impetuous folly –

FRED. – proposing unsuccessfully to a Parisian actress who – he discovered afterwards – had murdered her former husband.

FAREBROTHER. Illusions were at an end for him.

LYDGATE. I'll do good small work for Middlemarch, and great work for the world!

BULSTRODE. Meanwhile, Middlemarch counted on assimilating him very comfortably.

Scene Five

LYDGATE. Mr Bulstrode invited Lydgate to his office at the bank.

The bank. BULSTRODE *at his desk.*

BULSTRODE. I hope I may confide to you the superintendence of my new hospital, which is nearly finished. (*Points to it out of the window.*) I shall consider what you've said about its destination as a fever hospital. That decision will rest with me.

LYDGATE. A fine fever hospital, in addition to the old infirmary, might also be the nucleus of a medical school here, when once we get our medical reforms.

BULSTRODE. I shall rejoice to furnish your zeal with fuller opportunities, for I'm determined that so great an object shall not be shackled by our other medical men – Sprague and Wrench and so on… I hope you will not shrink from incurring a certain amount of jealousy and dislike from your professional brethren by presenting yourself as a Reformer?

LYDGATE. I acknowledge a good deal of pleasure in fighting. I should not care for my profession if I did not believe that better methods were to be found.

BULSTRODE. In my own imperfect health, I've consulted eminent men in the metropolis, and I'm painfully aware of the backwardness under which medical treatment labours here.

LYDGATE. Yes – as to all the higher questions which determine a diagnosis – these can only come from a scientific culture. Country practitioners have no more notion of that than the man in the moon.

BULSTRODE. Mmm…

BULSTRODE *considers* LYDGATE *closely.*

Now, Mr Lydgate. I hope we shall not vary in sentiment as to a measure in which your sympathetic concurrence may be an aid to me. You recognise, I hope, the existence of spiritual interests in your patients?

LYDGATE. Certainly. But those words are apt to cover different meanings to different minds.

BULSTRODE. Precisely. Now, as to clerical attendance at the old infirmary. The building stands in Mr Farebrother's parish. You know Mr Farebrother?

LYDGATE. I've seen him. He seems a bright, pleasant fellow. I understand he's a naturalist.

BULSTRODE. Mr Farebrother, my dear sir, is a man deeply painful to contemplate. (*Doubtfully*.) I suppose there is not a clergyman in the country who has greater talents...

Slight pause.

LYDGATE. I've not yet found any excessive talent in Middlemarch.

BULSTRODE. What I desire is that Mr Farebrother's attendance at the infirmary should be superseded by the appointment of a salaried chaplain, of Mr Tyke, in fact, and that no other spiritual aid should be called in.

LYDGATE. As a medical man I could have no opinion, unless I knew Mr Tyke.

BULSTRODE. Of course. But the subject is likely to be referred to the medical board, and what I trust I may ask of you is that, in virtue of the cooperation between us, which I now look forward to, you will not be influenced by my opponents in this matter.

LYDGATE. I hope I shall have nothing to do with clerical disputes.

BULSTRODE. With me, this question is one of sacred accountableness; whereas with my opponents, it is to gratify a spirit of worldly opposition. I shall not cease to identify with that Truth which an evil generation hates. I boldly confess to you, Mr Lydgate, that I should have no interest in hospitals if I believed that nothing more was concerned therein than the cure of mortal diseases – (*Intense whisper.*) I have another ground of action, and in the face of persecution, I will not conceal it.

LYDGATE. There we certainly differ.

Pause. BULSTRODE *smiles.*

BULSTRODE. Well, I shall be exceedingly obliged if you will look in on me here occasionally, Mr Lydgate. There will be many questions to discuss in private...

They shake hands. LYDGATE *goes.*

Mr Bulstrode's power was not due simply to his being a country banker who knew the secrets of most traders in Middlemarch.

VINCY. It was fortified by a beneficence, ready to confer obligations, and severe in watching the results.

MRS BULSTRODE. It was a principle with Mr Bulstrode to gain as much power as possible, that he might use it for the glory of God.

BULSTRODE. He went through a great deal of spiritual conflict and inward argument in order to adjust his motives and make clear to himself what God's glory required.

Scene Six

LYDGATE. It was not long before Lydgate was invited for an evening to the Vincys'.

The Vincys' drawing room. A sofa; a piano. A party in progress. We follow a group of men; SPRAGUE, VINCY *and* LYDGATE.

SPRAGUE. What line do you take, Vincy? Tyke or Farebrother?

VINCY. Farebrother. Mr Tyke's sermons are all doctrine. Farebrother's aren't. He's as good a fellow as ever breathed.

SPRAGUE. Mr Lydgate?

LYDGATE. I know little of either. But in general the fitter man for a post is not always the most agreeable.

VINCY. If I had my way, I wouldn't put disagreeable fellows anywhere. But the infirmary board must decide. Shall we join the ladies?

They turn to the ladies; MRS VINCY, ROSAMOND, MRS BULSTRODE, MRS PLYMDALE. LYDGATE *talks to* ROSAMOND.

LYDGATE. I'm sorry I didn't hear you sing the other day at Stone Court. The only pleasure I allowed myself in Paris was to go to the opera.

ROSAMOND. You'll find Middlemarch very tuneless. I know only two gentlemen who sing at all well.

LYDGATE. You'll let me hear some music tonight, I hope.

ROSAMOND. Papa is sure to insist on it. But I shall tremble before you, who've heard the best singers in Paris. I've heard very little – I've only once been to London.

LYDGATE. Tell me what you saw.

ROSAMOND. Very little. The ordinary sights such as raw country girls are always taken to.

LYDGATE. Do you call yourself a raw country girl?

ROSAMOND. I assure you my mind is raw. I pass at Middlemarch. But I'm really afraid of you.

MRS BULSTRODE. Rosamond could always say the right thing. She was clever.

MRS PLYMDALE. Happily she never attempted to joke and this perhaps was the most decisive mark of her cleverness.

LYDGATE. An accomplished woman almost always knows more than we men, though her knowledge is of a different sort. I'm sure you could teach me a thousand things, as an exquisite bird could teach a bear.

FRED *enters, opens the piano, and starts playing 'Cherry Ripe' with one hand.*

ROSAMOND. Ah, there is Fred. I must hinder him from jarring all your nerves. Fred, you'll make Mr Lydgate ill. He has an ear.

FRED *laughs and accelerates to the end.*

You perceive the bears will not always be taught.

FRED (*setting a chair at the piano*). Now then, Rosy, some good rousing tunes.

VINCY. Ay, Rosamond, sing for us.

General agreement. After a show of reticence, she goes to the piano.

ROSAMOND *sings 'Voi che sapete'.* VINCY *and* MRS VINCY *look on proudly.* LYDGATE *admires. Extra chairs are brought on and placed ready for whist. As the song ends,* FAREBROTHER *enters, greets everyone cheerfully, and then –*

FAREBROTHER. Mr Lydgate!

LYDGATE. Mr Farebrother!

FAREBROTHER. You promised to come to see me. Tomorrow evening? I can't let you off, you know, because I have some beetles to show you. We collectors feel an interest in every new man, till he's seen all we have to show him. Ah, whist! Come now and let us be serious. Cards, Mr Lydgate? Not play? Ah, you're too young and light for this sort of thing...

LYDGATE. I'm afraid it's time I left. I've some studies to pursue.

But he stays to see the whist begin. VINCY, MRS VINCY, FRED *and* FAREBROTHER *are playing for money.*

FRED. Punch?

FAREBROTHER. No, just water for me.

VINCY. Punch for me! It's the best inward pickle, preserves you against bad air. Don't you think, doctor?

SPRAGUE *smiles and nods.*

FRED (*calling*). Punch!

The game begins.

ROSAMOND. You'll not like us in Middlemarch I feel sure. We're very stupid and you've been used to something quite different.

LYDGATE. I suppose all country towns are pretty much alike. But I've made up my mind to take Middlemarch as it comes. I've certainly found some charms in it greater than I expected.

ROSAMOND. You mean the rides towards Tipton and Lowick? Everyone is pleased with those.

LYDGATE. No, I mean something much nearer to me.

ROSAMOND. Do you care about dancing at all? I'm not sure whether clever men ever dance.

LYDGATE. I would dance with you.

ROSAMOND. Oh! I was only going to say that we sometimes have dancing, and I wanted to know whether you'd feel insulted if you were asked to come.

LYDGATE. Not on the condition I mentioned.

Noise from the whist table.

Ah! Mr Farebrother seems to be winning!

ROSAMOND. He usually does.

FAREBROTHER. I have to earn money somehow! (*Sweeps up his winnings.*)

Scene Seven

LYDGATE. Lydgate walked home, in the starlight and brisk air, to his lodgings.

Lydgate's lodgings. He checks his notebook, then settles down to concentrate.

(*To himself.*) I do admire Rosamond exceedingly. But a wife is a pretty ornament I can't afford for at least five years. Where's that paper? (*Finds it in the table drawer.*) *On Fevers: The Specific Differences between Typhus and Typhoid.*

He starts to read, making notes.

FAREBROTHER. He was enamoured of that arduous invention which is the very eye of research, provisionally framing its object and correcting it to a more and more exactness of relation.

LYDGATE (*leaning back in delight*). I should never have been happy in any profession that didn't call forth the highest intellectual strain. And yet keep me in good warm contact with my neighbours. Nothing like the medical profession for that. (*Goes happily back to his work.*)

Light on ROSAMOND, *across the stage, dreaming.*

MRS VINCY. In Rosamond's romance, it was not necessary to imagine much about the inward life of the hero, or his serious business in the world.

ROSAMOND. How he looked at me! He's clever, of course, and sufficiently handsome. But above all, he's of good birth. I won't need to associate with vulgar people. His relatives must be quite equal to the county people round here.

MRS VINCY. All young men, might, could, would be or actually were, in love with her.

ROSAMOND. Lydgate could be no exception!

MRS VINCY. Poor Rosamond.

FAREBROTHER. Poor Lydgate.

Each lived in a world of which the other knew nothing.

Scene Eight

LYDGATE. The next evening, Lydgate went to see the Reverend Farebrother.

FAREBROTHER. After introducing his mother –

They shake hands.

– his aunt –

Likewise.

– and his sister –

All very different.

– who all depended on his meagre living, Farebrother took Lydgate to his den to show him his collection –

MRS FAREBROTHER. Though his mother declared there was nothing there – (*Calling after.*) but pickled vermin, drawers full of bluebottles, and no carpets on the floor!

FAREBROTHER*'s den.*

FAREBROTHER. Here we are. Smoke?

FAREBROTHER *offers a pipe.* LYDGATE *declines.*

No? (*Has one himself.*) I'm older than you and I've come to a compromise. I feed a weakness or two in case they get clamorous. Now, look! (*Takes a glass-fronted display of mounted insects from the table drawer.*) I fancy I've made an exhaustive study of the entomology of this district. We're singularly rich in orthoptera. (*Notices* LYDGATE *looking elsewhere.*) Ah, that glass jar. But perhaps you don't care about these things?

LYDGATE. Not by the side of anatomy. I was early bitten with an interest in the structure of tissues.

FAREBROTHER. How was that?

LYDGATE. As a child in a cyclopaedia I read a passage on the valves of the heart. I knew that 'valvae' were folding doors and I had my first notion of a finely adjusted mechanism in the human frame. I'm more and more convinced that it will be possible to demonstrate the single origin of all the body's separate tissues. I've no hobby besides. I've the sea to swim in there.

FAREBROTHER. Ah, you're a happy fellow. You don't know what it is to want spiritual tobacco. Oh, for a learned treatise on all the insects met with by the Israelites in their passage through the desert, or a monograph on the ant, by Solomon, showing its harmony with the results of modern research!

LYDGATE. It was clear that the vicar felt himself not altogether in the right vocation.

FAREBROTHER (*returning to his insects*). Suppose I ask you to look through these. You must learn to be bored. It's a good discipline for a young doctor who has to please his patients in Middlemarch.

LYDGATE (*going to look*). Don't you think men overrate the necessity for humouring everybody's nonsense? You must make your value felt, so that people must put up with you, whether you flatter them or not.

FAREBROTHER. But then you must be sure of having the value, and you must keep yourself independent. Very few men can do that. But do look at these! So delicate!

LYDGATE. What exquisite writing you have! No, I made up my mind some time ago to be as independent as possible. I didn't like what I saw in London when I was studying there, so much empty pretension and trickery. In the country, one can follow one's own course.

FAREBROTHER. Yes, well – you've got a good start. You're in the right profession. Some of us miss that and repent too late. But you mustn't be *too* sure of keeping your independence.

LYDGATE. You mean of family ties?

FAREBROTHER. Not altogether. Though I'm sure a good wife – a good unworldly woman – may really help a man. (*Slight pause.*) Mm... No, I was thinking that we Middlemarchers have our intrigues and our parties and they may threaten your independence. I'm of one party, for example, and Bulstrode is another. If you vote for me at the old infirmary, you will offend Bulstrode.

LYDGATE. What is there against Bulstrode?

FAREBROTHER. Nothing, except that if you vote against him, you will make him your enemy.

LYDGATE. I don't know that I need mind about that. But he seems to have good ideas about hospitals and he spends large sums on useful public objects. He might help me a good deal in carrying out my ideas.

FAREBROTHER. Very good. Then you mustn't offend him. (*Pause.*) If you vote against me, you'll not offend me, you know. I'm opposed to Bulstrode in many ways. I don't like the set he belongs to, Tyke and company, they're a narrow, ignorant set. They really look on the rest of mankind as a doomed carcass which is to nourish them for Heaven – (*Smiles.*) But I don't say that Bulstrode's new hospital is a bad thing. And as to his wanting to oust me from the old one – why, I'm not a model clergyman, only a decent makeshift.

Slight pause.

LYDGATE. What reason does Bulstrode give for superseding you?

FAREBROTHER. That I don't teach his opinions. But I should be glad of the forty pounds... I only wanted to tell you that if you vote for Tyke, you're not to cut me in consequence. I can't spare you. You're a sort of circumnavigator come to settle among us, and will keep up my belief in the Antipodes. Now, I want you to tell me more about your researches in Paris...

Scene Nine

VINCY. As the weeks passed, Lydgate's liking for the Vicar grew with growing acquaintanceship.

LYDGATE. He found he heartily wished for his friendship.

BULSTRODE. But he had a vexed sense that he must make up his mind on the question of the chaplaincy.

LYDGATE *alone.*

LYDGATE. I want to vote for Farebrother.

BULSTRODE. But he couldn't help feeling that Bulstrode would make voting for Tyke a question of office or no office for him in the new hospital.

LYDGATE. But I don't intend to be a vassal of Bulstrode.

FAREBROTHER. There were valid objections to Farebrother...

LYDGATE. He plays cards for money... He's even been seen in the billiards room at The Green Dragon... He seems only to care for the forty pounds.

FAREBROTHER. Lydgate had never felt poor, and had no power of imagining the part which want of money plays in the actions of men.

BULSTRODE. On the other hand there was Tyke.

LYDGATE. Nobody has anything against him. Except that they can't bear him and suspect him of cant.

But if I vote for him I shall be voting on the side obviously convenient for myself.

SPRAGUE. Whichever way Lydgate began to incline, there was something to make him wince, and he was a proud man.

LYDGATE. Confound their petty politics.

MRS BULSTRODE. For the first time, he felt the hampering pressure of small social conditions and their frustrating complexity.

Scene Ten

LYDGATE. The day of the vote had come.

BULSTRODE. And Lydgate –

LYDGATE. – undecided –

BULSTRODE. – was late in arriving.

The Town Hall. A meeting of the infirmary board. Those present are BULSTRODE, VINCY, PLYMDALE SNR, and the doctors SPRAGUE, WRENCH and MINCHIN. Extra chairs round the table.

SPRAGUE. I go for Farebrother. He has none too much, and has to keep house for his mother, his aunt and his sister.

VINCY. Put forty pounds in his pocket and you'll do no harm. He's a good fellow is Farebrother.

PLYMDALE SNR. What we have to consider is not anybody's income, Dr Sprague, but the souls of the poor sick people. He's a real Gospel preacher Mr Tyke. I should vote against my conscience if I voted against Mr Tyke.

SPRAGUE. Nobody is asked to vote against his conscience. But would any member of the committee have entertained the idea of displacing Mr Farebrother, if it had not been suggested by certain parties – (*Looking to* BULSTRODE.) who regard every institution of this town as machinery for carrying out their own views? Are we agreed, Mr Wrench?

MR WRENCH. We are, Dr Sprague.

SPRAGUE. There are influences at work here incompatible with genuine independence, and inspiring a crawling servility –

VINCY. Surely – Farebrother's been doing the work without pay, if pay is to be given it should be given to him –

PLYMDALE SNR. I shall vote for Mr Tyke, but I should not have known I was a servile crawler! –

SPRAGUE. If I may be allowed to conclude –

VINCY. Doctor – (*Turning to* MINCHIN.) I must have you on the side of Farebrother.

MINCHIN. I confess I have a divided esteem. Mr Farebrother is an amiable man, an able preacher, and has been longer among us. But I consider Mr Tyke an exemplary man.

PLYMDALE SNR. You don't set up Farebrother as a pattern of a clergyman, I hope. He's too lax.

Protests.

He'll make a little attendance go as far as he can –

VINCY. Better than too much. Sick people can't bear so much praying and preaching. Bad for the spirits – bad for the insides – eh, doctor?

Hubbub. Everyone talking at once.

BULSTRODE. Sit down, please, everyone.

Everyone sits and becomes quiet.

The vote. It is desirable that chaplaincies of this kind should be entered with a fervent intention. They are peculiar opportunities for spiritual influence. I propose Mr Tyke, a zealous, able man. Let us proceed to a vote. Let each person write Tyke or Farebrother on a piece of paper, and place it in this tumbler.

Silence while everybody votes. BULSTRODE, PLYMDALE SNR *and* MINCHIN *for Tyke;* SPRAGUE, WRENCH *and* VINCY *for* FAREBROTHER. BULSTRODE *then counts the votes out aloud, 'Tyke', 'Farebrother', etc. While he is doing so,* LYDGATE *enters.*

Ah, here is Mr Lydgate. I perceive the votes are equally divided at present. The casting vote is yours, Mr Lydgate. Will you be good enough to vote?

SPRAGUE. The thing is settled. We all know how Mr Lydgate will vote.

LYDGATE. You seem to speak with some peculiar meaning, sir?

SPRAGUE. I merely mean you are expected to vote with Mr Bulstrode. Is that offensive?

LYDGATE. It may be to others. But I shall not desist from voting with him on that account. (*Writes.*) Tyke.

The meeting breaks up.

Yet he knew that if he'd been quite free from indirect bias, he should have voted for Farebrother.

BULSTRODE. The petty medium of Middlemarch had been too strong for him

FAREBROTHER (*to* LYDGATE). The world has been too strong for *me*, I know. But then I'm not a mighty man – I shall never be a man of renown.

LYDGATE. Lydgate thought that there was a pitiable infirmity of will in Mr Farebrother.

Scene Eleven

VINCY. Not long after, in the Vincys' drawing room –

The Vincys' drawing room. MRS VINCY *and* ROSAMOND.
FRED, *groaning, throws himself on the sofa.*

MRS VINCY (*very concerned*). Fred?

FRED. Ugh. I feel very ill.

MRS VINCY. Oh, my poor boy.

FRED. Why is the doctor so slow? I feel much worse.

ROSAMOND (*by the window*). Mamma. There is Mr Lydgate
stopping to speak to someone. If I were you I would call him
in. They say he cures everyone.

MRS VINCY (*calling*). Mr Lydgate. Please. It's my son… He's
coming. Oh, he's here. (*As* LYDGATE *enters.*) It's Fred. Mr
Wrench is our usual doctor, but we saw you there and –

LYDGATE. Let me see.

He examines FRED, *lying on the sofa.* MRS VINCY *shows
him a small bottle.*

Mr Wrench sent these drugs?

MRS VINCY. Yes.

LYDGATE (*clearly disapproves*). Mr Wrench, you say. You
must go to bed immediately. I think it may be the early
stages of Typhoid fever. (*Writes a prescription.*)

MRS VINCY. Oh no. If anything should happen! Why Mr
Wrench should neglect my children…

LYDGATE. Mr Wrench may not be to blame. This form of
fever is very equivocal in its beginnings. Here's a
prescription, and I will write to Mr Wrench and tell him what
I've done.

MRS VINCY. But you must go on attending Fred. I can't have
my boy left to anybody who may come or not. Mr Wrench
shall know what I think, take it as he will…

WRENCH (*suddenly sits upright*). Mr Wrench did not take it at all well. He said afterwards that Lydgate paraded flighty foreign notions, and wrote to decline further attendance in the case. (*Lies down and is* FRED *again*.)

ROSAMOND. So Lydgate was installed as medical attendant on the Vincys.

A moment between LYDGATE *and* ROSAMOND.

Scene Eleven (A)

VINCY. Gradually, Lydgate's daily visits became more cheerful.

MRS VINCY (*at the bedside*). If only I can see my boy strong again – and who knows, master of Stone Court when your Uncle Featherstone dies – and you can marry – Mary, or anybody you like then.

FRED. Not if they won't have me, Mother.

MRS VINCY. Oh, take a bit of jelly, my dear.

She feeds him a spoonful.

Scene Twelve

ROSAMOND. As for Rosamond and Lydgate, that intimacy in which each feels the other is feeling something, having once existed, is not to be done away with.

VINCY. Soon there was once more music in the drawing room and all the extra hospitality of Mr Vincy's mayorality.

ROSAMOND *quietly plays piano, 'Voi che sapete'.*
LYDGATE *leans on the piano. They smile at each other.*

LYDGATE. For Lydgate, the preposterousness of the notion that he could set up a satisfactory establishment as a married man was a sufficient guarantee against danger. Flirtation was not necessarily a singeing process.

ROSAMOND. But Rosamond did not distinguish flirtation from love.

Scene Twelve (A)

NED. Now, young Ned Plymdale was one of the best matches in Middlemarch.

LYDGATE. Though not one of its leading minds…

NED *is having a tête-à-tête with* ROSAMOND *over a society magazine.*

NED. I think the honourable Mrs S is something like you.

ROSAMOND. Her back is very large.

NED. I didn't say she was as beautiful as you.

ROSAMOND. I suspect you of being a flatterer – ah, Mr Lydgate.

LYDGATE (*approaches*). Miss Vincy.

They shake hands.

ROSAMOND. How did you find Fred?

LYDGATE. Going on well.

ROSAMOND. Poor fellow. (*To* NED.) We've looked to Mr Lydgate as our guardian angel during his illness.

NED *smiles nervously.* LYDGATE *looks at the magazine and laughs.*

What are you laughing at so profanely?

LYDGATE. How silly. (*Flicks through.*) Oh, do look at this bridegroom coming out of church. Did any haberdasher ever look so smirking! I will answer for it, the story makes him one of the first gentlemen in the land.

ROSAMOND (*amused*). You're so severe I'm frightened at you.

NED. There are a great many celebrated people in *The Keepsake* at all events. This is the first time I've heard it called silly.

ROSAMOND (*to* LYDGATE). I think I shall accuse you of being a barbarian. You know nothing of the celebrated Mrs S –

NED. But Sir Walter Scott – I suppose Mr Lydgate knows him.

LYDGATE. Oh, I read no literature now. (*Shuts the magazine.*) I read so much when I was a lad, it will last me all my life.

ROSAMOND. I should like to know when you left off. Then I might be sure I knew something you didn't know.

NED. Mr Lydgate would say *that* was not worth knowing.

LYDGATE. On the contrary. It would be worth knowing by the fact that Miss Vincy would tell it me.

NED. I shall go to look at the whist.

After he's gone, there is a slight pause.

ROSAMOND. You've given offence.

LYDGATE. What – is this Mr Plymdale's? (*Puts the magazine down.*) I didn't think –

ROSAMOND. I shall begin to think that you *are* a bear, and want teaching by the birds.

LYDGATE. Well, there is a bird who can teach me what she will. Don't I listen to her willingly?

ROSAMOND. To Rosamond it seemed as if she and Lydgate were as good as engaged.

LYDGATE. Lydgate had the counter idea of remaining unengaged.

MRS VINCY. But Rosamond's idea looked through watchful blue eyes.

VINCY. Whereas Lydgate's idea lay blind.

Scene Thirteen

LYDGATE. That evening he worked with undisturbed interest, and wrote out his daily notes with as much precision as usual.

Lydgate's study. LYDGATE *at work.*

SPRAGUE. Moreover he was beginning to feel some zest for the growing feud between him and the other medical men.

BULSTRODE. And he was beginning to be called in to houses of some importance.

LYDGATE. Only a few days later he was called to Lowick Manor to attend to the Reverend Mr Casaubon's sudden illness.

Scene Fourteen

DOROTHEA. Afterwards he saw Dorothea Casaubon in the library.

The library at Lowick Manor. LYDGATE *with* DOROTHEA.

LYDGATE. He may possibly live for fifteen years or more…

DOROTHEA. You mean if we are very careful.

LYDGATE. Yes, careful against mental agitation of all kinds. But it is one of those cases in which death is sometimes sudden.

DOROTHEA (*low voice*). Help me. Tell me what I can do?

LYDGATE. What do you think of foreign travel? You've been lately in Rome on your wedding journey I think?

DOROTHEA. Oh, that would be worse than anything. (*Tearful.*) Nothing will be of any use that he does not enjoy…

LYDGATE. Lydgate was deeply touched, wondering about her marriage. It was something of which he had –

ROSAMOND. – as yet –

LYDGATE. – no personal experience.

Scene Fifteen

The Vincys' drawing room.

LYDGATE. She appears to feel strongly for him.

ROSAMOND. Of course she is devoted to her husband.

But at the same time Rosamond thought that it was not so very melancholy to be mistress of Lowick Manor with a husband likely to die soon.

But how your practice is spreading! You were called in to Sir James Chettam, I think, and now the Casaubons.

LYDGATE. Yes. But I don't really like attending such people so well as the poor. One has to go through more fuss, and listen more to nonsense.

ROSAMOND. At least you go through broad corridors and have the scent of rose leaves.

LYDGATE (*smiling*). That's true, Mademoiselle de Montmorency… (*Lifts her hand to kiss it.*)

Scene Sixteen

VINCY. But this persistent flirtation could not continue indefinitely…

MRS BULSTRODE. Mrs Bulstrode was the Mayor's sister and was on her way to see her niece Rosamond, when she met Ned Plymdale's mother.

In the street.

Mrs Plymdale – I can't stop, I'm going to see poor Rosamond.

MRS PLYMDALE. Why do you say 'poor Rosamond'?

MRS BULSTRODE. She's so pretty and has been brought up in such thoughtlessness. Her mother has always had that levity about her which makes me anxious for the children.

MRS PLYMDALE. Well, Harriet, if I'm to speak my mind, anybody would suppose you and Mr Bulstrode would be delighted. You've done everything to put Mr Lydgate forward.

MRS BULSTRODE. Selina, what do you mean?

MRS PLYMDALE. Not but what I am truly thankful for my Ned's sake. He could certainly better afford to keep a wife than some people can, but I should wish him to look elsewhere. Still, I should say I was not fond of strangers coming into a town.

MRS BULSTRODE. I don't know. My husband Mr Bulstrode was a stranger here at one time. Abraham and Moses were strangers in the land, and the Bible tells us to entertain strangers.

MRS PLYMDALE. I was not speaking in a religious sense, Harriet. I spoke as a mother.

MRS BULSTRODE. I'm sure you've never heard me say anything against a niece of mine marrying your son.

MRS PLYMDALE. Oh, it's pride in Miss Vincy, I'm sure. No young man in Middlemarch was good enough for her. But now she's found a man as proud as herself.

Slight pause.

MRS BULSTRODE. You don't mean there's anything between Rosamond and Mr Lydgate.

MRS PLYMDALE. Is it possible you don't know, Harriet?

MRS BULSTRODE. Oh, I'm not fond of gossip. Your circle is rather different from ours.

MRS PLYMDALE. Well, but your own niece.

MRS BULSTRODE. I don't believe there can be anything serious at present. My brother would certainly have told me.

MRS PLYMDALE. Well, I understand that nobody can see Miss Vincy and Mr Lydgate together without taking them to be engaged.

Scene Seventeen

The Vincys' drawing room.

MRS BULSTRODE. I've just heard something about you that has surprised me very much, Rosamond.

ROSAMOND. What's that, Aunt?

MRS BULSTRODE. I can hardly believe it – that you should be engaged without my knowing it – without your father telling me.

ROSAMOND. I'm not engaged, Aunt.

MRS BULSTRODE. How is it that everyone says so then?

ROSAMOND (*gratified*). The town's talk is of very little consequence.

MRS BULSTRODE. Oh, my dear, be more thoughtful. You are turned twenty-two now and you will have no fortune. Your father, I'm sure, will not be able to spare you anything. Mr Lydgate is very intellectual and your uncle finds him very useful, but the profession is a poor one here. And you're not fit to marry a poor man.

ROSAMOND. Mr Lydgate is not a poor man, Aunt. He has very high connections.

MRS BULSTRODE. He told me himself that he was poor.

ROSAMOND. That's because he's used to people who have a high style of living.

MRS BULSTRODE. My dear Rosamond, you must not think of living in high style. (*Slight pause.*) Then it is really true? You are thinking of Mr Lydgate. Be open, my dear Rosamond. Mr Lydgate has really made you an offer?

ROSAMOND (*her pride hurt*). Pray excuse me, Aunt. I'd rather not speak on the subject.

MRS BULSTRODE. You'd not give your heart to a man without a decided prospect, I trust. Ned Plymdale is a nice young man – and a large business of that kind is better than a profession. Not that marrying is everything – I would have you seek first the kingdom of God – but a girl's heart –

ROSAMOND. I should never give my heart to Ned Plymdale.

MRS BULSTRODE. I see how it is, my dear. You have allowed your affections to be engaged without return.

ROSAMOND. No indeed, Aunt, I have not.

MRS BULSTRODE. Then you are quite confident that Mr Lydgate has a serious attachment to you?

ROSAMOND *is mortified. She stares at the floor.*

Oh, Rosamond…

Scene Seventeen (A)

MRS BULSTRODE. Mrs Bulstrode spoke to Mr Bulstrode.

You must find out Mr Lydgate's intentions.

BULSTRODE. Mr Bulstrode spoke to Mr Lydgate.

Do you have any intention of marrying soon?

LYDGATE (*laughing*). Decidedly not.

MRS BULSTRODE. Mrs Bulstrode spoke to Mr Lydgate.

I think it's a heavy responsibility, Mr Lydgate, to interfere with the prospects of any girl.

LYDGATE. On the other hand, a man must be a great coxcomb to think that he mustn't pay attention to a young lady lest she should fall in love with him.

MRS BULSTRODE. Oh, Mr Lydgate, you know what your advantages are.

LYDGATE. Mr Lydgate spoke to Mr Farebrother.

I must give up going out in the evening!

FAREBROTHER. Well, if you don't mean to be won by the sirens, you're right to take precautions.

LYDGATE (*to himself*). I've been making a fool of myself, behaving so as to be misunderstood.

He resolved not to go to the Vincys', except on business.

ROSAMOND. Rosamond became very unhappy.

MRS VINCY. Her uneasiness grew into terror at the blank to come.

MRS BULSTRODE. She felt as forlorn as Ariadne – a charming stage Ariadne –

MRS PLYMDALE. Left behind with all her boxes full of costumes and no hope of a coach.

Scene Eighteen

LYDGATE. But ten days later, Mr Lydgate was obliged to call at the Vincys'.

The Vincys' drawing room. ROSAMOND *is on her own.*

(*Formally.*) I've come with a message for your father.

ROSAMOND. Oh yes. But he's not at home. Pray sit down.

He sits.

LYDGATE. There's a marked change for the worse in your Uncle Featherstone's health. He's not expected to live more than a few hours. I thought your family should know. (*Slight pause.*) That's all.

ROSAMOND. Thank you.

Silence. LYDGATE *gets up to go, and she gets up too, dropping her embroidery. They both stoop to pick it up, rise close together. Looking at each other, suddenly she is in tears.*

LYDGATE. What's the matter? You're distressed. Tell me – pray.

Silence. Gently, he kisses each of her eyes in turn. They sit.

ROSAMOND. She made her little confession…

LYDGATE. He poured out words of gratitude…

MRS VINCY. And in half an hour he left the house an engaged man…

ROSAMOND. Whose soul was not his own.

Scene Nineteen

ROSAMOND *and* VINCY.

VINCY. But what has he got to marry on?!

ROSAMOND. Mr Lydgate is not poor, Father. He bought a practice worth eight or nine hundred a year.

VINCY. Stuff and nonsense! He might as well buy next year's swallows, it'll all slip through his fingers.

ROSAMOND. On the contrary, Papa, he will increase the practice. See how he's been called in by the Chettams and Casaubons.

VINCY. I hope he knows I shan't give anything – with this disappointment about Fred getting *nothing* in Uncle Featherstone's will – and Parliament going to be dissolved, and machine-breaking everywhere and an election coming on –

ROSAMOND. Dear Papa – what can that have to do with my marriage?

VINCY. A pretty deal to do with it! We may all be ruined for what I know – the country's in that state! Some say it's the end of the world and be hanged if I don't think it looks like it. Anyhow, it's not a time for me to be drawing money out of my business and I should wish Lydgate to know that.

ROSAMOND. I'm sure he expects nothing, Papa. And he has such very high connections. He is sure to rise in one way or another. He is engaged in making scientific discoveries. (*Pause*.) I cannot give up my only prospect of happiness, Papa. Mr Lydgate is a gentleman. I could never love anyone who was not a perfect gentleman. You would not like me to go into a consumption. (*Slight pause*.) And you know that I never change my mind.

Silence.

Promise me, Papa, that you will consent.

Silence.

We shall never give each other up.

VINCY. Well, well, child, he must write to me.

Mr Vincy, bluster as he would, had as little of his own way as if he had been a prime minister.

Scene Twenty

LYDGATE *with* ROSAMOND.

LYDGATE. Dear, your eyelids are red.

ROSAMOND. Are they?

LYDGATE. As if you could hide it from me. Things trouble you and you don't tell me.

ROSAMOND. Papa is not pleased about our engagement.

LYDGATE. He wants us to give it up?

ROSAMOND. I never give up anything I choose to do.

LYDGATE. God bless you! (*Kisses her*.) It's too late. You're of age, and I claim you as mine. Why should we delay? I've taken the large house you like at Lowick Gate. You'll not mind about new clothes. They can be bought afterwards.

ROSAMOND (*smiling*). What original notions you clever men have! This is the first time I ever heard of wedding clothes being bought after marriage.

LYDGATE. But you'd not insist on my waiting months for the sake of clothes? Remember, we're looking forward to a better sort of happiness – being continually together, independent of others and ordering our lives as we will. Come, dear, tell me how soon you can be altogether mine?

ROSAMOND (*after a moment*). Six weeks?

Scene Twenty-One

Lydgate's study. FAREBROTHER *brings cloudy pond water in a jar.*

LYDGATE. Farebrother!

FAREBROTHER. I've brought you some pond products, which I need to examine under a better microscope than mine.

LYDGATE. By all means.

He brings his microscope, while FAREBROTHER *looks round.*

FAREBROTHER. Eros has brought chaos to your bachelor lodging, I see.

LYDGATE. A better order will begin after.

FAREBROTHER. Soon?

LYDGATE. I think so. This unsettled state of affairs uses up time, and when one has notions in science, every moment is an opportunity. I feel sure marriage must be the best thing for a man who wants to work steadily. He can get calmness and freedom.

FAREBROTHER. You're an enviable dog, to have such a prospect. Rosamond, calmness and freedom. I'm left with nothing but my pipe and my pond life. Now, are we ready?

They examine the jar.

Scene Twenty-Two

The Vincys' drawing room. LYDGATE *and* ROSAMOND *go to sit on the sofa together.* MRS VINCY *sits at a distance.*

ROSAMOND. There is still house linen and furniture to be bought.

MRS VINCY. And it's a very large house. It will take a deal of furniture.

ROSAMOND. Still, Mamma can see to some things while we are away.

MRS VINCY. To be sure.

ROSAMOND. And cousin Mary will be useful. Her sewing is exquisite. It's the best thing I know about Mary.

LYDGATE. I suppose we must be away a week or so.

ROSAMOND. Oh, more than that! We might go to visit your family on our wedding journey. Which of your uncles do you like best?

LYDGATE. My Uncle Godwin, I think. He's a good-natured old fellow.

ROSAMOND. You were constantly at his house at Quallingham when you were a boy, were you not? I should so like to see the old spot and everything you were used to. Does he know you're going to be married?

LYDGATE. No.

ROSAMOND. Do send him word, you naughty, undutiful nephew. He'll perhaps invite us to Quallingham. (*Looking around her*.) You see me in my home as it's been since I was a child, it's not fair that I should be ignorant of yours…

LYDGATE. I will write to him then. But my cousins are bores.

ROSAMOND. It seemed magnificent to Rosamond to be able to speak so slightly of a baronet's family. But her mother was near spoiling all.

MRS VINCY. I hope your uncle Sir Godwin won't look down on Rosy, Mr Lydgate. I should think he would do something handsome. A thousand or two can be nothing to a baronet.

ROSAMOND. Mamma! How could you!

LYDGATE. Lydgate had to confess he was descending a little in relation to Rosamond's family.

Scene Twenty-Three

LYDGATE *alone*.

ROSAMOND. Meanwhile, the requisite things must be bought for the new house –

LYDGATE. And Lydgate found his sum of eight hundred pounds had been considerably reduced since he had come to Middlemarch.

MRS PLYMDALE. But he supposed that if things were done at all, they must be done properly.

MRS BULSTRODE. He saw a dinner service in Brassing, which struck him as exactly the right thing. (*Shows off a fine cup and saucer.*)

LYDGATE. It was expensive china, but that might be in the nature of dinner services.

MRS VINCY (*to* LYDGATE). It's lovely. I trust in Heaven it won't be broken.

LYDGATE (*to* MRS VINCY). One must hire servants who won't break things.

FAREBROTHER. It never occurred to Lydgate to live other than what he would have called an ordinary way, with green glasses for hock, and excellent waiting at table.

VINCY. And Rosamond never thought of money except as something necessary, which other people would always provide.

ROSAMOND (*stepping forward to join him*). She thought that no one could be more in love than she was.

LYDGATE. He thought that after all the wild mistakes and absurd credulity of his past, he had found perfect womanhood.

SPRAGUE. He held it as one of the prettiest attributes of the feminine mind, to adore a man's pre-eminence, without too precise a knowledge of what it consisted in.

VINCY. He relied much on the psychological difference between the goose and the gander.

BULSTRODE. Especially on the innate submissiveness of the goose as beautifully corresponding to the strength of the gander.

FAREBROTHER. So Lydgate and Rosamond were safely married.

They stand before FAREBROTHER, *while everyone gathers behind them. Wedding bells.*

I now pronounce you man and wife.

They kiss and then pass down an archway of congratulatory Middlemarchers. At the end, they turn. Everyone cheers.

Scene Twenty-Four

LYDGATE. When they returned from their wedding journey, Lydgate returned to his work at the new hospital.

SPRAGUE. But opposition to Lydgate was growing…

The new hospital. LYDGATE *is working. On the table he has some anatomical drawings. In the street,* MRS PLYMDALE *and* FRIENDS *refer to him and gossip.*

MRS PLYMDALE. I think he means to let people die in that hospital, for the sake of cutting them up.

MRS SPRAGUE. If a doctor's good for anything, he should know what's the matter before you die, not pry into your insides after you've gone.

MRS PLYMDALE. He says if doctors only get paid for their work by overdosing people with drugs, that makes them as mischievous as quacks.

MRS SPRAGUE. Does he mean to say there's no use in taking medicines?

MRS BULSTRODE. How will he cure his patients then?

MRS PLYMDALE. I wouldn't employ him. Others may do as they please.

MRS SPRAGUE. I prefer Mr Wrench, bleeding, blistering, starving –

MRS PLYMDALE. Slow to arrive, but at least he *does* something.

They leave.

LYDGATE. It's as useless to fight ignorance as to whip the fog…

Now it is the DOCTORS' *turn.*

SPRAGUE. Untried notions, Mr Wrench.

WRENCH. He ignores experience, Dr Sprague.

SPRAGUE. The strengthening system –

WRENCH. The lowering system –

SPRAGUE. It's his arrogance, Mr Wrench.

WRENCH. His pretension, Dr Sprague.

SPRAGUE. Reckless innovation –

WRENCH. That's the essence of the Charlatan.

BULSTRODE *joins* LYDGATE.

LYDGATE (*to* BULSTRODE). I must work the harder, that's all. This hospital will flourish in spite of them, and then they'll be glad to come in. Things can't last as they are. There must be all sorts of reforms soon.

BULSTRODE. I shall not flinch, you may depend on it, Mr Lydgate. While I see you carrying out high intentions with vigour, you shall have my unfailing support. I have confidence that the blessing, which has attended my efforts against the spirit of evil in this town – (*Turns toward the* DOCTORS.) will not be withdrawn.

SPRAGUE. Charlatans both!

Scene Twenty-Five

DOROTHEA. One day, Mrs Casaubon came to the hospital to ask about her husband's health, and Lydgate was not willing to let slip an opportunity.

LYDGATE. This hospital is a capital piece of work. But the whole medical profession here have set themselves against it, and hinder subscriptions.

DOROTHEA. How very petty.

LYDGATE. There's no stifling the offence of being young and a newcomer, and happening to know something more than the old doctors. Still, I believe I can pursue certain observations, which may be a lasting benefit to medical practice. I should be a base truckler if I allowed any consideration of personal comfort to hinder me. And the course is all the clearer from there being no salary to put my persistence in an equivocal light.

DOROTHEA. I'm glad you've told me this, Mr Lydgate – I feel sure I can help.

Scene Twenty-Six

LYDGATE. And when he returned home, to his new town house…

The Lydgates' drawing room. ROSAMOND *welcomes her husband after the day's work.*

ROSAMOND. Mrs Casaubon was here asking for you, so I directed her to the hospital. What did she want to say to you?

LYDGATE. Merely to ask about her husband's health. (*Warms himself at the fire.*) But I think she's going to be splendid to our new hospital. I think she will give us two hundred a year.

ROSAMOND. She's very aristocratic and beautiful.

LYDGATE. I never thought about it.

ROSAMOND. Our new friend Mr Ladislaw was here teaching me some music when Mrs Casaubon came in. He seemed vexed. Do you think he disliked her seeing him at our house? Surely your position is more than equal to his – however he may be related to the Casaubons.

LYDGATE. No, no. Ladislaw is a sort of gypsy, he thinks nothing of the niceties of social rank. It must be something else if he were really vexed.

ROSAMOND. Music apart, he is not always very agreeable to me. Do you like him?

LYDGATE. Yes, I think he's a good fellow. Rather miscellaneous and bric-a-brac but likeable.

ROSAMOND. Do you know, I think he adores Mrs Casaubon.

LYDGATE. Poor devil! (*Pinches her ears.*)

ROSAMOND. Why so?

LYDGATE. Why, what can a man do when he takes to adoring one of you mermaids? He only neglects his work.

ROSAMOND. I'm sure you don't neglect your work. You're always at the hospital or seeing poor patients, and then at home you always want to pore over your microscopes and phials. Confess, you like those things better than me.

LYDGATE. Haven't you ambition enough to wish that your husband should be something better than a Middlemarch doctor? What I want, Rosy, is to be worthy of something exceptional. A man must work to do that, my pet.

ROSAMOND. Of course I wish you to make discoveries – no one could more wish you to attain a high position in some better place than Middlemarch. (*Goes to the piano.*) You cannot say that I've ever tried to hinder you from working. But we cannot live like hermits. (*Plays quietly.*) I like to meet people…

Rosamond felt herself beginning to discover that women, even after marriage, might make conquests.

She hums along, as she plays 'Lungi dal caro bene'. LYDGATE *puts his feet up on the sofa.*

You're not discontented with me, Tertius?

LYDGATE. No, dear, no. I am too entirely contented.

He contemplates.

ROSAMOND. Is that enough music for you, my lord?

LYDGATE. Yes, dear, if you're tired.

She comes to sit close to him.

ROSAMOND. What's absorbing you?

LYDGATE. I'm thinking of a great fellow, who was about as old as I am, three hundred years ago – and he'd already begun a new era in anatomy.

ROSAMOND. I can't guess. We used to play at guessing historical characters at school, but not anatomists.

LYDGATE. I'll tell you. His name was Vesalius. And the only way he could get to know anatomy as he did, was by going to snatch bodies at night from graveyards and places of execution.

ROSAMOND. Ugh! I'm very glad you're not Vesalius. I should have thought he might find some less horrible way than that.

LYDGATE. No, he couldn't. He could only get a complete skeleton by snatching the whitened bones of a criminal from the gallows, and burying them, and fetching them away by bits, secretly in the dead of night.

ROSAMOND (*half-playful*). I hope he's not one of your great heroes, else I shall have you getting up in the night to go to St Peter's churchyard. You have enemies enough.

LYDGATE. So had Vesalius, Rosy. No wonder the medical fogies in Middlemarch are jealous when some of the greatest doctors living were fierce upon Vesalius, because he showed the old ideas were wrong. But the facts of the human frame were on his side, so he got the better of them.

ROSAMOND (*interested*). And what happened to him afterwards?

LYDGATE. Oh, he had a great deal of fighting to the last. At one time they made him burn a good deal of his work. He died rather miserably.

Slight pause.

ROSAMOND. Do you know, Tertius, I often wish you'd not been a medical man.

LYDGATE. Nay, Rosy, don't say that. That's like saying you wish you'd married another.

ROSAMOND. Not at all. You're clever enough for anything. You might easily have been something else. And your cousins at Quallingham all think that you've sunk below them in your choice of a profession.

LYDGATE. The cousins at Quallingham may go to the Devil. What impudence to say that to you!

ROSAMOND (*quietly persevering*). Still, I don't think it's a nice profession, dear.

LYDGATE. It is the grandest profession in the world, Rosamond. And to say you love me without loving the medical man in me, is the same as to say that you like eating a peach but don't like its flavour. It pains me.

ROSAMOND (*smiles*). Very well, Doctor Grave-face. I will declare in future that I dote on skeletons, and body-snatchers, and bits of things in phials, and quarrels with everybody that end in your dying miserably.

LYDGATE (*petting her*). No, no, not as bad as that…

Scene Twenty-Seven

WILL. One of the most frequent visitors to their new house was Will Ladislaw.

BROOKE. Who had recently become editor of Mr Brooke's newspaper – *The Pioneer*.

WILL. He was often uncomplimentary to Rosamond.

ROSAMOND. But was gradually becoming necessary to her entertainment.

WILL *lying on the floor by the fire*, LYDGATE *reading* The Pioneer, *and* ROSAMOND *on the sofa with her embroidery*.

WILL (*to* LYDGATE). You're struggling for medical Reform, and I for political Reform.

LYDGATE. But it's no good your puffing up Brooke as a Reformer in *The Pioneer*, Ladislaw.

WILL. He's good enough for the occasion.

LYDGATE. That's the way with you political writers, Ladislaw. Crying up the men who are part of the very disease that wants curing.

WILL. Are we to try for nothing till we find immaculate men to work with?

LYDGATE. Oh... I see – of course. Suppose the worst opinion about Bulstrode were true, that wouldn't make it less true that he has the resolution to do what ought to be done in respect to the hospital. But he's nothing to me otherwise. I wouldn't cry him up on any personal ground.

WILL (*nettled*). Do you mean that I cry up Brooke on any personal ground? (*Starts to get up*.)

LYDGATE. Not at all. I was simply explaining my own actions. I meant that a man may work with others whose motives are equivocal, if he's quite sure of his personal independence, and that he's not working for his private interest – either place or money.

WILL. You've no more reason to imagine that I have personal expectations from Brooke, than I have to imagine that you have personal expectations from Bulstrode!

LYDGATE. You quite mistake me, Ladislaw. I beg your pardon. In fact I should rather attribute to you a romantic disregard of your own interests. I referred simply to intellectual bias in general.

ROSAMOND. How very unpleasant you both are this evening. I cannot conceive why money should have been referred to. Politics and medicine are sufficiently disagreeable.

LYDGATE. Poor Rosy! Disputation is not amusing to cherubs. Have some music. Ask Ladislaw to sing with you.

ROSAMOND *starts to sing 'Lungi dal caro bene'*. WILL *joins in*.

Scene Twenty-Eight

WILL. And later – when Will Ladislaw had gone back to his lodgings –

ROSAMOND. What put you out of temper this evening, Tertius?

LYDGATE. Me? It was Ladislaw who was out of temper.

ROSAMOND. I mean before that. Something had vexed you before you came in. You hurt me when you look so.

LYDGATE. Do I? Then I'm a brute. (*Caresses her penitently.*)

ROSAMOND. What vexed you?

LYDGATE. Oh, outdoor things… business…

FAREBROTHER. It was really a letter insisting on the payment of a bill for furniture.

LYDGATE. But Lydgate wished to save her from any perturbation.

ROSAMOND. Rosamond was expecting to have a baby.

Scene Twenty-Nine

WILL. That summer, Lydgate had to suffer a visit from his cousin, Captain Lydgate –

SPRAGUE. Which he had drawn down, because they had visited Uncle Godwin at Quallingham on the wedding tour.

ROSAMOND *arranging her hair at the mirror.*

ROSAMOND. I wish you would talk more to the Captain at dinner, Tertius. You really look so absent sometimes. You seem to be seeing through his head instead of looking at him.

LYDGATE. If he got his head broken I might look at it with interest, not before. He's a vapid fop. (*Slight pause.*) Parts his hair in a despicable fashion.

ROSAMOND. I cannot conceive why you should speak of your cousin so contemptuously.

LYDGATE. Ask Ladislaw if he doesn't think your Captain the greatest bore he ever met with.

MRS VINCY. Rosamond thought she knew perfectly well why Mr Ladislaw disliked the Captain.

ROSAMOND. He was jealous, and she liked his being jealous.

In my opinion, Captain Lydgate is a thorough gentleman, and I think you ought not, out of respect to Sir Godwin, to treat him with neglect.

LYDGATE. No, dear, but we've had dinners for him. He comes in and out as he likes. He doesn't want me.

ROSAMOND. Still, when he's in the room you might talk a little on his subjects. I think his conversation is quite agreeable. Yesterday he took me riding –

LYDGATE. Rosy!

ROSAMOND. He's assured me the grey is gentle –

LYDGATE. No!

ROSAMOND. And trained to carry a lady –

LYDGATE. You're with child! –

ROSAMOND. I feel so much better for a ride. I thought you might let me go riding again…

Silence.

LYDGATE. You will not go again, Rosy, that is understood. There would always be the chance of an accident. You know very well that I wished you to give up riding.

ROSAMOND. But there's the chance of an accident indoors, Tertius.

LYDGATE. My darling, don't talk nonsense. Surely I'm the person to judge for you. I say you are not to go again.

ROSAMOND (*after a moment*). I wish you'd help me fasten up my plaits, dear…

He does, and kisses her neck.

LYDGATE. I shall tell the Captain that he ought to have known better.

ROSAMOND. I beg you not to. It will be treating me as if I were a child. Promise that you'll leave the subject to me.

Slight pause.

LYDGATE. Very well.

MRS VINCY. But the gratification of riding on a fine horse, with Captain Lydgate – Sir Godwin's son – riding by her side, and of being met by anyone but her husband, was as good as her dreams before marriage.

ROSAMOND. And she was riveting the connection with Quallingham, which must be a wise thing to do.

BULSTRODE. But the gentle grey, unprepared for the crash of a tree being felled, took fright –

FAREBROTHER. – caused a worse fright to Rosamond –

MRS VINCY. – leading finally to the loss of her baby.

ROSAMOND. All the embroidered robes and caps had to be laid by in darkness.

SPRAGUE. And the Captain's visit naturally soon came to an end.

Scene Twenty-Nine (A)

ROSAMOND *sits*. LYDGATE *kneels by her, holding her hand*.

ROSAMOND (*mildly*). The ride made no difference, Tertius. If I'd stayed at home the same symptoms would have come on and it would have ended the same way, because I'd felt something like them before.

LYDGATE. Oh, my poor, poor darling!

But he secretly wondered over the terrible tenacity of this mild creature and his powerlessness over her.

Scene Thirty

LYDGATE. And he was also aware of the biting presence of a petty degrading care, such as casts the blight of irony over all higher effort.

Evening. LYDGATE *is looking at accounts.*

Dear Rosy, lay down your work and come and sit by me.

She obeys.

Dear. I'm obliged to tell you what will hurt you, Rosy. But there are things which husband and wife must think of together. I dare say it has occurred to you already, that I'm short of money.

ROSAMOND *looks away.*

My household expenses amount to nearly a thousand pounds, while the proceeds of the practice make hardly five hundred. The consequence is, there is a large debt at Brassing – three hundred and eight pounds – and, in fact, we are getting deeper every day.

ROSAMOND (*neutrally*). What can *I* do, Tertius?

LYDGATE. It's necessary for you to know, because I have to give security, and a man must come to make an inventory of the furniture.

Slight pause.

ROSAMOND. Have you not asked Papa for money?

LYDGATE. No.

ROSAMOND. Then I must ask him! (*Stands and moves away.*)

LYDGATE. No, Rosy, it's too late. The inventory will be
   tomorrow. It's a mere security, it will make no difference, it's
   temporary. I insist your father shall not know, unless I
   choose to tell him.

Despite herself, ROSAMOND *begins to cry. She faces away
from him.*

   Try not to grieve, darling. I have been at fault. I ought to
   have seen that I could not afford to live in this way. But
   many things have told against me in my practice and it really
   has ebbed to a low point. We must change our way of living.
   Come, dear, sit down and forgive me.

She comes back to him.

ROSAMOND. Why can't you put off the inventory? You can
   send the men away tomorrow.

LYDGATE. I shall not send them away.

ROSAMOND. If we left Middlemarch, there would be a sale,
   and that would do as well.

LYDGATE. But we're not going to leave Middlemarch.

ROSAMOND. Why can't we go to London? Or near
   Quallingham, where your family is known?

LYDGATE. We can go nowhere without money, Rosamond.

ROSAMOND. Your family wouldn't wish you to be without
   money. And surely these odious tradesmen might be made to
   understand that and to wait.

LYDGATE (*angrily*). This is idle, Rosamond. I've made
   arrangements and they must be carried out. As to my family,
   I have no expectations whatever, and shall not ask them for
   anything.

Silence.

   There are some details I want to consider with you. We can
   give a good deal of the plate back, and any jewellery we like.

ROSAMOND (*thinly*). Are we to go without spoons or forks,
   then?

LYDGATE. Oh no, dear. But look – (*Produces a list.*) I've marked a number of articles, which, if we returned them, would reduce the debt by thirty pounds and more. I've not marked any of the jewellery. (*Offers it to her.*)

ROSAMOND. It's useless for me to look, Tertius. You will return what you please.

LYDGATE lowers the list. ROSAMOND leaves the room. He rises, at a loss. After a while she returns with a jewellery box.

This is all the jewellery you ever gave me. Return what you like, and the plate. You'll not expect me to stay at home tomorrow. I shall go to Papa's.

LYDGATE (*bitterly*). And when shall you come back?

ROSAMOND. Oh, in the evening. Of course I shall not mention the subject to Mamma.

Slight pause.

LYDGATE. Now we've been united, Rosy, you should not leave me to myself in the first trouble.

ROSAMOND. I shall do everything it becomes me to do.

LYDGATE. It's not right that the thing should be left to servants. And I shall be obliged to go out on my rounds – I don't know how early. I understand your shrinking from these money affairs, but it's surely better to manage the thing ourselves, and let the servants see as little as possible.

ROSAMOND. Very well – I will stay at home.

LYDGATE. I shall not touch these jewels, Rosy. Take them away again. But I'll write out a list of plate that can be packed up.

ROSAMOND (*slightest touch of sarcasm*). The servants will know *that*.

LYDGATE. Well, we must meet some disagreeables. Where's the pencil, I wonder?

She brings him the pencil. As she turns away, he puts his arm around her.

Come, darling, let's make the best of things. It will only be
for a time, I hope. Kiss me.

She receives and returns his kiss faintly.

But Lydgate looked forward with dread to future discussions.

Scene Thirty-One

In the street outside the Vincys'. A winter's night.

FAREBROTHER. Ah, Lydgate – just the man I was going to
look for. You see, I can leave the whist table easily enough
now I don't need the money. I owe that to you, Mrs
Casaubon says.

LYDGATE. How?

FAREBROTHER. When Casaubon died, you recommended me
warmly for the church at Lowick, but you didn't mean me to
know it. I call that ungenerous. You should let a man have
the pleasure of feeling you've done him a good turn.

LYDGATE. I can't tell what you mean – I spoke of you to Mrs
Casaubon, that's all.

FAREBROTHER. Well, I am very glad to have the living and
you've done me a service. It's rather a strong check on one's
self-complacency to find out how much of one's right doing,
depends on not being in want of money. A man will not be
tempted to say the Lord's Prayer backward, if he doesn't
want the Devil's services. I've no need to hang on the smiles
of chance now.

LYDGATE. I don't see there's any money-getting without
chance. In a profession, it's pretty sure to come by chance.

FAREBROTHER. Ah, there's patience wanted with the way of
the world. But it's easier for a man to wait patiently when he
has friends who love him, and ask for nothing better than to
help him through.

LYDGATE. Oh, yes. (*Looks at his pocket watch.*)

> Lydgate knew this was an offer of help from Mr Farebrother and he could not bear it. Suicide seemed easier.

FAREBROTHER. What time are you?

LYDGATE. After eleven. (*Leaves.*)

Scene Thirty-Two

LYDGATE. Lydgate made many efforts to draw Rosamond into sympathy with him. He dreaded a future without affection.

The Lydgates' drawing room.

(*Draws her onto his knee.*) We can do with only one servant and live on very little. There must be many in our rank who manage with much less – there's Wrench –

ROSAMOND (*with disgust*). Oh, if you think of living as the Wrenchs do –

LYDGATE. I only meant that he avoids expenses.

Pause.

ROSAMOND. But why should you not have a good practice, Tertius? You should be more careful not to offend people, and you should prescribe more medicines as the others do. It cannot answer to be eccentric, you should think what would be generally liked.

LYDGATE (*controlling anger*). What I am to do in my practice, Rosy, is for me to judge.

Pause.

ROSAMOND. My Uncle Bulstrode ought to allow you a salary for the hospital. It's not right that you should work for nothing.

LYDGATE. It was understood from the beginning that my services would be gratuitous. (*Pause.*) I think I see one resource. I hear that young Ned Plymdale is going to be married to Miss Sophie Toller. They are rich, and it's not often that a good house like ours is vacant in Middlemarch. I feel sure they would be glad to take this house with most of the furniture and they'd be willing to pay handsomely. I shall employ Trumbull as an agent. No time must be lost.

ROSAMOND *rises and walks away. She is in tears*.

I am very sorry, Rosamond. I know this is painful.

ROSAMOND. I thought at least when I had borne to have that man taking an inventory – *that* would suffice.

LYDGATE. I explained it to you at the time, dear. That was only a security, and behind that security there is a debt. If young Plymdale will take our house and most of the furniture, we shall be able to pay some debts. We might take a smaller house. Trumbull, I know, has a very decent one to let at thirty pounds a year and this is ninety.

ROSAMOND. I could never have believed that you would like to act in this way.

LYDGATE (*rising*). Like it? Of course I don't like it – it's the only thing I can do.

ROSAMOND. I should have thought there were many other means. Let's have a sale and leave Middlemarch altogether.

LYDGATE. What's the use of leaving my work in Middlemarch to go where I have none? We should be just as penniless.

ROSAMOND. That's entirely your own doing, Tertius. You will not behave as you ought to do to your own family. You offended Captain Lydgate. Sir Godwin was very kind to me when we were at Quallingham, and I'm sure if you told him your affairs, he would do anything for you. But rather than that, you like giving up our house and furniture to Mr Ned Plymdale.

LYDGATE (*violently*). Well then, if you will have it so, I *do* like it. I like it better than making a fool of myself by going to beg where it's no use. Understand, then, that it's what *I like to do*!

ROSAMOND *walks out in silence*.

FAREBROTHER. It was as if a fracture in delicate crystal had begun.

Scene Thirty-Three

ROSAMOND. Next day, Rosamond went to see Mrs Plymdale to congratulate her on her son's marriage.

MRS PLYMDALE. Mrs Plymdale's view was that Rosamond might now have retrospective glimpses of her folly in rejecting him.

Mrs Plymdale's house. MRS PLYMDALE *has placed a chair for* ROSAMOND.

Yes, Ned is most happy I must say. And Sophie Toller is all I could desire in a daughter-in-law. She is a very nice girl – no airs, no pretensions.

ROSAMOND. I've always thought her very agreeable.

MRS PLYMDALE. I look on it as a reward for Ned, that he should have got into the very best connection in the town.

ROSAMOND. I'm sure he's a very deserving young man.

MRS PLYMDALE. Oh, he has not the style of a captain in the army, as if everybody was beneath him, but I'm thankful he has not. It's a poor preparation both for here and hereafter.

ROSAMOND. Oh dear, yes, appearances have very little to do with happiness; I think there is every prospect of their being a happy couple. What house will they take?

MRS PLYMDALE. Oh, as for that, they must put up with what they can get. They've been looking at a house in St Peter's Place. (*Goes to the window*.) I suppose they're not likely to hear of a better. Indeed, I think Ned will decide the matter today.

ROSAMOND. I like St Peter's Place.

MRS PLYMDALE (*looking out*). Well, it's a genteel situation, near the church, but the windows are narrow and it's all ups and downs. (*Turning.*) You don't happen to know of any other?

Slight pause.

ROSAMOND. Oh no. I hear so little of these things.

Scene Thirty-Four

MRS VINCY. Rosamond was now obliged to do what she intensely disliked, but she must act according to her judgement.

ROSAMOND. If her judgement were not right, she would not have wished to act on it.

Trumbull's office.

Mr Trumbull, has my husband called about disposing of our house?

TRUMBULL. Yes, ma'am, yes, he did; he did so. I was about to fulfil his order, if possible this afternoon. He wished me not to procrastinate.

ROSAMOND. I called to tell you not to go any further, Mr Trumbull, and I beg you not to mention what has been said on the subject. Will you oblige me?

TRUMBULL. Certainly, Mrs Lydgate. Confidence is sacred with me. I am to consider the commission withdrawn?

ROSAMOND. Yes, I find that Mr Ned Plymdale has taken a house already – the one in St Peter's Place. And, besides, there are other circumstances which render the proposal unnecessary.

TRUMBULL. Very good, Mrs Lydgate, very good. Rely on me. The affair shall go no further.

Scene Thirty-Five

The Lydgates' drawing room. ROSAMOND *idly plays a few notes on the piano.* LYDGATE *lies on the sofa, absorbed.*

ROSAMOND. Mr Ned Plymdale has taken a house already.

LYDGATE (*startled*). How do you know?

ROSAMOND. I called at Mrs Plymdale's this morning, and she told me he'd taken the house in St Peter's Place.

> LYDGATE *reacts with a bitter spasm of vexation. Then –*

LYDGATE. Perhaps someone else may turn up. I told Trumbull to be on the lookout if he failed with Plymdale.

Pause.

ROSAMOND. How much money is it that those disagreeable people want?

LYDGATE. Oh, if I could have got six hundred from Plymdale I might have managed to make our creditors wait patiently.

ROSAMOND. But, I mean, how much should you want if we stayed in this house?

LYDGATE. More than I'm likely to get anywhere…

ROSAMOND. Why should you not mention the sum?

LYDGATE. Well, it would take at least a thousand to set me at ease. But that's impossible… (*Angered.*) I wish you – (*Goes.*)

Alone, ROSAMOND *goes to the table drawer and finds a letter. She reads it back.*

ROSAMOND. Dear Sir Godwin, thank you for your letter expressing condolences at the loss of my baby. Erm – (*Skipping through.*) desirable that Tertius should quit Middlemarch… professional success hindered… his great regard for you, his uncle… always his best friend… money difficulties… requiring… (*Fills in the amount.*) one… thousand… pounds… (*Takes the letter, and goes.*)

Scene Thirty-Six

SPRAGUE. But in a few days.

Breakfast. ROSAMOND *brings two cups; they sit either side of the table.*

LYDGATE. Trumbull seems to have got no bite at all on the house. I shall have to see him this morning and tell him to advertise in *The Pioneer* and *The Trumpet*.

ROSAMOND. Ah. (*The inevitable moment.*) But I ordered him not to enquire further.

LYDGATE *stares at her in amazement.*

LYDGATE. May I ask why?

ROSAMOND. I knew it would be very injurious to you if it were known you wished to part with your house and furniture and I had a very strong objection to it. I think that was reason enough.

LYDGATE. It was of no consequence, then, that I had told you imperative reasons of another kind, and had given an order accordingly?

ROSAMOND (*becomes ever more cold and calmly correct*). I think I had a perfect right to speak on a subject which concerns me at least as much as you.

LYDGATE. You had a right to speak, but only to me. You had no right to contradict my orders secretly and treat me as if I were a fool. Is it of any use to tell you again why we must try to part with the house?

ROSAMOND. It's not necessary. I remembered what you said. You spoke just as violently as you do now. But that does not alter my opinion that you ought to try every other means rather than take a step, which is so painful to me. As for advertising the house, I think it would be perfectly degrading to you.

LYDGATE. And suppose I disregard your opinion as you do mine?

ROSAMOND. You can do so, of course. But I think you ought
to have told me before we married that you would place me
in the worst position, rather than give up your own will.

*Silence. He has moved away from the table. She quietly
brings him his cup.*

When we were married, everyone felt your position was very
high. I could not have imagined then that you would want to
sell our furniture and take a house in Bride Street, where the
rooms are like cages. If we are to live in that way, let us at
least leave Middlemarch.

LYDGATE. These would be very strong considerations if I
didn't happen to be in debt.

ROSAMOND. Many persons must have been in debt in the
same way, but if they are respectable, people trust them.
(*With serene wisdom.*) It cannot be good to act rashly.

LYDGATE *starts to go.*

I may at least request that you will not go to Trumbull at
present – until it has been seen that there are no other means.
(*Slight pause.*) Promise you will not go to him without
telling me.

LYDGATE (*short laugh*). I think it is you who should do
nothing without telling me!

He had a growing dread of Rosamond's elusive obstinacy,
which could not allow any assertion of power to be final.

He hesitates and then leaves.

ROSAMOND. I'm sure I've acted in every way for the best.
But Tertius is so disappointing. (*Resentfully.*) And now even
Will Ladislaw has left. (*Sighs deeply.*)

WILL. She felt some resentment towards Will Ladislaw, for his
exaltation of Mrs Casaubon.

Scene Thirty-Seven

LYDGATE, *alone*.

LYDGATE. What am I to do? Perhaps I should appeal to Sir
Godwin after all. (*Winces*.) I can't depend on a letter. A
journey north? Oh no! Have I fallen so low?

ROSAMOND *enters, full of hope*.

ROSAMOND. Tertius. Here's a letter. From Quallingham!

She hands it to him; he opens it, puzzled.

LYDGATE. My Uncle Godwin… (*Reads*.)

SIR GODWIN (*his voice from the shadows*). Dear Tertius –
Don't set your wife to write to me when you have anything
to ask. It is a roundabout wheedling sort of thing, which I
should not have credited you with. As to my supplying you
with a thousand pounds, I can do nothing of the sort. My
own family drains me to the last penny. You seem to have
made a mess where you are and the sooner you go
somewhere else the better. But I have nothing to do with men
of your profession. You might have gone into the Army or
the Church. I have always wished you well, but you must
consider yourself on your own entirely now. Your
affectionate uncle – Godwin.

LYDGATE. It will be impossible to endure life with you, if you
will be always secretly meddling, interfering in ignorance in
affairs, which it belongs to me to decide on.

Silence.

I had nearly resolved on going to Quallingham. It would
have cost me pain, yet it might have been of some use. But I
am at the mercy of your devices. If you mean to resist every
wish I express, say so and defy me. I shall at least know
what I'm doing then.

Silence.

ROSAMOND. Rosamond wished she had never seen him.

SIR GODWIN. Sir Godwin's rudeness –

BULSTRODE. – disagreeable creditors –

VINCY. – even her father was unkind and might have done more for them.

MRS VINCY. There was but one person in the world she did not blame.

ROSAMOND. Herself.

LYDGATE. Can't you see, Rosamond, that nothing can be so fatal as a want of openness between us? It's happened again and again, that I've expressed a decided wish, and you've seemed to assent, yet after, you have secretly disobeyed. In that way, I can never know what I have to trust to. There'd be some hope for us, if you'd admit this… Am I such an unreasonable brute?

Silence.

May I depend on your not acting secretly in future?

ROSAMOND. I cannot possibly make promises in answer to such words. 'Secret meddling', 'interfering ignorance' – I think you ought to apologise. You spoke of it's being impossible to live with me. Certainly you've not made my life pleasant to me of late. I think it was to be expected that I should try to avert some of the hardships which our marriage has brought on me. (*A tear, pressed away.*)

Pause.

LYDGATE. Lydgate felt checkmated.

FAREBROTHER. Was he not only to sink from his highest scientific resolve, but to sink into the hideous fettering of domestic hate?

LYDGATE (*softening*). Rosamond. You should allow for a man's words when he's disappointed and provoked. How could I wish to make anything hard to you? When I hurt you, I hurt part of my own life. I should never be angry with you, if you would be quite open with me.

ROSAMOND. I've only wished to prevent you from hurrying us into wretchedness without any necessity. (*Tears again since he has softened*.) It is so very hard to be disgraced here among all the people we know and to live in such a miserable way. I wish I had died with the baby...

FAREBROTHER. Such words and tears are omnipotent over a loving-hearted man.

LYDGATE *draws her to him, and comforts her as she weeps*.

LYDGATE. He wished to excuse everything in her if he could. As if she were an animal of another and feebler species.

ROSAMOND (*calmly*). Nevertheless, she had mastered him.

Slow fade.

End of Act One.

ACT TWO

Scene Thirty-Eight

Outside Stone Court. A fine summer's evening.

BULSTRODE. Mr Bulstrode the banker had recently bought Mr Featherstone's old residence at Stone Court. (*Looks at the house.*)

MRS BULSTRODE. As a retreat, which he might gradually enlarge and beautify –

BULSTRODE. – until it should be conducive to the divine glory that he should enter on it as a residence.

He surveys his land.

MRS BULSTRODE. The evenings were delicious in that quiet spot –

BULSTRODE. The odours of the new hayricks…

MRS BULSTRODE. The breath of the rich old garden…

BULSTRODE (*to himself*). What's that fellow coming up the lane?

After a moment, RAFFLES *appears.*

RAFFLES. By Jove, Nick Bulstrode, it's you! How are you, eh? You didn't expect to see *me* here. Come, shake us by the hand.

BULSTRODE. I did not indeed expect you in this remote country place.

RAFFLES. I came out of love to you, Nick. Found your address – (*Takes out a crumpled paper.*) 'The Shrubs' – (*Looks back down the lane.*) You live near at hand, eh? (*Then looks at Stone Court.*) Have another rural mansion to invite me to? Your old lady must have been dead a pretty while – gone to glory without the pain of knowing how poor her daughter was, eh? But by Jove you're very pale and pasty.

BULSTRODE. I was going home. (*Starts to go.*)

RAFFLES. I'll come back with you, Nick. What a pleasant surprise it must be to see me, old fellow.

BULSTRODE. Our acquaintance, many years ago, had not the sort of intimacy which you are now assuming, Mr Raffles.

RAFFLES. You don't like being called Nick? Why, I've always called you Nick in my heart. By Jove, my feelings have ripened for you like fine old cognac. I hope you've got some in the house now.

BULSTRODE. You had some business to transact with me? I have little time to spare, Mr Raffles.

RAFFLES. Nick... I must call you Nick, we always did call you Young Nick when you meant to marry the old widow. Some said you had a likeness to Old Nick, but that was your mother's fault, calling you Nicholas.

BULSTRODE. May I ask why you returned from America. I considered, when an adequate sum was furnished, you would remain there for life.

RAFFLES. I did stay ten years. And I'm not going again, Nick. (*Slow wink.*)

BULSTRODE. Do you wish to be settled in any business?

RAFFLES. I don't care about working. I want an independence.

BULSTRODE. That could be supplied, if you would engage to keep at a distance.

RAFFLES. That must be as it suits my convenience.

BULSTRODE. If you intend to rely on me, Mr Raffles, you will meet my wishes.

RAFFLES. Ah, didn't I always? I've often thought that I might have done better by telling your old woman that I'd found her daughter and grandchild. But you've buried the old lady by this time. And you've got the fortune you wanted out of that profitable business. Still in the dissenting line, eh? Still godly? (*Slow wink.*)

BULSTRODE. You will do well to reflect, Mr Raffles, that it is possible for a man to overreach himself. If you insist on remaining here I shall decline to know you.

RAFFLES. Ha! That reminds me of the droll dog of a thief who declined to know the constable. (*Paces*.) I'll tell you what. Give us a couple of hundred and – honour bright – I'll go away. But I shall come and go where I like. Have you the money?

BULSTRODE. No, I have one hundred. (*Indicates Stone Court*.)

RAFFLES. I'll wait here till you bring it. I did have another look after Sarah again – what was her married name? – But I didn't find her. If I hear of her and her family, you shall know, Nick. What *was* her husband's name? (*Opens a pocketbook*.)

BULSTRODE. I'll fetch the money. (*Starts to go back to the house*.)

RAFFLES. Oh yes… (*Lowering the book*.) It was Ladislaw.

They turn to each other.

Scene Thirty-Nine

BULSTRODE. Though Raffles left Middlemarch, Bulstrode felt a cold certainty that he would come back.

BULSTRODE *alone*.

MRS BULSTRODE. Night and day, without interruption, save of brief sleep –

FAREBROTHER. – he felt certain scenes of his earlier life coming between him and everything else…

RAFFLES. He had once married a rich widow in a dishonourable business and had displaced her daughter's inheritance.

SPRAGUE. A daughter who had fled dishonour and could not be found.

RAFFLES. Only one man besides Bulstrode knew where that daughter had gone and he was Raffles, paid to keep silent.

BULSTRODE *kneels in prayer.*

LYDGATE. Bulstrode was not a coarse hypocrite.

MRS BULSTRODE. His soul had become saturated with the belief that he did everything for God's sake, being indifferent to it for his own.

BULSTRODE (*looking up*). Who would use money and position better than I mean to use them?

FAREBROTHER. But now he was in danger of seeing his past disclosed to the scorching judgement of his neighbours –

MRS BULSTRODE. – and the wife he loved.

BULSTRODE. How can I recover peace? My wife believes in me. How can I restore trust? By what sacrifice can I stay the rod, oh Lord. How can I make restitution?...

A realisation, and he rises slowly to his feet.

At last he came to a difficult resolve –

WILL. – and wrote to Will Ladislaw.

Scene Forty

BULSTRODE*'s house at The Shrubs.*

BULSTRODE. I begged you to come to my house, Mr Ladislaw, because I have a communication of a very private – indeed of a sacredly confidential nature to make to you. Nothing, I dare say, has been farther from your thoughts than that there had been important ties in the past, which could connect your history with mine.

WILL. No indeed.

BULSTRODE. You see before you, Mr Ladislaw, a man who is deeply stricken. But for the knowledge that I am before the bar of One who seeth not as man seeth, I should be under no compulsion to make any disclosure. So far as human laws go you have no claim on me...

Silence. He motions WILL *to sit.*

I am told that your mother's name was Sarah Dunkirk and that she ran away from her family to go on the stage. Can you confirm this?

WILL. Yes, it's true.

BULSTRODE. Did she ever mention *her* mother to you?

WILL. I heard her say she thought her mother did not know the reason of her running away.

BULSTRODE. That mother was my first wife. You have a claim on me, Mr Ladislaw. I was enriched by that marriage – which I probably would not have been if my wife could have discovered her daughter. That daughter, I gather, is no longer living?

WILL (*rising*). No

BULSTRODE. Pray be seated, Mr Ladislaw. I entreat your patience with one who is already bowed down by inward trial.

WILL *sits again.*

It is my wish, Mr Ladislaw, to make amends for the deprivation, which befell your mother. I know that you are without fortune, and I wish to supply you adequately from a store which would have been yours had my wife been able to find her daughter.

Pause.

Bulstrode felt he was performing a strikingly penitential act in the eyes of God.

WILL. I suppose you knew of my mother's existence, and where she might have been found?

BULSTRODE. I will not deny it. I wish to make atonement.
I'm ready to allow you five hundred pounds yearly during
my life, and the capital at my death.

WILL. Were you connected with the business by which that
fortune was originally made?

BULSTRODE (*after a moment*). Yes.

WILL. And was that business a thoroughly dishonourable one?
One that might have ranked those concerned with it with
thieves and convicts?

BULSTRODE (*angrily*). The business was established long
before I became acquainted with it, sir, nor is it for you to
institute an enquiry of that kind.

WILL (*stands*). Yes it is. It is eminently mine when I have to
decide whether I will accept your money. My unblemished
honour is important to me. It is important to me to have no
stain on my birth and connections. And now I find there is a
stain which I can't help. My mother felt it, and tried to keep
clear of it, and so will I. You shall keep your ill-gotten
money. Goodnight, sir.

He goes. After a moment, BULSTRODE *breaks down.*

MRS BULSTRODE. Bulstrode wept.

BULSTRODE. But it was of comfort that Will Ladislaw was
not likely to repeat what had taken place that evening.

Scene Forty-One

LYDGATE. Meanwhile, Lydgate had no longer free energy
enough for his own research.

LYDGATE *alone*.

WILL. Under the first galling pressure of difficulties, he had
once or twice tried a dose of opium.

LYDGATE. And his thought began to turn upon gambling.

FAREBROTHER. He even found himself in the billiard room at The Green Dragon –

Instantly the company are gathered low around the billiards table, cues poised, as if playing intensely. The sound of billiard balls and the noise of the billiards room.

LYDGATE. – excited by gleaming visions of buying his rescue – (*Putting money down feverishly.*)

FRED. – but he was shocked by the sight of Rosamond's brother Fred there, watching him gravely…

FRED *is standing, staring at* LYDGATE.

LYDGATE. And the next day he felt unmixed disgust.

The billiards room dissolves. LYDGATE *is alone again.*

Perhaps we should quit Middlemarch after all. But would any man buy the practice for as little as it's worth? And is it not contemptible to relinquish worthy work? And afterwards… Rosamond in poor lodgings?

FAREBROTHER. There is no incompatibility between scientific insight and poor lodgings.

ROSAMOND. The incompatibility is between scientific ambition and a wife who objects to that kind of residence.

LYDGATE. I have to ask help from somebody. Mr Vincy?

VINCY. But Mr Vincy had suffered one bad year after another, and was trading more and more on capital borrowed from Bulstrode. He couldn't afford a single hundred…

LYDGATE. Mr Bulstrode? If I spoke to him I could always make a retreat if… Oh no, the humiliation of dependence on Bulstrode…

BULSTRODE. Then opportunity came –

Scene Forty-Two

BULSTRODE*'s house at The Shrubs*.

BULSTRODE. It's my health. I can't sleep and I'm afraid of insanity.

LYDGATE (*starting to examine him*). Any mental strain may affect a delicate frame like yours. I'm naturally strong, yet I myself have been thoroughly shaken lately.

BULSTRODE. Am I more liable to cholera, if it visited our district?

LYDGATE. We have taken good practical precautions for the town. The arrangements in the new hospital –

BULSTRODE. Ah, yes! With regard to my health, I am contemplating withdrawal from the management of much business – I think I may take up some place near the coast. You would recommend that?

LYDGATE (*absently*). Oh... yes.

BULSTRODE. In case of my ultimate decision to leave Middlemarch, I must withdraw my support for the hospital.

Silence. LYDGATE *is shocked*.

LYDGATE. The loss to the hospital can hardly be made up, I fear.

BULSTRODE. The only person who may be counted on to increase her contribution is Mrs Casaubon. You might enter into the subject with her. And we might win more general support by a change of system. (*Slight pause*.) I mean the amalgamation of the new hospital with the old infirmary. The medical management of the two shall be combined. The benevolent interests of the town will cease to be divided.

LYDGATE. I can't be expected to rejoice in that since the other medical men will interrupt my methods, if only because they are mine.

BULSTRODE. Yes, the original plan was one I had much at heart. But since providential indications demand renunciation... I renounce.

Pause.

LYDGATE. I'm much obliged to you for giving me full notice. The highest object to me is my profession and I had identified the hospital with the best use I can make of my profession. But the best use is not always the same with monetary success. Everything which has made the hospital unpopular has helped to make me unpopular as a practitioner. I get chiefly patients who can't pay me. I should like them best, if I had nobody to pay on my own side. (*Takes the plunge.*) I have slipped into money difficulties, which I can see no way out of, unless someone who trusts me and my future will advance me a sum without other security. I have no prospects from my own family. My expenses, in consequence of my marriage, have been much greater than I expected. The result is that it would take a thousand pounds to clear me. I find that it is out of the question that my wife's father should make such an advance. That's why I mention my position to... to the only other man who may be held to have some personal connection with my prosperity or ruin.

BULSTRODE. I am grieved, though not surprised. For my own part, I regretted your alliance with my brother-in-law's family, which has always been of prodigal habits and which has already been much indebted to me. My advice would be, that you should simply become a bankrupt.

Silence.

LYDGATE (*bitterly*). That would not improve my prospect.

BULSTRODE. It is a trial, but trial is our portion here, and a needed corrective. I recommend you to weigh my advice.

LYDGATE. Thank you. I've occupied you too long. Good day. (*Leaves.*)

Scene Forty-Three

MRS BULSTRODE. Now, Mrs Bulstrode believed in her husband as an excellent man.

BULSTRODE. She knew little of his former connections.

MRS BULSTRODE. His influence had turned her own mind towards seriousness.

BULSTRODE. In some respects he was rather afraid of her –

MRS BULSTRODE. – who had nothing to be ashamed of –

BULSTRODE. – and whom he had married out of a thorough inclination still subsisting.

MRS BULSTRODE *at the sofa, looking out of the window nervously.*

MRS BULSTRODE. Nicholas – there has been such a disagreeable man – it's made me quite uncomfortable.

BULSTRODE. What kind of man, my dear.

MRS BULSTRODE. A drunken, red-faced man. He declared he was an old friend of yours, and you would be sorry not to see him. Most impudent he was – stared at me and said his friend Nick had luck in his wives. Do you really know anything of such a man?

BULSTRODE. I believe I know, my dear. An unfortunate dissolute wretch whom I helped too much in days gone by.

MRS BULSTRODE. You look very ill. Is there anything the matter?

BULSTRODE. I've a good deal of pain in my head.

MRS BULSTRODE. Lie down, and let me sponge it.

BULSTRODE (*lying on the sofa*). You're very good, Harriet.

She sponges his head.

Scene Forty-Four

RAFFLES. But Raffles soon insisted on staying in the house.

As BULSTRODE *rises,* RAFFLES *takes his place, lying on the sofa.*

BULSTRODE (*to* MRS BULSTRODE). There's a family tie which binds me to this case, but I urge caution. There are signs of a certain mental alienation in him. I think it's safer if no one but myself should enter this room, even with food and drink.

FAREBROTHER. Bulstrode shrank from a direct lie with an intensity disproportionate to the number of his more indirect misdeeds.

SPRAGUE. But it is only what we are vividly conscious of, that we can vividly imagine to be seen by Omniscience.

MRS BULSTRODE *leaves.*

Early morning. BULSTRODE *watches* RAFFLES *asleep.* RAFFLES *suddenly becomes aware of* BULSTRODE *standing over him, and sits up in terror.*

BULSTRODE. I came to call you, Mr Raffles, because I've ordered the carriage at half-past seven to conduct you to the railway – Be silent, sir, and hear what I have to say. I shall supply you with one hundred pounds now, but if you return to Middlemarch – if you use your tongue in a manner injurious to me, you will have to live without help from me. I know the worst you can do, and I shall brave it. Get up, sir, and do as I order.

RAFFLES *rises and leaves.*

RAFFLES. Raffles left. (*Stops and turns.*) But he would return.

BULSTRODE. For Bulstrode it was as if, on all the pleasant surroundings of his life, a dangerous reptile had left his slimy traces...

(*Kneels.*) Surely, Lord, it must be more for your Divine Glory that I should escape dishonour.

He made preparations to leave Middlemarch, but leaving an opening for return.

Scene Forty-Five

RAFFLES (*as he becomes* GARTH). Now, Bulstrode had been consulting Mr Garth, the land agent, on how to let Mr Featherstone's old property at Stone Court. But one day Mr Garth came to his house at The Shrubs.

GARTH. I've just come away from Stone Court, Mr Bulstrode.

BULSTRODE. You found nothing wrong there I hope?

GARTH. Why, yes – a stranger – who is very ill, I think. He wants a doctor and I came to tell you. His name is Raffles.

Slight pause.

BULSTRODE. I see. Poor wretch. Do you know how he came there?

GARTH. I saw he was ill and it seemed right to carry him under shelter.

BULSTRODE. Perhaps you will oblige me by calling at Mr Lydgate's. I'll ride myself to Stone Court. (*Slight pause.*) Perhaps you had some other business?

GARTH. Yes. I must request you to put your business into some other hands.

BULSTRODE. This is sudden.

GARTH. It is but it's fixed.

Slight pause.

BULSTRODE. You've been led to this by some slanders, uttered by that unhappy creature?

GARTH. I can't deny that.

BULSTRODE. You're a conscientious man, Mr Garth, accountable to God. You wouldn't believe a slander.

GARTH. I'm obliged to believe that this Raffles has told me the truth. I can't be happy working with you. I must beg you to seek another agent.

BULSTRODE. Very well. But I must at least know the worst he's told you.

GARTH. What he has said to me will never pass my lips. If you led a harmful life for gain, and kept others out of their rights by deceit, I dare say you repent. You'd like to go back, but can't. That must be a bitter thing. It's not for me to make your life harder.

BULSTRODE. But you do – you do make it harder, by turning your back on me.

GARTH. I'm sorry. I don't judge you. But I have that feeling that I can't go on working with you. Everything else is buried. And I wish you good day. (*Starts to leave*.)

BULSTRODE. One moment, Mr Garth. I may trust then that you will not repeat, either to man or woman –

GARTH. Why should I have said it if I didn't mean it?

BULSTRODE. Excuse me. I am the victim of this man. You're wronging me by too readily believing him.

GARTH. No, I'm ready to believe better when better is proved. And what I say I've no need to swear. I wish you good day.

BULSTRODE. The deep humiliation under Mr Garth's rejection alternated with the sense of safety that the upright Mr Garth and no other, had been the man to whom Raffles had spoken.

(*Looking to Heaven*.) Oh God, if I could breathe in perfect liberty, my life will be more consecrated to you than it has ever been before.

Scene Forty-Six

BULSTRODE. He rode to Stone Court, anxious to arrive there before the doctor.

Stone Court upstairs. RAFFLES *on the bed*. BULSTRODE *approaches*.

RAFFLES (*intense vague terror*). I've only come because I'm ill. The money's all gone – I've been robbed – half of it taken. And I'm ill – somebody's hunting me – they're after me. But I haven't told anybody anything. I've kept my mouth shut – I've not –

BULSTRODE. That's untrue. You told the man who brought you here – my agent, Garth.

RAFFLES. No no – I was seeing things. I swear to God – I wasn't – I didn't –

BULSTRODE. Who else have you told?

RAFFLES. No, no, I've not... I've not... (*Sinks back.*)

MRS ABEL (*entering*). Sir? The doctor's here.

BULSTRODE. Thank you, Mrs Abel. What has this man been saying to you?

MRS ABEL. He's only asked for beer and hasn't spoken to me since. He's been very ill.

BULSTRODE (*as* LYDGATE *enters*). Ah, doctor...

MRS ABEL *steps back a little*.

I've called you in because –

LYDGATE (*goes to examine the patient*). Let me see...

BULSTRODE. He's an unfortunate man who was once in my employment many years ago. Afterwards he went to America and returned, I fear, to an idle dissolute life. Being destitute, he has a claim on me... I believe he's seriously ill; his mind is affected, I feel bound to do the utmost for him...

LYDGATE. What's his name?

BULSTRODE. Raffles. (*Slight pause.*) You may go, Mrs Abel.

MRS ABEL. Sir…

She goes. LYDGATE *continues his examination.*

BULSTRODE. Is it a serious case?

LYDGATE. It's difficult to decide. The man had a robust constitution to begin with. I should not expect this attack to be fatal. But he should be well watched.

BULSTRODE. I will remain here myself, for the night.

LYDGATE. I should think that is hardly necessary.

BULSTRODE. The housekeeper can relieve me if needed.

LYDGATE. Very well then. I need give my directions only to you. (*Writes instructions.*) I shouldn't wonder if he got better in a few days by adhering to my treatment. But there must be firmness. In cases of alcoholic poisoning such as this, the prevalent practice is to allow alcohol. But I've repeatedly acted on a contrary conviction with a favourable result. If he calls for alcoholic liquors of any kind, you are *not* to give them to him. In my opinion, men in his condition are oftener killed by treatment than by the disease. (*Starts to leave.*)

I suppose Bulstrode has some test by which he finds out whom Heaven cares for. He's made up his mind it doesn't care for me.

SPRAGUE. As he rode home, Lydgate thought –

LYDGATE. I must tell Rosamond my application to Bulstrode failed. I must prepare her for the worst.

Scene Forty-Seven

BAILIFF. But the bailiffs were already in the house.

The Lydgates' drawing room. Two BAILIFFS *put chairs on the table, ready for removal.* ROSAMOND *lies on the sofa, which may be out of position.* LYDGATE *enters, sees what has happened and runs to* ROSAMOND. *Kneels beside her.*

LYDGATE (*almost a cry of prayer*). Oh, forgive me, my poor Rosamond. Let us only love one another.

She looks at him in blank despair and he breaks down.

ROSAMOND. Papa says he can do nothing about the debt. He wants me to go home with them till you have a comfortable home for me. Do you object, Tertius?

LYDGATE. Surely there's no hurry?

ROSAMOND. I should not go till tomorrow. I shall want to pack.

LYDGATE. Oh, wait a little longer. There's no knowing what may happen. (*Rises, and speaks with sudden, bitter irony.*) I may get my neck broken and that may make things easier.

ROSAMOND (*chill mildness*). I see you don't wish me to go. Why can't you say so, without violence? I shall stay till you request otherwise.

Scene Forty-Eight

BULSTRODE. Meanwhile, Bulstrode prepared to sit up alone with Raffles throughout the night.

Stone Court upstairs. RAFFLES *half-raving on the bed.* BULSTRODE *looks through his pockets.*

Mmm... pocketbook... nothing much... bills...

RAFFLES. Give me brandy, please. I'm sinking away, the earth's sinking from under me...

BULSTRODE. Would you like some food?

RAFFLES. No, brandy. You're starving me. You want revenge on me. I swear by God and all his saints, I never told any mortal a word against you. (*Sinks back. Pause. Then, staring.*) Doctor?

BULSTRODE (*startled*). Where's the doctor?

RAFFLES. He wants to starve me to death, doctor, in revenge for telling, when I never told...

BULSTRODE. There's no doctor.

RAFFLES *drifts into unconsciousness, muttering from time to time.*

Should providence award death to this wretched creature, surely there is no sin in contemplating death as desirable... Provided I keep my hands from hastening it. But Thy will be done, Lord.

RAFFLES (*suddenly*). Brandy! Give me brandy...

BULSTRODE. Why should Lydgate's treatment be better than any other... (*Pause*). But of course, I must do what is prescribed...

RAFFLES *mutters.*

Suppose Lydgate listens to his raving... I've probably made him my enemy by refusing him. (*An idea is dawning.*) It would have been better to create in him a sense of obligation.

MRS BULSTRODE. This unhappy man had longed for years to be better than he was.

SPRAGUE. He had taken his selfish passions into discipline and clad them in severe robes, so that he had walked with them as a devout choir –

FAREBROTHER. But now that a terror had risen among them, they could chant no longer, but threw out their cries for safety...

Scene Forty-Nine

LYDGATE. Next day, Lydgate came again.

> LYDGATE *examines* RAFFLES *with his stethoscope.*
> RAFFLES *stirs fitfully.*

> The symptoms are worse…

BULSTRODE. You are less hopeful?

LYDGATE. No, I still think he will recover.

BULSTRODE. You have some fresh instructions?

LYDGATE. Yes, if he continues to be sleepless, you may give him this opium. (*Produces a small bottle.*) It's a very small dose and must not be given above twice in the course of the night.

> BULSTRODE *nods.*

> And no alcohol. Alcohol is the one thing I should be much afraid of. He should wear through. There's a good deal of strength in him.

BULSTRODE. You look ill yourself, Mr Lydgate. Most unprecedented. I fear you are harassed.

LYDGATE (*brusquely*). Yes I am.

BULSTRODE. Something new, I fear? Pray be seated.

LYDGATE. No thank you. I mentioned yesterday the state of my affairs. There is nothing to add except that the bailiffs have, since then, been put into my house. I will say good morning.

BULSTRODE. Stay, Mr Lydgate, stay. I have been reconsidering. I was lately taken by surprise and saw it superficially. Mrs Bulstrode is anxious for her niece, I know, and I myself should grieve at a calamitous change in your position. You said, I think, that a thousand pounds would suffice entirely to free you from your burdens?

LYDGATE. Yes. (*With joy.*) That would pay all my debts and leave a little on hand.

BULSTRODE. I will write a cheque to that amount. I am aware that help, to be effectual in these cases, should be thorough.

He writes the cheque.

LYDGATE. Lydgate thought of his good start in life saved from frustration, his good purposes unbroken.

BULSTRODE. I have great pleasure in thinking that you will be released from further difficulty.

LYDGATE. I am deeply obliged to you. You have restored to me the prospect of working with some happiness and some chance of good.

BULSTRODE *hands him the cheque.*

MRS BULSTRODE. Though as Lydgate returned home to tell the good news to Rosamond –

LYDGATE. – there crossed his mind – as a dark-winged flight of evil augury –

FAREBROTHER. – what contrast a few months had brought –

WILL. – that he should be overjoyed at being under a strong obligation to Bulstrode.

Scene Fifty

MRS BULSTRODE. Yet Bulstrode was scarcely the easier.

He sits by RAFFLES.

BULSTRODE (*to himself*). How can I wish for his recovery? Raffles dead is the image that brings release…

RAFFLES. Give me brandy…

BULSTRODE. Lord, if it is possible, release me from the threat of ignominy. Thou knowest it would break me utterly as an instrument of Thy service… Save Thy faithful servant, Lord, from disgrace.

RAFFLES. I'm sinking. I'm sinking away –

BULSTRODE (*rising, irritated*). Such persistent life.

RAFFLES. Down. I'm sinking down through the earth. I'm
sinking...

BULSTRODE. Into death, into death. But not my will, but
Thine be done, Lord.

MRS BULSTRODE. The day slowly advanced into evening...

It grows darker.

BULSTRODE (*calling*). Mrs Abel.

MRS ABEL (*appears with a candle*). Sir?

BULSTRODE. I find myself unfit for further watching. I must
consign the patient to your care tonight. If he's too watchful,
give him a dose of this opium.

She takes the bottle.

MRS ABEL. What must I do besides?

BULSTRODE. Nothing at present. Unless there is any
important change, I shall not come into the room again
tonight. I must go to bed.

MRS ABEL. You've much need, sir, I'm sure. And take
something strengthening.

BULSTRODE *takes the candle and stands apart.* MRS
ABEL *sits in the dark by* RAFFLES.

BULSTRODE. I wish I'd sent again for Lydgate. No, what's the
use? He'll only say again that Raffles may recover... (*Starts
to go. Turns back.*) Oh I forgot to tell Mrs Abel not to give
above two doses of opium in the night. (*Stands motionless.*)
It's excusable. I'm weary.

RAFFLES *can be heard* – 'I'm sinking' – 'Brandy' –
'Sinking down'.

He's still not sleeping. Who knows if Lydgate's prescription
would not be better disobeyed, than followed...?

Pause. MRS ABEL *rises and calls.*

MRS ABEL. Sir? (*Goes across to meet* BULSTRODE.) If you
please, sir, should I have no brandy nor nothing to give the
poor creetur? He feels sinking away, and nothing else will he
swaller, only the opium. And he says more and more he's
sinking down through the earth...

Pause. BULSTRODE *makes no reply.*

I think he must die for want o' support, if he goes on in that
way. When I nursed my poor master, Mr Robisson, I had to
give him port wine and brandy constant, and a big glass at a
time.

Silence.

It's not a time to spare when people are at death's door, nor
would you wish it, sir, I'm sure. Else I should give him our
own little bottle o' rum as we keep by us. But a sitter-up so
as you've been, and doing everything as laid in your power –

BULSTRODE (*takes a key from his pocket*). That is the key of
the wine cooler. You'll find plenty of brandy there...

They turn away from each other as the lights fade.

Scene Fifty-One

Lights slowly up. RAFFLES *is still.* BULSTRODE *apart.*

FAREBROTHER. About six in the morning, Bulstrode rose to
pray.

MRS ABEL. He listened in the passage.

MRS BULSTRODE. He walked in the garden.

MRS ABEL. He looked at the fresh spring leaves.

MRS ABEL *approaches* BULSTRODE.

Sir?

BULSTRODE. How is your patient? Asleep I think?

MRS ABEL. He's gone very deep, sir. He went off gradual between three and four o'clock. Would it please to go and look at him?

BULSTRODE *goes to* RAFFLES' *side.*

WILL. Bulstrode knew at a glance that Raffles was not in the sleep, which brings revival –

SPRAGUE. But the sleep, which streams deeper and deeper into the gulf of death.

BULSTRODE *picks up a large bottle with very little brandy in it, and the opium bottle, almost empty. He hides them away, and then returns to* RAFFLES.

MRS ABEL. As he beheld the enemy of his peace going irrevocably into silence, he felt more at rest than he had done for months.

FAREBROTHER. His conscience was soothed by the enfolding wing of secrecy, an angel sent down for his relief.

LYDGATE. Lydgate arrived at half-past ten in time to witness the final breaths.

(*Uneasy.*) I had not expected this. I thought he'd recover... When did this change begin?

BULSTRODE. I did not watch by him last night. I was overworn and left him under Mrs Abel's care. When I came in before eight he was nearly in this condition –

They stop and look to RAFFLES. RAFFLES *takes his last breath.*

LYDGATE. It's all over.

A moment of stillness.

BULSTRODE. He'll need a grave.

LYDGATE. Did he have any connections?

BULSTRODE. So far as I know, none...

Scene Fifty-Two

The Lydgates' drawing room. LYDGATE *may be putting the last of his furniture straight.* FAREBROTHER *has just arrived.*

FAREBROTHER. How are you, Lydgate? I came to see you because I heard something, which made me anxious about you.

LYDGATE. That there were bailiffs in the house?

FAREBROTHER. Yes. Is it true?

LYDGATE. It was true, but the danger is over. The debt is paid. The house and the furniture are safe. I'm out of difficulties.

FAREBROTHER. I'm very thankful to hear it. I like that better than all the news in *The Times*… I confess I was coming to you with a heavy heart.

LYDGATE. Thank you for coming. I can enjoy the kindness all the more because I'm happier. I've certainly been feeling a good deal crushed. (*Smiling sadly.*) I'm afraid I shall find the bruises still painful by and by. But just now I can only feel that the torture-screw is off…

FAREBROTHER. My dear fellow – one question – forgive me if I take a liberty…

LYDGATE. I don't believe you can offend me.

FAREBROTHER. You haven't – in order to pay your debts – incurred another debt, which may harass you worse hereafter?

LYDGATE. No. (*Uncomfortably.*) There's no reason why I shouldn't tell you. The person to whom I'm indebted is Bulstrode. He made me a very handsome advance – a thousand pounds.

FAREBROTHER. Well, that is generous. And Bulstrode must feel an interest in your welfare, after you've worked with him in a way which has probably reduced your income instead of adding to it. I'm glad.

LYDGATE. I shall set up a surgery to dispense drugs and take a percentage. I really think I made a mistake in that respect.

And if Rosamond won't mind, I shall take an apprentice. I don't like these things, but if one carries them out faithfully, they're not really lowering. I've had a severe galling. I hope now I'll be able to start afresh.

FAREBROTHER. Congratulations! I'm so glad.

They embrace.

Scene Fifty-Two (A)

ROSAMOND *alone*.

ROSAMOND. Though the creditors were paid, Rosamond was not joyous. There still was no outlook anywhere.

WILL. Except in an occasional letter from Will Ladislaw who had quit the town.

ROSAMOND. Rosamond fancied that Will exaggerated his admiration for Mrs Casaubon in order to pique her.

She fancied him always to be a bachelor and live near her, always at her command –

WILL. – and have an understood, though never fully expressed, passion for her –

ROSAMOND. – which would be sending out lambent flames every now and then in interesting scenes.

Scene Fifty-Three

MRS DOLLOP. But gossip had begun at The Green Dragon –

MRS PLYMDALE. – and spread through Middlemarch like the smell of fire.

The bar at The Green Dragon. MRS DOLLOP *behind the bar serving drinks.*

FIRST MAN. Do you know how Bulstrode came by his early fortune?

SECOND MAN. Dishonestly, I dare say.

FIRST MAN (*nods*). I had it from an old chum of his over a stiff glass at The Saracen's Head.

SECOND MAN. Really?

FIRST MAN. Tells me he can tap Bulstrode to any amount, knows all his secrets.

SECOND MAN. What's his name?

FIRST MAN. Raffles.

SECOND MAN. Raffles? He was buried yesterday at Lowick.

FIRST WOMAN. He died at Stone Court. The housekeeper says –

SECOND WOMAN. – Bulstrode sat up with him alone one night.

FIRST WOMAN. He died the day after.

SECOND MAN. Did any doctor attend him?

SECOND WOMAN. Yes, Mr Lydgate.

SECOND MAN. Have you heard? Mr Lydgate's suddenly able to pay off all his debts.

FIRST WOMAN. If Bulstrode wanted to get rid of Raffles, that might have something to do with his munificence towards Lydgate.

SECOND WOMAN. Yes indeed.

FIRST WOMAN. Put two and two together…

ALL (*together*). Oh yes.

FIRST WOMAN. The scandal required dinners to feed it, and many invitations were issued on the strength of it.

SECOND WOMAN. It melted into a mass of mystery, as so much lively metal to be poured out in dialogue –

FIRST WOMAN. – and to take such fantastic shapes as Heaven pleased.

MRS DOLLOP (*as if in one breath*). When a man's bee 'ticed to a lone house, and there's them can pay for hospitals and nurses for half the countryside choose to be sitters-up night and day, and nobody come near but a doctor as is known to stick at nothink, and as poor as he can hang together, and after that so flushed o' money as he can pay off Mr Byles the butcher (as his bill has been running on for the best o' joints since last Michaelmas was a twelvemonth) – I don't need anybody to come and tell me as there's been more going on nor the prayer books got a service for – I don't need to stand winking and blinking and thinking.

FIRST WOMAN. They're all of one mind to get rid of Bulstrode. There's gentlemen says they'd as soon dine with a fellow from the Hulks.

SECOND WOMAN. And this Lydgate. He's been for cutting up everybody, it's plain enough what use he wanted to make o' looking into respectable people's insides.

Scene Fifty-Four

LYDGATE. At that time a meeting was held in the Town Hall
because of a cholera case in the town.

*The Town Hall. Men gather round the table as for the
meeting of the Infirmary Board.* PLYMDALE SNR *now as
Chairman.*

BULSTRODE. Bulstrode now felt himself providentially
secure.

MRS BULSTRODE. And he felt he should, this morning,
resume his old position as a man of influence in the public
affairs of the town. (*Becomes* MINCHIN *as they all sit.*)

PLYMDALE SNR. This meeting has been convened for the
adoption of sanitary measures in Middlemarch as authorised
by the recent Act of Parliament.

BULSTRODE. May I express my opinion, Mr Chairman? –

SPRAGUE. Mr Chairman. I request that before anyone deliver
his opinion, I may be permitted to speak on a question of
public feeling.

PLYMDALE SNR. You may, Dr Sprague.

SPRAGUE. I am speaking at the express request of no fewer
than eight of my fellow townsmen. Am I not, Mr Wrench?

WRENCH. You are, Dr Sprague.

SPRAGUE. It is our united sentiment that Mr Bulstrode should
be called upon to resign all public positions as a gentleman
among gentlemen.

A murmur of agreement.

I call upon him, either publicly to deny statements made
against him by a man now dead and who died in his house,
that he was for many years engaged in nefarious practices,
and that he won his fortune by dishonest procedures, or else
to withdraw from all his positions.

Silence. All look at BULSTRODE.

BULSTRODE. I protest against proceedings which are dictated
by virulent hatred. Say that the evil-speaking of which I am
to be made the victim accuses me of malpractices – who
shall be my accuser? (*Slight pause*.) Not men whose own
lives are unchristian – (*Points them out*.) nay, scandalous –

Murmurs and hisses grow.

– and who have been spending their income on sensual
enjoyments, while I have been devoting mine to advance the
best objects, with regard to this life and the next.

Several rise to their feet to protest.

SPRAGUE (*topping them*). I repudiate your canting
Christianity. It is not *my* principle to maintain thieves and
cheat offspring of their true inheritance. Again I call you to
enter into satisfactory explanation or else to withdraw from
all posts.

Cries of 'Withdraw!' PLYMDALE SNR *tries to calm the
meeting.*

PLYMDALE SNR. Allow me.

SPRAGUE *is the last to sit.*

Mr Bulstrode, it is not desirable to prolong the present
discussion. I for my part, should be willing to give you full
opportunity and hearing. But I must say that your present
attitude is painfully inconsistent with those principles, which
you have sought to identify yourself with, and I recommend
you to quit the room and avoid further hindrance to business.

Slight pause.

BULSTRODE *rises to his feet, staggers,* LYDGATE *goes to
support him, leads him away. They turn.*

LYDGATE. Lydgate's act of support, was unspeakably bitter to
him. He now felt the conviction –

BULSTRODE. – that Bulstrode had given him the thousand
pounds as a bribe –

LYDGATE. – and that somehow the treatment of Raffles had
been tampered with.

Scene Fifty-Five

FAREBROTHER. It was Mr Farebrother who took the story to
   Mrs Casaubon at Lowick Manor.

The library at Lowick Manor.

DOROTHEA. Oh, Mr Farebrother…

FAREBROTHER. What is the truth? It's a delicate matter, Mrs
   Casaubon. I confess I should shrink from opening the subject
   with Lydgate. He'd probably take it as a deadly insult.

DOROTHEA. I'm convinced he's not guilty.

FAREBROTHER. It's possible he is. I've often felt so much
   weakness in myself that I can conceive even a man of
   honourable disposition succumbing to such a temptation as
   that… Accepting money offered more or less indirectly –

DOROTHEA. No! –

FAREBROTHER. To ensure his silence –

DOROTHEA. Oh, how cruel –

FAREBROTHER. Under the pressure of hard circumstance – as
   I'm sure Lydgate has been –

DOROTHEA. But there's a man's character beforehand –

FAREBROTHER. My dear Mrs Casaubon, character is not cut
   in marble. It's something living and changing and may
   become diseased as our bodies do.

DOROTHEA. Then it may be rescued and healed. I shall not be
   afraid to ask him. People are almost always better than their
   neighbours think them. And what do we live for if not to
   make life less difficult to each other. Let's find out the truth
   and clear him.

FAREBROTHER. I do think it would be better to wait…

Scene Fifty-Five (A)

LYDGATE *alone*.

LYDGATE. Lydgate felt violent and unreasonable, raging as if under the pain of stings.

(*Crying out*.) I didn't take the money as a bribe!

But who would believe me? They'll all feel warranted in making a wide space between me and them, as if I were a leper.

My practice and reputation are utterly damned.

(*Determined*.) But I shall do as I think right and explain to nobody.

FAREBROTHER. He had no impulse to tell Rosamond his troubles. In his morbid state of mind, almost all contact was pain.

Scene Fifty-Six

MRS BULSTRODE. And in Middlemarch, nobody wants to tell any wife that the town holds a bad opinion of her husband.

The street. MRS PLYMDALE *and* MRS SPRAGUE *are gossiping, when* MRS BULSTRODE *comes by. They stop talking abruptly.* MRS BULSTRODE *is unnerved, but passes on*.

MRS PLYMDALE (*watching her go*). Poor Harriet. She's been a good wife to Bulstrode. She thinks her husband the best of men.

She draws up a chair for MRS SPRAGUE, *and they are in –*

MRS PLYMDALE'*s house*.

MRS SPRAGUE. Well, but she ought to separate from him. Do you think any hint has reached her?

MRS PLYMDALE. I hardly think so. We hear that he's ill and
has never stirred out of the house since the meeting on
Thursday. (*Looking out of the window*.) But she was at
church yesterday with a new Tuscan bonnet and feather.

MRS SPRAGUE. I suppose the Bulstrodes will go abroad
somewhere. That's what's generally done when there's
anything disgraceful in a family –

MRS PLYMDALE. If ever a woman was crushed she will be –

MRS SPRAGUE. Dr Sprague says that's what he should
recommend the Lydgates to do. A thousand pounds he took,
just at that man's death. It really makes one shudder.

MRS PLYMDALE. Pride must have a fall –

MRS SPRAGUE. He says Lydgate should have kept among the
French.

MRS PLYMDALE. That would suit Rosamond well enough, I
dare say. But she got that lightness from her mother, she
never got it from her Aunt Bulstrode, who to my knowledge
– (*Low voice*.) would rather have had her marry elsewhere…

Scene Fifty-Six (A)

MRS BULSTRODE. But poor Mrs Bulstrode felt sure that
something had happened.

MRS BULSTRODE *at* MRS PLYMDALE*'s*.

Oh, Selina, do you know what has…? (*Slight pause*.) Mr
Bulstrode was taken so ill at the meeting on Thursday, that
I've not liked to leave the house… I wonder if…?

MRS PLYMDALE *remains silent*.

Yet I always think Middlemarch such a healthy spot. (*Looks
out of the window*.) I never saw a town I should like to live at
better.

MRS PLYMDALE. I'm sure I'd be glad you should always live at Middlemarch, Harriet. Still, we must learn to resign ourselves, wherever our lot is cast. I'm sure there'll always be people in the town who will wish you well.

Scene Fifty-Six (B)

MRS BULSTRODE. She went straight to her brother, Mr Vincy.

MRS BULSTRODE *with* VINCY.

VINCY. God help you, Harriet, you know all?

MRS BULSTRODE. I know *nothing*, brother! What is it?

VINCY. And he told her everything...

The scandal goes much beyond proof – especially as to the end of Raffles. But people will talk. And nod, and wink. It damages Lydgate as much as Bulstrode. I don't pretend to say what is the truth. I only wish we'd never heard the name of either Bulstrode or Lydgate. You'd better have been a Vincy all your life, and so had Rosamond. (*Slight pause.*) But you must bear up as well as you can, Harriet. And I'll stand by you, whatever you make up your mind to do.

MRS BULSTRODE. I must go home. I feel very weak.

He gives her his arm.

Scene Fifty-Six (C)

BULSTRODE. At home she locked herself in her room.

> BULSTRODE*'s house at The Shrubs*. MRS BULSTRODE *sits apart*.

MRS BULSTRODE (*remembering particular moments*). When I think of… (*Cries out in pain.*) Twenty years I've believed in him. Twenty years of odious deceit.

MRS VINCY. She needed time to get used to her poor lopped life –

FAREBROTHER. – before she could walk steadily to the place allotted to her.

MRS BULSTRODE. Yet he's always cherished me…

> *She stands and prepares to join him.*

MRS PLYMDALE. She had begun a new life in which she must embrace humiliation.

> *Now there is light on* BULSTRODE, *across the stage*.

DOROTHEA. Bulstrode awaited his wife in anguish.

BULSTRODE. Perhaps I shall never see my wife's face with affection in it again.

> *She goes to him. He dares not look at her.*

MRS BULSTRODE. Look up, Nicholas.

> *He does.*

> I know.

> *He bursts into tears, and they cry together.*

> But she could not ask: 'How much is false?'

BULSTRODE. And he could not say: 'I am innocent.'

Scene Fifty-Seven

BULSTRODE. At Lydgate's house –

LYDGATE. – the silence between Lydgate and Rosamond had become intolerable.

The Lydgates' drawing room.

LYDGATE (*at last*). Rosamond. Have you heard anything that distresses you?

ROSAMOND. Yes. (*Stops sewing.*)

LYDGATE. What have you heard?

ROSAMOND. Everything, I suppose. Papa told me.

LYDGATE. That people think me disgraced?

ROSAMOND. Yes. (*Starts sewing again.*)

Silence.

LYDGATE. If she has any trust in me she will say she doesn't believe I deserve disgrace.

ROSAMOND. If he's innocent, why doesn't he say something to clear himself…

Silence. LYDGATE rises angrily and paces the room.

(*At last.*) I wish you would sit down.

He sits; is about to speak.

Surely, Tertius…

LYDGATE. Well?

ROSAMOND. Surely now at last you have given up the idea of staying in Middlemarch. I can't go on living here. Let's go to London. Papa, and everyone else, says you'd better go. Whatever misery I have to put up with, it will be easier away from here.

LYDGATE. The old round to be gone through again. I can't bear it.

He leaves the room.

ROSAMOND (*to herself*). It's of no use saying anything more to him.

WILL. But Will Ladislaw was coming to visit Middlemarch.

MRS VINCY. She was determined to tell him everything…

ROSAMOND. I need someone who'll recognise my wrongs.

Scene Fifty-Eight

LYDGATE. Then one day Lydgate was summoned to Lowick Manor.

The library at Lowick Manor. DOROTHEA *and* LYDGATE.

DOROTHEA. I've wished very much to see you about the new hospital. I know so much there depends on you.

LYDGATE. Mrs Casaubon, I cannot advise you to increase your support in dependence on me… I may be obliged to leave the town.

DOROTHEA. Not because there is no one to believe in you? I know the unhappy mistakes about you. You would not do anything dishonourable.

LYDGATE (*after a deep breath*). Thank you.

DOROTHEA. I beseech you to tell me how everything was. I'm sure that the truth would clear you. Then we can consult together.

LYDGATE. I should like to tell you everything. It will be a comfort to me to speak where belief has gone beforehand.

DOROTHEA. Do trust me.

LYDGATE. And Lydgate gave himself up, for the first time in his life, to the exquisite sense of leaning entirely on a generous sympathy, without any check of proud reserve.

DOROTHEA. And he told her everything.

LYDGATE. How my orders came to be disobeyed I don't know. It is still possible that Bulstrode was innocent of any criminal intention. But all that has nothing to do with the public belief. I'm simply blighted.

DOROTHEA. Oh, it is hard. And that all this should have come to you who had meant to lead a higher life than the common. I remember what you said when you first spoke to me about the hospital. There is no sorrow I have thought about more than that – to love what is great, and try to reach it, and yet to fail.

LYDGATE. Yes, I had some ambition. I meant everything to be different with me. But the most terrible obstacles are such as nobody can see except oneself.

DOROTHEA. Suppose we kept on the hospital and you stayed, the evil feeling towards you would gradually die out. You may still win a great fame, and we shall all be proud of you.

LYDGATE. If only it could be done… (*Looks away. Suddenly.*) Why should I not tell you? You know what sort of a bond marriage is. It's impossible for me to do anything without considering my wife's happiness. I can't see her miserable. She married me without knowing what she was going into, and it might have been better for her if she had not married me.

DOROTHEA (*thinking of her own life*). I know, I know. You couldn't give her pain.

LYDGATE. And she wishes to go. The troubles she has had here have wearied her.

DOROTHEA. But when she saw the good that might come of staying –

LYDGATE. She wouldn't see it. (*Slight pause.*) The fact is – we've not been able to speak to each other about it. She may fear that I've really done something base. It's my fault. I ought to be more open.

DOROTHEA. May I go and see her? I would tell her you shall be cleared in every fair mind. I would cheer her heart. Will you ask her if I may see her?

LYDGATE. I'm sure you may. She would feel honoured –
   cheered I think by the proof that you at least have some respect
   for me. I'll not speak to her about your coming, that she may
   not connect it with my wishes. I know I ought to – but…

DOROTHEA. How well Dorothea knew the invisible barriers
   to speech between husband and wife.

   And if Mrs Lydgate knew there were friends who would
   support you, she might then be glad that you should stay in
   your place at the hospital and recover your hopes? (*Pause*.)
   You need not decide immediately…

   Pause.

LYDGATE (*makes his decision*). No. I prefer there should be no
   wavering. No. I can think of nothing for a long while but
   getting an income.

DOROTHEA. It hurts me to hear you speak so hopelessly.
   Think how much money I have since my husband died. It
   would be like taking a burden from me if you took some of it
   every year till you got free of this fettering want of income.
   Why should not people do these things? It's so difficult to
   make shares all even –

LYDGATE. God bless you, Mrs Casaubon. It's good you have
   such feeling but I'm not the man to benefit by them, to be
   pensioned for work I've never achieved. It's very clear to
   me, I must not count on anything else, but getting away from
   Middlemarch as soon as I can manage it. I must do as other
   men do, and think what will please the world and bring in
   money. Look for a little opening in London and push myself
   – set up in a watering place – or go to some southern town
   where there are plenty of idle English – and get myself
   puffed – that's the sort of shell I must creep into, and try to
   keep my soul alive in.

DOROTHEA. Now that's not brave.

LYDGATE. No, it's not brave. Yet you have made a great
   difference in believing in me. If you can clear me in a few
   others' minds, especially in Farebrother's, I shall be deeply
   grateful.

DOROTHEA. Oh, Mr Farebrother will believe. Others will believe. It's stupidity to suppose that you would be bribed to do a wickedness.

LYDGATE. I don't know. I've not taken a bribe yet. But there's a pale shade of bribery which is sometimes called prosperity. (*Slight pause.*) You'll do me another great kindness then, and come and see my wife?

DOROTHEA. Yes, I will. I remember how pretty she is. I hope she will like me.

Dorothea immediately formed a plan of relieving Lydgate from his obligation to Bulstrode.

FAREBROTHER. She wrote a cheque for a thousand pounds –

MRS PLYMDALE. Which she determined to take when she went to see Rosamond.

Scene Fifty-Nine

WILL. Meanwhile, Rosamond had written a letter to Will Ladislaw –

ROSAMOND. – written with a charming discretion –

WILL. – but intended to hasten his arrival by a hint of trouble.

The Lydgates' drawing room. ROSAMOND *and* WILL *on the sofa.* ROSAMOND *flushed and tearful,* WILL *fervently trying to calm her.*

I can give you no assurance –

ROSAMOND. But I've been so unhappy –

WILL. You cannot allow yourself –

ROSAMOND. Won't you understand me –

WILL. – to make your happiness depend on me.

ROSAMOND. But you must have some love for me –

WILL. No – (*Takes her hands firmly.*)

ROSAMOND. If only a little –

WILL. My love is deeply committed to –

> DOROTHEA *enters*.

DOROTHEA. Oh, I –

> ROSAMOND *and* WILL *stand guiltily.*

> Excuse me, Mrs Lydgate. The servant didn't know you were here. I had a letter for Mr Lydgate, which I wished to put into your own hands.

> *She puts down the letter, and leaves.* ROSAMOND *looks to* WILL, *who is motionless.*

MRS VINCY. Rosamond had been little used to imagining other people's states of mind –

MRS PLYMDALE. – except as a material cut into shape by her own wishes.

> ROSAMOND *touches* WILL*'s sleeve.*

WILL. Don't touch me!

> *She suddenly sits, folding her cold hands.*

ROSAMOND. You can easily go after Mrs Casaubon and explain your preference.

WILL. Go after her! Explain! How can a man explain at the expense of a woman?

ROSAMOND. You can tell her what you please.

WILL. Do you suppose she would like me better for sacrificing you? (*Moves about restlessly.*) I had no hope before. But I had one certainty – that she believed in me. That's gone. (*New fury.*) Explain my preference! I never had a *preference* for her, any more than I have a preference for breathing. No other woman exists by the side of her. I'd rather touch her hand if it were dead, than I would touch any other woman's living.

> *Silence.*

ROSAMOND. Rosamond seemed to be waking into some new terrible existence. She had no sense of self-justification now – only a terrified recoil under a lash.

Silence. He moves to go, then stops. Her mute misery.

WILL (*at length*). Shall I come and see Lydgate this evening?

ROSAMOND. If you like.

He goes. She curls up on the sofa in apparent torpor.

Later. LYDGATE *enters, picks up* DOROTHEA'*s letter, then notices* ROSAMOND'*s state.*

LYDGATE. My poor Rosamond! Has something agitated you?

She falls into hysterical sobbing. He goes to comfort her.

Scene Fifty-Nine (A)

WILL. When Will came that evening he found he could not mention his earlier visit.

As WILL *enters,* ROSAMOND *leaves quickly.*

LYDGATE. Poor Rosamond is ill.

WILL. Not seriously, I hope.

LYDGATE. No, only a nervous shock. She's been overwrought lately. The truth is, Ladislaw, I'm an unlucky devil.

WILL. I heard something.

LYDGATE. Your name is mixed up with the disclosures.

WILL. Yes. I know.

BULSTRODE. But Will said nothing about Bulstrode's offer of money to him.

WILL. He shrank from saying he'd rejected the money –

LYDGATE. – when it was Lydgate's misfortune to have accepted it.

Scene Sixty

DOROTHEA. Next day, Dorothea was again at Lydgate's door.

DOROTHEA *and* LYDGATE.

Do you think Mrs Lydgate can receive me this morning?

LYDGATE. I've no doubt. She's not been very well since you
were here yesterday, but she's better this morning. (*Takes a
letter from his pocket.*) Oh, I wrote this last night, and was
going to carry it to Lowick in my ride. When one is
grateful –

DOROTHEA. You have let me take the banker's place? You
have consented?

LYDGATE. Yes. The cheque is going to Bulstrode today –

ROSAMOND *appears*.

Oh, Rosy dear, Mrs Casaubon is come to see you again.
You'd like to see her, would you not?

ROSAMOND (*dares not say no*). Oh... yes.

LYDGATE (*feeling a little foolish*). I'm going out
immediately... (*Goes.*)

ROSAMOND *bows coldly*.

ROSAMOND. Will prefers her. Why has she come back? To
press her advantage?

DOROTHEA *comes forward to shake her hand*.
ROSAMOND *motions for her to sit*.

DOROTHEA. I had an errand yesterday I didn't finish. I came
to talk to you about the injustice that's been shown to Mr
Lydgate. You'll let me speak of this?

ROSAMOND. She is not going to speak of Will.

MRS VINCY. The relief was a warm stream over her shrinking
fears.

ROSAMOND. I know you've been very good. I shall like to
hear anything about my husband.

DOROTHEA. I'd asked him to come to Lowick about the hospital. He told me everything about this sad event. He told me because I was very bold, and asked him. The truth is, he knew nothing of this man Raffles and he thought that Mr Bulstrode offered him the money because he repented of having refused it before. All his anxiety about the patient was to treat him rightly. And I've told Mr Farebrother and Mr Brooke and Sir James Chettam – they all believe in your husband. That will cheer you, will it not?

ROSAMOND. Thank you. You're very kind.

DOROTHEA. He felt he'd been wrong not to pour out everything to you. It was because he feels so much more about your happiness than anything else – he feels his life bound into one with yours and it hurts him more than anything that his misfortunes must hurt you. That's why I came yesterday. Trouble is so hard to bear, is it not? (*Takes* ROSAMOND*'s hand.*) How can we live, and think that anyone has trouble – piercing trouble – and we could help them and never try.

ROSAMOND, *'as if a wound has been probed', bursts into tears.*

MRS VINCY. An unknown world had broken in on Rosamond.

MRS BULSTRODE. The dream world in which she had been easily confident of herself and critical of others had been shattered.

DOROTHEA (*at last, timidly*). We were talking about your husband. He said he'd been feeling very lonely in his trial, but I think he would have borne it better if he'd been able to be quite open with you.

ROSAMOND. He is so angry and impatient if I say anything. He ought not to wonder that I object to speak to him on painful subjects.

DOROTHEA. It was himself he blamed. He refused my proposal that he should keep his position at the hospital, because that would bind him to stay in Middlemarch, and he would not undertake anything that would be painful to you.

ROSAMOND*'s 'faint pleasure'*.

He could say that to me, because he knows that I had much
trial in my marriage, and I've felt how hard it is to walk always
in fear of hurting another who's tied to us. (*Slight pause.*)
Marriage is so unlike everything else. There's something even
awe-ful in the nearness it brings. Even if we loved someone
else better than – than those we were married to, it would be no
use – (*Low voice.*) I mean, marriage drinks up all our power of
giving or getting any blessedness in that sort of love. I know it
may be very dear – but it murders our marriage – and then the
marriage stays with us like a murder – and everything else is
gone. And then our husband – if he loved and trusted us and
we've not helped him, but made a curse in his life... (*Takes*
ROSAMOND*'s hand again.*) I know, I know that the feeling
may be very dear – it's taken hold of us unawares – it's so hard
– it may seem like death to part with it – and we are weak – I
am weak... (*Stops, too upset.*)

ROSAMOND *kisses her forehead. They clasp each other as*
if in a shipwreck.

ROSAMOND (*whispers*). You're thinking what is not true.
(*Moves apart.*) When you came in yesterday – it was not as
you thought... He was telling me how he loved another
woman, that I might know he could never love me. And now
I think he hates me because you mistook him yesterday. He
has never had any love for me – I know he has not – he's
always thought slightly of me. He said yesterday that no
other woman existed for him besides you. But now I've told
you and he can't reproach me any more.

DOROTHEA. No, he can't reproach you any more.

Silence.

You're not sorry I came this morning?

ROSAMOND. No. You've been very good to me. I didn't think
you'd be so good. I was very unhappy. I'm not happy now.
Everything's so sad.

DOROTHEA. But better days will come. Your husband
depends on you for comfort. He loves you best. The worst
loss would be to lose that – and you have not lost it.

ROSAMOND. Tertius didn't find fault with me then?

DOROTHEA (*smiles*). No indeed. How can you imagine it?

Scene Sixty (A)

Later. LYDGATE *has returned.*

LYDGATE. Well, Rosy, what do you think of Mrs Casaubon, now that you've seen so much of her.

ROSAMOND. I think she must be better than anyone. And she's beautiful. If you go to talk to her so often –

LYDGATE *laughs.*

– you will be more discontented with me than ever!

LYDGATE. But has she made you any less discontented with me?

ROSAMOND. I think she has. How heavy your eyes are, Tertius.

He joins her on the sofa.

And do push your hair back.

MRS VINCY. Lydgate felt thankful for this little mark of interest in him.

MRS BULSTRODE. Poor Rosamond's vagrant fancy had come back terribly scourged.

She goes into his arms.

DOROTHEA. Lydgate had chosen this fragile creature.

MRS VINCY. And had taken the burden of her life upon his arms.

MRS BULSTRODE. He must walk as best he could, carrying that burden…

Epilogue

LYDGATE. In after years, Lydgate gained an excellent practice –

SPRAGUE. – alternating, according to the season, between London and a continental bathing place.

WRENCH. He wrote a treatise on gout –

MRS BULSTRODE. – a disease which has a great deal of wealth on its side.

VINCY. He was what was called a successful man –

ROSAMOND. – and Rosamond had a more thorough conviction of his talents.

FAREBROTHER. His acquaintances thought him enviable to have so charming a wife.

DOROTHEA. She continued mild in her temper –

MRS PLYMDALE. – inflexible in her judgement –

LYDGATE. – but he opposed her less and less –

ROSAMOND. – whence Rosamond concluded he had learnt the value of her opinions.

BULSTRODE. Though to the last he occasionally let slip a bitter speech.

LYDGATE. You're my basil plant.

ROSAMOND. What does that mean?

LYDGATE. It flourished wonderfully on a murdered man's brains.

ROSAMOND. Then why did you choose me? Why not Dorothea Ladislaw?

MRS VINCY. But Rosamond never committed another compromising indiscretion.

ROSAMOND. And she always remembered Dorothea's generosity, which had come to her in the sharpest crisis of her life.

LYDGATE *alone*.

BULSTRODE. In the multitude of middle-aged men, there is always a good number who once meant to alter the world a little.

FAREBROTHER. The story of their coming to be shapen after the average, and fit to be packed by the gross –

VINCY. – is hardly ever told, even in their consciousness.

DOROTHEA. Lydgate had not meant to be one of those failures.

SPRAGUE. But he had not done what he once meant to do.

MRS VINCY. That element of tragedy is not unusual.

MRS PLYMDALE. And we do not expect to be moved by what is not unusual.

MRS BULSTRODE. Though if we had a keen vision, and feeling of all ordinary life –

WILL. – it would be like hearing the grass grow, and the squirrel's heartbeat –

LYDGATE. – and we should die of that roar which lies on the other side of silence...

Silence. Slow fade.

The End.

FRED AND MARY'S STORY

Characters

MR VINCY, *Mayor of Middlemarch*
MRS VINCY, *the Mayor's wife*
FRED VINCY, *their son*
ROSAMOND VINCY, *their daughter*
MR GARTH, *land agent and builder*
MRS GARTH, *his wife*
MARY GARTH, *their daughter*
BEN, *their child, seven-ish*
LETTY, *their child, four-ish*
MR FEATHERSTONE, *rich landowner*
MRS WAULE, *his sister*
SOLOMON, *his brother*
JONAH, *another of his brothers*
MARTHA, *another of his sisters*
THE REV MR FAREBROTHER, *vicar*
MRS FAREBROTHER, *his mother*
FAREBROTHER'S AUNT AND SISTER
MR LYDGATE, *doctor*
MR BULSTRODE, *banker*
MRS BULSTRODE, *his wife*
MR TRUMBULL, *auctioneer and agent*
DOROTHEA BROOKE
CELIA BROOKE, *her sister*
MR BROOKE , *their uncle*
SIR JAMES CHETTAM, *Brooke's neighbour*
MRS CADWALLADER
MR STANDISH, *a lawyer*
TIM, *a labourer*
HIRAM, *a labourer*
MR GARTH'S ASSISTANT

Plus: two railway surveyors, labourers in the fields, billiards players.

Ben and Letty were represented by life-sized dolls, manipulated and voiced by the member of the cast most conveniently at hand.

Suggested Doubling

FRED

MARY / CELIA

VINCY / GARTH

MRS VINCY / MRS GARTH

ROSAMOND / MR GARTH'S ASSISTANT

FAREBROTHER / TRUMBULL / SIR JAMES

FEATHERSTONE / JONAH / TIM

BULSTRODE / SOLOMON / HIRAM / BROOKE

MRS WAULE / MRS FAREBROTHER / FAREBROTHER'S
AUNT AND SISTER / MRS CADWALLADER / MRS
BULSTRODE

LYDGATE / STANDISH

DOROTHEA / MARTHA

ACT ONE

Prologue

The cast are gathered around the acting area.

MARY. Middlemarch.

FEATHERSTONE. In 1829 –

BULSTRODE. – before Reform had done its part –

GARTH. – those who would make their living from the land –

MRS GARTH. – were asked to make true choices…

FRED. The Story of Fred –

MARY. – and Mary.

VINCY. Who of any consequence in Middlemarch was not acquainted with the Vincy family.

Mr Vincy the manufacturer was about to be Mayor of Middlemarch.

MRS VINCY. He had descended a little in having taken an inkeeper's daughter to wife.

MRS BULSTRODE. But his sister had made a wealthy match in accepting –

BULSTRODE. – Mr Bulstrode, the banker –

FEATHERSTONE. – and Mrs Vincy's sister had been second wife to rich, childless Mr Featherstone.

MRS VINCY. So that nephews and nieces might be supposed to touch the affections of the widower.

FRED. Especially the Vincy's children – Fred –

ROSAMOND. – and Rosamond.

Scene One

The Vincys' drawing room. After breakfast. MRS VINCY *sits on the sofa with some mending,* ROSAMOND *with embroidery.*

ROSAMOND. Mamma. When Fred comes down, I wish you would not let him have herrings. I can't bear the smell of them all over the house at this hour of the morning.

MRS VINCY. Oh, my dear, you're so hard on your brother –

ROSAMOND. Brothers are so unpleasant.

MRS VINCY. Be thankful if they have good hearts. A woman must learn to put up with little things. You'll be married some day –

ROSAMOND. Not to anyone like Fred!

MRS VINCY. I wonder you're not glad to have such a gentlemanly young man for a brother, although he couldn't take his degree – I'm sure I can't understand why, for he seems to me most clever, and you know yourself he was thought equal to the best society at college. And you'll not find any Middlemarch young man who hasn't something against him.

ROSAMOND. But I shall not marry any Middlemarch young man.

MRS VINCY. So it seems, my love, for you've as good as refused the pick of them.

FRED (*entering*). Have you nothing else for breakfast? (*Calling back.*) Bring me a grilled bone.

ROSAMOND. Really, Fred. If you must have hot things for breakfast, I wish you'd come down earlier. You can get up at six o'clock to go hunting.

FRED. That's because I like it.

ROSAMOND. What would you think of me if I came down two hours after everyone else and ordered grilled bone?

FRED. I should think you were uncommonly fast.

ROSAMOND. I can't think why brothers are to make themselves disagreeable.

FRED. Disagreeable is a word that describes your feelings, and not my actions.

ROSAMOND. I think it describes the smell of grilled bone.

FRED. Look at Mother – you don't see her objecting. She's my notion of a pleasant woman.

MRS VINCY. Bless you, my dears, don't quarrel. Come, Fred, tell us about the new doctor. How is your Uncle Featherstone pleased with him?

FRED. Pretty well I think.

MRS VINCY. And what do you think of him? They say he's of excellent family.

ROSAMOND. It always makes a difference to be of good family.

FRED. He's tallish, dark, clever –

ROSAMOND. I suppose Mary Garth admires Mr Lydgate.

FRED. Really, I can't say. If you're jealous, go oftener to Stone Court yourself, and eclipse her.

ROSAMOND. I wish you wouldn't be so vulgar, Fred.

MRS VINCY (*to* FRED). Are you going to Stone Court today to see your Uncle Featherstone?

FRED. Yes, after breakfast. (*Calls off.*) Where is breakfast? (*Throws himself on to the sofa with a book.*)

MRS VINCY (*to* ROSAMOND). It's true though what your brother says. It's a thousand pities you haven't patience to go and see your uncle more. There's no knowing what he might have done for you as well as for Fred. And now it stands to reason that your Uncle Featherstone will do something for Mary Garth – because she's also his niece, and she lives there.

ROSAMOND. Mary Garth can bear being at Stone Court because she likes that better than being a governess. I would rather not have anything left to me, if I must earn it by enduring my uncle's cough, and his ugly relations.

MRS VINCY. He can't be long for this world, my dear. I wouldn't hasten his end, but what with asthma and that inward complaint, let's hope there's something better for him in another. And I've no ill-will towards Mary Garth, but there's justice to be thought of. Mr Featherstone's first wife brought him no money, as my sister did. That side of the family really can't have so much claim as ours. And I must say I think Mary Garth a dreadful plain girl – more fit for a governess.

FRED (*from his book*). Everyone would not agree with you there, Mother.

MRS VINCY. Well, my dear, if she had some fortune left her, she might be a match for someone. But the Garths are so poor and live in such a small way. I shall leave you to your studies, my dear, for I must go and do some shopping.

ROSAMOND. Fred's studies are not very deep. He's only reading a novel.

MRS VINCY. Well, by and by he'll go to his Latin and things. There's a fire in the smoking room on purpose. It's your father's wish, you know – Fred, my dear – and I always tell him you will be good, and go back to college again to take your degree.

FRED *kisses his mother's hand, but says nothing, and* MRS VINCY *leaves*.

ROSAMOND. I suppose you're not going out riding today?

FRED. Why?

ROSAMOND. Papa says I may have the chestnut to ride now.

FRED. I'm going to Stone Court, remember.

ROSAMOND. It's indifferent to me where we go. I can see Mary. (*Slight pause*.) Though I hope none of my uncle's horrible relations are there.

FRED. They will be. They hang about my uncle like vultures. I believe he hates them all.

Scene Two

MRS WAULE. Meanwhile, at Mr Featherstone's house, Stone Court, Mrs Jane Waule – Mr Featherstone's sister – was already by his bedside.

Stone Court upstairs. FEATHERSTONE *ill in bed.* MARY *seated in a corner, darning.*

It's a pity Mrs Vincy's family can't be better conducted.

FEATHERSTONE. Tchah! What are you driving at, sister?

MRS WAULE. It's the talk up and down in Middlemarch how unsteady young Fred Vincy is, and has been at The Green Dragon forever gambling at billiards, since he came home.

FEATHERSTONE. Nonsense! What's a game of billiards?

MRS WAULE. If it's true, and he's losing hundreds of pounds, it must be found somewhere else than out of his father's pocket, for they say Mr Vincy's been losing money for years, though nobody would think so, to see him keeping open house. And it's openly said that young Vincy has raised money on his Expectations. I don't say what Expectations. Mary Garth hears me, and is welcome to tell again.

MARY. No thank you, Mrs Waule.

FEATHERSTONE (*rubs the gold knob of his stick and makes a brief convulsive laugh*). And who says Fred Vincy hasn't got Expectations? A fine spirited fellow is like enough to have them…

MRS WAULE (*tearfully*). It's painful to me and my brother Solomon to hear your name made free with, and your complaint being such as may carry you off sudden, and people who are not Featherstones openly reckoning on your property coming to them. And me your own sister, and Solomon your own brother.

FEATHERSTONE. Out with it, Jane. You say Fred Vincy's been getting somebody to advance him money on what he says he knows about my will, eh?

MRS WAULE. I never said so, brother. But Solomon had it from most undeniable authority.

FEATHERSTONE. Stuff and nonsense. It's all a got-up story. Go to the window, Mary, I thought I heard a horse. See if the doctor's coming.

MARY *crosses to the window.*

MRS WAULE. Not got up by me, brother, nor yet by Solomon who has made his will. He makes it no secret what he intends to do with his property.

FEATHERSTONE. The more fool he.

FEATHERSTONE *coughs severely.* MARY *goes to him.*

ROSAMOND *enters. Bows to* MRS WAULE, *who greets her coldly.*

MRS WAULE. How do you do, Miss Vincy.

FEATHERSTONE (*overcoming his cough*). Heyday, miss. You have a fine colour. Where's Fred?

ROSAMOND. Seeing about the horses. He'll be in presently.

FEATHERSTONE. Sit down, sit down.

MARY *offers her seat to* ROSAMOND.

(*Dismissively.*) Mrs Waule, you'd better go.

MRS WAULE (*rising*). Mrs Waule accepted that, included in the Almighty's intentions about families, was the freedom from the necessity of behaving agreeably.

(*In an undertone.*) Brother, I hope the new doctor will be able to do something for you. I'm sure it's my wish you should be spared. And there's none more ready to nurse you than your own sister, if you'd only say the word. And there's my girls, Rebecca and Joanna, and then there's John...

FEATHERSTONE. Ay, ay, I remember – you'll see, I've remembered them all – all dark and ugly. They'd need some money, eh? Ay, ay. Money's a good egg, and if you've got money to leave behind you, lay it in a warm nest. Goodbye, Mrs Waule.

MRS WAULE *goes, with a suspicious look at* MARY *and* ROSAMOND, *and* FRED *as he enters.*

MRS WAULE. Notwithstanding her jealousy of the Vincys and Mary Garth, there remained –

FRED. – as the nethermost sediment in her mental shallows –

MRS WAULE. – a persuasion that her brother Peter could never leave his chief property away from his brother and sister.

FEATHERSTONE. You two misses, go away. I want to speak to Fred.

MARY. Come up to my room, Rosamond, you'll not mind the cold for a little while.

They go. FEATHERSTONE *waits till they've gone.*

FEATHERSTONE. So, sir. You've promised to pay off your debts with my land when I'm dead and gone, eh?

FRED. I've certainly never borrowed money on such an insecurity. Please to explain.

FEATHERSTONE. No, sir, it's you who must explain. I can alter my will yet, let me tell you. I'm of sound mind, can reckon compound interest in my head and remember every fool's name as well as twenty years ago. What the deuce? I say you must contradict this story.

FRED. I have, sir. The story's a silly lie.

FEATHERSTONE. Nonsense. You must bring dockiments. It comes from authority.

FRED. Name the authority.

FEATHERSTONE. It's pretty good authority I think – a man who knows most of what goes on in Middlemarch. (*Thinks quickly.*) It's that fine religious, charitable uncle of yours. Come now. (*Inward shake of merriment.*)

FRED. Mr Bulstrode?

FEATHERSTONE. Who else, eh?

FRED. Then the lie's grown out of some sermonising words he may have let fall about me.

FEATHERSTONE. Bulstrode 'ud know. You bring me a writing
from Bulstrode to say he doesn't believe you've ever
promised to pay your debts out o' my land. Come now!
(*Grimaces with silent triumph.*)

FRED. You must be joking, sir. Mr Bulstrode has a prejudice
against me. I could hardly ask him that – it's hardly a thing
for a gentleman to ask.

FEATHERSTONE. Ay, I know. You'd sooner offend me than
Bulstrode. And what's he? A speckilating banker fellow. His
religion is nonsense. There's one thing pretty clear. God
A'mighty sticks to the land. He promises land, and He gives
land, and He makes chaps rich with corn and cattle. But you
take the other side. You like Bulstrode and speckilation
better than Featherstone and land.

FRED. I beg your pardon, sir, I like neither Bulstrode, nor
speculation.

FEATHERSTONE. Well, well, you can do without me, that's
clear. You neither want a bit of land to make a squire out of
you, nor a lift of… a hundred pound, by the way…? It's all
one to me. I can make five wills if I like and I shall keep my
banknotes for a nest egg. It's all one to me.

FRED. I'm not ungrateful, sir. I never meant to show disregard
for any kind intentions you might have towards me.

FEATHERSTONE. Very good. Then prove it. You bring me a
letter from Bulstrode, and then, if there's any scrape you've
got in to, we'll see if I can back you a bit. Come now! That's
a bargain. Here, give me your arm. I'll try and walk to the
bookshelves. What have you been bringing Missy books for?

FRED. She's very fond of reading.

FEATHERSTONE. I can't abide her reading to herself. You're
not to bring her any more books, do you hear?

FRED. Would you like her to come down?

FEATHERSTONE. No, I can ring the bell when I want her. I
might want Miss Rosy to sing.

Scene Three

MARY. The two girls were in Mary's room.

ROSAMOND. They had known each other since childhood and school.

MARY*'s room.* ROSAMOND *is seated in front of a mirror.* MARY *stands behind her.*

MARY. What a brown patch I am by the side of you, Rosy.

ROSAMOND. Oh no, no one thinks of your appearance – you're so sensible and useful, Mary. What have you been doing lately?

MARY. Oh, minding the house, pouring out syrup, pretending to be amiable and contented.

ROSAMOND. It may become different. You may have an offer.

MARY (*alert*). Has anyone told you he means to make me one?

ROSAMOND. Of course not. I mean, there's a gentleman who may fall in love with you, seeing you every day.

MARY (*determined not to reveal anything*). That seems to me as often a reason for people to detest each other.

ROSAMOND. Not when they're interesting and agreeable. I hear Mr Lydgate is both.

MARY (*lapsing into indifference*). Oh, Mr Lydgate. (*Direct.*) You want to know about him?

ROSAMOND. Merely how you like him.

MARY. I don't like people who speak to me without seeming to see me.

ROSAMOND. Is he so haughty? I rather like a haughty manner.

MARY. If any girl can choose the particular conceit she'd like, it's you, Rosy.

ROSAMOND. Haughtiness is not conceit. I call Fred conceited.

MARY. I wish no one said any worse of him. Mrs Waule has been telling Uncle that Fred is very unsteady.

ROSAMOND. Oh, Fred is horrid.

MARY. What do you mean?

ROSAMOND. He's so idle and makes Papa so angry and says he'll not take holy orders.

MARY. I think he's right. He's not fit to be a clergyman.

ROSAMOND. But when Papa has been at the expense of educating him for it. And only suppose if he should have no fortune left him by Uncle Featherstone.

MARY. I can suppose that very well.

ROSAMOND. Then I wonder you can defend Fred.

MARY (*laughs*). I don't defend him. I'd defend any parish from having him as a clergyman.

ROSAMOND. But if he were a clergyman, he'd be different.

MARY. Yes, he'd be a great hypocrite, and he's not that yet.

ROSAMOND. It's no use saying anything to you, Mary. You always take Fred's part.

MARY. Why shouldn't I? He'd take mine. He's the only person who takes the least trouble to oblige me.

Slight pause.

ROSAMOND. You make me feel very uncomfortable. I wouldn't tell Mamma for the world.

MARY (*angrily*). What wouldn't you tell her?

ROSAMOND (*mildly*). Pray don't go into a rage, Mary.

MARY. If your mamma is afraid that Fred will make me an offer, tell her that I'll not marry him if he asked me. But he's not going to, that I'm aware. He certainly never has asked me.

ROSAMOND. Mary, you're always so violent.

MARY. And you're so exasperating.

ROSAMOND. What can you blame me for?

MARY. Oh, blameless people are always the most exasperating.

Distant ring of a bell.

There's the bell – I think we must go down. He'll want you to sing.

ROSAMOND. I didn't mean to quarrel.

MARY. Nonsense, if one's not to get into a rage sometimes what's the use of being friends?

ROSAMOND. I'm sure he'll want 'Flow On, Thou Shining River'.

She starts to sing as we move into the next scene.

Scene Four

Stone Court upstairs. ROSAMOND *sings unaccompanied a verse of 'Flow On, Thou Shining River', while keeping an eye on the window.* FEATHERSTONE *is coughing. She breaks off singing as* LYDGATE *enters.*

FEATHERSTONE. Ah, doctor, you're late. You've met Fred. This is my niece, Rosamond Vincy.

LYDGATE *greets her briefly, then examines* FEATHERSTONE.

Miss Rosy has been singing me a song – you've nothing to say against that, eh, doctor? I like it better than your physic.

ROSAMOND (*after a moment*). How the time is going on. Fred, we must really go.

FRED. Very good.

LYDGATE. Miss Vincy is a musician then?

FEATHERSTONE. The best in Middlemarch I'll be bound, eh, Fred? (*Slight pause.*) Speak up for your sister.

FRED. My evidence would be good for nothing, sir.

ROSAMOND. Middlemarch has not a very high standard, Uncle.

FRED. Goodbye, sir.

ROSAMOND. Goodbye, Uncle. Oh –

She has forgotten her whip. LYDGATE *passes it to her.*

LYDGATE. Your whip.

ROSAMOND (*bowing*). Thank you.

Their eyes meet.

Scene Five

ROSAMOND. In riding home, both brother and sister were inclined to be silent.

Open country. Two chairs, reversed, become their horses, walking.

FRED. Fred saw the old man wanted to exercise his power by tormenting him a little.

Rosy, did Mary tell you Mrs Waule had said anything about me?

ROSAMOND. Yes, that you were very unsteady.

FRED. Was that all?

ROSAMOND. Mary mentioned nothing else. But really, Fred, I think you ought to be ashamed to –

FRED. Oh, fudge! Don't lecture me. What did Mary say?

ROSAMOND. I'm not obliged to tell you. You care so very much what Mary says, and you're too rude to allow me to speak.

FRED. Of course I care what Mary says. She's the best girl I know.

ROSAMOND. I should never have thought she was a girl to fall in love with.

FRED. How do you know what men would fall in love with? Girls never know.

ROSAMOND. Fred – let me advise you not to fall in love with her, for she says she wouldn't marry you if you asked her.

FRED. She might have waited till I did ask her. (*Nudges his horse into a trot.*)

ROSAMOND. I knew it would nettle you. (*Follows.*)

FRED. Not at all. She wouldn't have said it if you hadn't provoked her.

Scene Six

FRED. Fred decided he would tell his father about Featherstone's demand.

VINCY. And as he hoped, his father took on himself the unpleasant business of speaking to Bulstrode at the bank.

FRED *pats his father on the shoulder encouragingly as* VINCY *moves into the scene.*

The bank. BULSTRODE *behind his desk. He has a stick of celery or small sandwich in a box. He eats.*

BULSTRODE. I cannot persuade you to adopt my regimen, Vincy?

VINCY. No, no. Life wants padding. However, what I came to talk about this lunchtime was a little affair of my young Fred's... (*Resolved to be good humoured.*) The fact is, it's about a whim of old Featherstone's. Somebody's been cooking up a story out of spite to try to set the old man against Fred. He's as good as told Fred that he means to leave him his land, and that makes other people jealous.

BULSTRODE. Vincy, you'll not get any concurrence from me
as to the course you've pursued with your eldest son. It was
entirely from worldly vanity that you destined him for the
Church. You were not warranted in devoting money to an
expensive education which has succeeded in nothing but in
giving him extravagant idle habits.

To point out other people's errors was a duty that Mr
Bulstrode rarely shrank from.

VINCY. Well, it's no good going back. There wasn't a finer
business in Middlemarch than cloth manufacture at the time,
and the lad was clever. It's a good British feeling to try to
raise your family a little.

BULSTRODE. I act as your friend when I say that what you
have just said is worldliness.

VINCY (*reacts*). Very well, I'm worldly. I don't suppose you
conduct business on unworldly principles. The only
difference is that my worldliness is more honest than yours.

BULSTRODE (*wearily*). This is unfruitful, Vincy. You had
some particular business?

VINCY. Yes, yes. Somebody's told old Featherstone, giving you
as the authority, that Fred has been trying to borrow on the
prospect of Featherstone's land. Of course you never said
any such nonsense. But the old man will insist that Fred
bring him a denial in your handwriting. Just a bit of a note
saying you don't believe a word of such stuff. I suppose you
can have no objection.

BULSTRODE. Pardon me, I have an objection. I'm by no
means sure that your son in his recklessness and ignorance –
I'll use no severer word – has *not* tried to raise money on his
future prospects.

VINCY. But Fred gives me his honour. He's not a liar. And I
should have thought that there was no religion to hinder a
man from believing the best of a young fellow. It would be a
poor sort of religion to put a spoke in his wheel by refusing.

BULSTRODE. I'm not at all sure I should be befriending your
son by smoothing his way to the future possession of

Featherstone's property. I cannot regard wealth as a blessing to those who use it simply as a harvest for this world. It will not tend to the glory of God.

VINCY. If you mean to hinder everybody from having money but saints, you must give up some profitable partnerships – that's all I can say. It may be for the glory of God that Plymdale uses those blue dyes from Brassing – but they rot the silk, that's all I know – oh, I could get up a pretty row if I chose!

Pause.

BULSTRODE. You pain me very much. You must remember, if you please, that I stretch my tolerance towards you as my wife's brother. It little becomes you to complain of me withholding material help from your family. I must remind you it's not your own prudence or judgement that has enabled you to keep your place in the trade.

VINCY. You've been no loser by my trade yet. And when you married Harriet, you could expect that our families should hang by the same nail. But if you want my family to come down in the world, you'd better say so. If you want –

BULSTRODE. Shall you come down in the world for want of this letter about your son?

VINCY. Well, whether or not, I consider it very unhandsome of you to refuse it. It's the sort of thing – this tyrannical spirit – wanting to play bishop and banker everywhere – it's this sort of thing makes a man's name stink!

BULSTRODE. Vincy, if you insist on quarrelling with me, it will be exceedingly painful to Harriet, as well as myself.

VINCY. I don't want to quarrel. We should be friends. You like to be master, there's no denying that – you must be first chop in Heaven, else you won't like it much. But you're my sister's husband, and we ought to stick together. And if I know Harriet, she'll consider it your fault if you refuse to do Fred a good turn. And I don't say I shall bear it well. I consider it unhandsome.

BULSTRODE (*uncomfortably*). I will reflect a little, Vincy. I'll mention the subject to Harriet... I shall probably send you a letter.

VINCY. Very well. As soon as you can, please. Before tomorrow!

BULSTRODE (*sighing*). Bulstrode wrote the letter.

BULSTRODE *takes a letter from his pocket, passes it to* VINCY, *who passes it to* FRED, *who pats* VINCY *on the shoulder in thanks.*

Scene Seven

FRED. Early next morning, Fred carried the letter to Mr Featherstone.

Stone Court upstairs. FRED *passes the letter to* FEATHERSTONE *in bed.*

FEATHERSTONE (*reading*)....'my conviction that your son Frederick has not obtained any advance of money on bequests promised by Mr Featherstone' – Tchah! Promised? Who said I ever promised? I promise nothing – I shall change my will as often as I like – 'Accrue'... 'Demise'... He couldn't speak finer if he wanted to borrow! (*Throws the letter down.*) You don't suppose I believe a thing because Bulstrode writes it fine, eh?

FRED. You wished to have the letter, sir...

Slight pause.

FEATHERSTONE. And now what d'you expect?

FRED. I expect nothing, sir. I came to bring you the letter. If you like, I'll bid you good morning.

FEATHERSTONE. Not yet, not yet. Ring the bell. I want Missy to come.

FRED *rings*. MARY *enters, looking as if she's been crying*.

Why couldn't you sit still here, till I told you to go. I want my waistcoat. I told you always to put it on the bed.

MARY *goes to fetch the waistcoat.* FRED *tries to anticipate her – 'Allow me' –*

Let it alone! You bring it, Missy. Lay it down here. Now, go away again till I call you!

MARY *goes*.

It was usual with Featherstone to season his pleasure in showing favour to one person, by being especially disagreeable to another –

MARY. And Mary was always on hand to furnish the seasoning.

FEATHERSTONE *has taken keys from his waistcoat and a tin box from under his bedclothes.*

FEATHERSTONE. You expect I'm going to give you a little fortune, eh?

FRED. Not at all, sir. You were good enough to speak of making me a present the other day, else, of course, I should not have thought of the matter. (*But he has hopes.*)

FEATHERSTONE *opens the box, fingers many twenty-pound banknotes. Finally gives* FRED *a few.* FRED *tries to put them in his pocket without looking.*

FEATHERSTONE. Don't you think it's worth your while to count 'em?

FRED. I thought… But I shall be happy to…

He counts five notes, and is disappointed.

It's very handsome of you, sir.

FEATHERSTONE. I should think it is. (*Locks the box and tucks it under the bedclothes.*)

FRED. I assure you I'm very grateful.

FEATHERSTONE. So you ought to be. You want to cut a figure in the world, and I reckon Peter Featherstone is the only one you've got to trust to.

FRED. Yes indeed. I was not born to very splendid chances. It really seems a little too bad to have to ride a broken-winded hunter and see men, not half such good judges, able to throw away any amount of money on buying bad bargains.

FEATHERSTONE. Well, you can buy yourself a fine hunter now, and have a little over to get yourself out of any little scrape.

FRED. You're very good, sir.

FEATHERSTONE. I'm a better uncle than your Uncle Bulstrode. You won't get much out of his speckilations I think. He's got a pretty strong string round your father's leg, from what I hear, eh?

FRED. My father never tells me anything about his affairs, sir.

FEATHERSTONE. *He'll* never have much to leave you, let 'em make him Mayor of Middlemarch as much as they like. You won't get much by his dying.

FRED. Shall I destroy this letter of Mr Bulstrode's, sir?

FEATHERSTONE. Ay, ay, it's worth no money to me.

FRED *tears it up*.

Well, come again soon.

FRED *is dismissed*.

FRED. Sir.

Scene Eight

FRED. Fred had longed to be set free from his uncle –

MARY. – to go downstairs, to see Mary Garth.

Stone Court downstairs. MARY sits on the sofa, sewing.

(*Rising, as* FRED *enters.*) Am I wanted upstairs?

FRED. No, only I'm dismissed.

MARY *sits again, resumes her work.*

May I stay a little, Mary, or shall I bore you.

MARY. Pray sit down. You'll not be so heavy a bore as Mrs Waule's son, John, who was here yesterday.

FRED. Poor fellow – I think he is in love with you.

MARY (*angrily*). It's one of the most odious things in a girl's life, that there must always be some supposition of falling in love coming between her and any man who is kind to her. I should have thought I at least might have been safe from all that. I've no ground for the vanity of fancying everybody who comes near me is in love with me.

FRED. I didn't mean to make you angry.

MARY. Oh, I'm not angry, except with the ways of the world. I do like to be spoken to as if I had some common sense. I feel as if I could understand a little more than I ever hear – (*Undercurrent of laughter.*) even from young gentlemen who have been to college.

FRED. I don't care how merry you are at my expense. I thought you looked so sad when you came upstairs. It's a shame you should stay here to be bullied in that way.

MARY. Oh, I've tried being a governess but I'm not fit for that – my mind is too fond of wandering. Everything here I can do as well as anyone else – perhaps better than some – Rosy, for example.

FRED (*brotherly scepticism*). Well, Rosy!

MARY. Come, Fred. You've no right to be critical.

FRED. Oh, because I'm idle and extravagant? Well, I'm not fit
to be poor. I should not have made a bad fellow if I'd been
rich. And I couldn't do my duty as a clergyman any more
than you could do yours as a governess.

MARY. There are other sorts of work. It's very miserable not to
resolve on some course.

FRED. You want to quarrel with me.

MARY. How can I want to quarrel with you? However naughty
you may be to others, you're good to me.

FRED. Because I like you better. But you despise me.

MARY (*nods and smiles*). A little.

FRED. You'd admire a stupendous fellow, who'd have opinions
about everything.

MARY. Yes, I should.

FRED (*awkwardly*). I suppose a woman is never in love with
anyone she's always known, ever since she can remember.
It's always some new fellow.

MARY. Let me see. I must go back on my experience. There is
Juliet – she seems an example of what you say. But then
Ophelia had probably known Hamlet a long while, and then
there are… mm… altogether my experience is rather mixed.

FRED. When a man is not loved, it's of no use for him to say he
could be a better fellow – could do anything –

MARY. Not in the least use. Might, could, would…

FRED. I don't see how a man is to be good for much unless he
has some one woman to love him dearly.

MARY. I think the goodness should come before he expects
that.

FRED. It's hardly fair to say I'm bad.

MARY. I said nothing at all about you.

FRED (*commits himself*). I shall never be good for anything,
Mary, if you'll not say that you love me – if you'll not
promise to marry me – I mean, when I'm able to marry…

MARY. If I did love you, I'd certainly not promise to marry you.

FRED. I think that's quite wicked, Mary. If you love me –

MARY. – I think it would be wicked of me to marry you. My father says an idle man ought not to exist, much less be married.

FRED. Then I'm to blow my brains out?

MARY. No – on the whole I think you'd do better to pass your examination. I've heard the Reverend Mr Farebrother say it's disgracefully easy. And he always speaks the truth.

FRED. Anything's easy to him. Not that cleverness has anything to do with it. I'm ten times cleverer than many who pass.

MARY. That only shows you're ten times more idle.

FRED. Well, if I did pass, you wouldn't want me to go into the Church?

MARY. That's not the question – what I want you to do. You've a conscience of your own, I suppose.

The bell rings.

There's my uncle.

FRED (*seizes her hand*). Mary. If you'll not give me some encouragement, I shall get worse instead of better.

MARY. I'll not give you encouragement. Your family would dislike it and so would mine. My father would think it a disgrace if I accepted a man who got into debt and wouldn't work.

He is stung, and releases her hand.

Fred, you've always been so good, so generous to me. I'm not ungrateful. But never speak to me in that way again.

FRED. Very well.

Fred was thoroughly in love with a girl who had no money.

FEATHERSTONE. But there was Featherstone's land in the background.

FRED. And let Mary say what she would, he felt she really did care for him.

MARY. At six years old he had made her his wife with a brass ring from an umbrella…

FRED. He was not utterly in despair.

Scene Nine

FRED (*giving his mother the money*). Mother. Keep this for me till I need it. There's eighty pounds. I want it to pay a debt with.

MRS VINCY. Bless you, my dear.

FRED. But he owed twice as much – a hundred and sixty pounds – and worse –

GARTH. – it had been guaranteed in the shape of a bill signed by Mary's father, Caleb Garth…

MRS VINCY. The Vincys had the belief in life as a merry lot –

FRED. – the rejection of all anxiety –

LYDGATE. – which made the house exceptional at that time –

MRS BULSTRODE. – when Evangelicalism had cast a certain suspicion over amusements.

VINCY. Now that Mr Vincy was Mayor of Middlemarch, he must give dinner parties, whatever the expense.

The Vincys' drawing room. A party in progress.

(*Calling.*) Fred! Bring the whist table.

FRED. We can't play till Mr Farebrother arrives.

VINCY. We can be ready… (*Before* FRED *can leave*.) And open the piano, Fred, so Rosy can give us some music.

Meanwhile LYDGATE *has been talking quietly to* ROSAMOND. *We may only catch snatches of their conversation.* 'Do you call yourself a raw country girl?' … 'I'm really afraid of you'. FRED *goes over to the piano.*

LYDGATE (*to* ROSAMOND). I'm sure you could teach me a thousand things, as an exquisite bird could teach a bear…

FRED has opened the piano, and starts playing 'Cherry Ripe' with one hand.

ROSAMOND. Ah, there is Fred. I must hinder him from jarring all your nerves. Fred, you'll make Mr Lydgate ill. He has an ear.

FRED laughs and accelerates to the end.

You perceive the bears will not always be taught.

FRED (*setting a chair at the piano*). Now then, Rosy. Some good rousing tunes first.

VINCY. Rosamond, sing for us.

MRS VINCY. Yes, sing for us.

General agreement. After a show of reticence, ROSAMOND *goes to the piano. She sings 'Voi che sapete'.*

FRED. I wish I could play that on my flute.

FAREBROTHER *enters cheerfully.*

LYDGATE. The Reverend Mr Farebrother came in like a pleasant change in the light.

FRED. Ah, Mr Farebrother. We were awaiting you.

He goes off to bring two extra chairs for whist, while FAREBROTHER *greets others.*

LYDGATE. Mr Farebrother.

FAREBROTHER. Lydgate! You promised to come to see me. Tomorrow evening? I can't let you off, you know, because I have some beetles to show you. We collectors feel an interest in every new man till he's seen all we have to show him.

FRED *has returned and placed the chairs ready for whist.*

Ah, whist. Come now and let us be serious. Cards, Mr Lydgate? Not play? Ah, you're too young and light for this sort of thing.

FAREBROTHER *joins* FRED *at the whist.* VINCY *and* MRS VINCY *too.*

LYDGATE. I'm afraid it's time I left. (*But he stays.*)

FRED (*to* FAREBROTHER). Punch?

FAREBROTHER. No, just water for me.

VINCY. Punch for me! It's the best inward pickle – preserves you against bad air, don't you think, doctor?

LYDGATE *smiles but shakes his head.*

FRED (*calling off*). Punch!

ROSAMOND. You'll not like us in Middlemarch I feel sure.

LYDGATE. I suppose all country towns are pretty much alike. I've made up my mind to take Middlemarch as it comes...

They talk quietly over the piano. We follow the game of whist until –

FAREBROTHER. Mine I think.

LYDGATE. Ah. Mr Farebrother seems to be winning.

ROSAMOND. He usually does!

FAREBROTHER. I have to earn money somehow. (*Sweeps up his winnings.*)

FRED. Come. Another hand!

FAREBROTHER. Indeed. Shall I deal?

Scene Ten

FAREBROTHER*'s house*. FAREBROTHER, MRS FAREBROTHER, LYDGATE.

FAREBROTHER. The Reverend Mr Farebrother lived in an old parsonage with his sister –

She shakes hands with LYDGATE.

– his aunt –

Likewise.

– and his mother –

All very different.

– who all depended on his meagre living.

VINCY. And perhaps partly on his winnings at cards.

MRS FAREBROTHER. I am proud to say my son will compare with any preacher in the kingdom.

FAREBROTHER (*to* LYDGATE). A mother is never partial. I'm not a model clergyman, only a decent makeshift.

MRS FAREBROTHER. My son always undervalues himself. I tell him he is undervaluing the God who made him –

FAREBROTHER. I must take Mr Lydgate away to my study, Mother. I promised to show him my collection – shall we go?

MRS FAREBROTHER. Oh, there's good tea in the pot – and there's nothing there – (*Calling after.*) but pickled vermin, drawers full of bluebottles and no carpets on the floor.

FAREBROTHER*'s den.*

FAREBROTHER. Here we are. (*Brings out a glass-fronted display of insects from the table drawer.*) Do look at these.

There, they spoke of personal independence.

LYDGATE. I made up my mind some time ago to be as independent as possible. In London there's so much empty pretension and trickery. In the country one can follow one's own course.

FAREBROTHER. Yes, well – you've got a good start. You're in the right profession. Some of us miss that, and repent too late. But you mustn't be too sure of keeping your independence.

LYDGATE. You mean of family ties?

Lydgate conceived these might press rather tightly on Mr Farebrother.

FAREBROTHER. Not altogether. Of course they make many things more difficult. But a good wife – a good unworldly woman – may really help a man. There's a parishioner of mine – a fine fellow, but who would hardly have pulled through as he has done without his wife. Do you know the Garths?

LYDGATE. No, but there's a Miss Garth at old Featherstone's.

FAREBROTHER. Ah. Their daughter. An excellent girl.

LYDGATE. She's very quiet. I've hardly noticed her.

FAREBROTHER. She'll have taken notice of you, though, depend on it. She gauges everybody. I prepared her for confirmation – (*Slight pause.*) She's a favourite of mine.

Silence.

Mm.

But Mr Farebrother, like Mr Lydgate, was a bachelor who could hardly afford to keep a wife, however strong his inclination…

Scene Eleven

FRED. Meanwhile, Fred's debt was on his mind.

FRED, *alone, in an agony of remorse.*

FEATHERSTONE. After an unfortunate attempt to make money on a horse –

MRS BULSTRODE. – he was left with only fifty pounds.

FRED. And I owe a hundred and sixty! In five days' time! I daren't tell my father. Not now. I must explain it all to Mr Garth.

VINCY (*as he becomes* GARTH). To Mary's father, who had guaranteed the debt and would have to pay it.

FRED. Now through all his education, Fred had kept his affection for the Garths, and his habit of going to their house as a second home –

The Garths' back parlour.

GARTH. – though intercourse between the elders of the families had long since ceased –

MRS GARTH. – and the acquaintance was carried on between the children rather than the parents.

GARTH. Mr Garth had no ambition for profit, and was living narrowly.

MRS GARTH. His honourable exertions had won him due esteem –

ROSAMOND. – but in no part of the world is genteel visiting founded on esteem, in the absence of suitable furniture and a complete dinner service.

MARY. And Mrs Vincy was alarmed lest Fred should engage himself to this 'plain girl' whose parents lived in 'such a small way'.

FRED. So Fred never spoke at home of his visits to the Garths.

MRS GARTH *is sorting out the washing on the kitchen table, when* FRED *enters, pestered by* BEN *and* LETTY, *two of the Garths' children.*

BEN. Look!

LETTY. Fred's here!

FRED. Mrs Garth.

MRS GARTH. You, Fred, so early in the day? You look quite pale. Has anything happened?

FRED. I want to speak to Mr Garth – and to you also.

MRS GARTH. Caleb'll be in again in a few minutes. He's some work at his desk that must be done. Do you mind staying with me, while I finish matters here?

BEN. But we needn't do our grammar yet, need we? (*Taken* FRED's *whip and is trying it out*.)

MRS GARTH. No, go out now. But put that whip down. Don't whip the cat!

The cat squeals, and everyone watches it as it races off.

Pray take the whip from him, Fred.

FRED. Come, old boy, give it me.

BEN (*handing over the whip*). Will you let me ride your horse today?

FRED. Another time. I'm not riding my own horse.

BEN. Shall you see Mary today?

FRED. Oh. (*An 'unpleasant twinge'.*) Yes, I think so.

BEN. Tell her to come home soon and play forfeits and make fun.

MRS GARTH. Enough, Ben! Run away, and take Letty with you. Letty, you go too.

BEN. Come on, Letty…

The CHILDREN *go. Pause.* FRED *is unsure whether to confess now, or wait for* GARTH.

FRED. Do you still teach pupils, now, Mrs Garth?

MRS GARTH. Only one. Fanny Hackbutt comes at half-past eleven. I'm at a low ebb with pupils. (*Pleased.*) But I've saved my little purse for Alfred's apprenticeship – I have ninety-two pounds. He can go to Mr Hanmer's now. He's just at the right age.

FRED. Ah.

Slight pause.

This didn't lead well towards the news that Mr Garth was on the brink of losing ninety-two pounds and more.

MRS GARTH. Caleb thinks that Alfred will turn out a distinguished engineer. He wants to give the boy a good chance. There's Caleb now. I hear him coming in.

GARTH *enters, carrying* LETTY *in his arms.*

Letty, don't bother your father…

GARTH. What, Fred my boy. You're here betimes. (*Sees* FRED's *face.*) Is anything the matter?

FRED. Yes, Mr Garth.

GARTH (*to* LETTY). Then you run along and play with Ben in the garden.

LETTY *goes.*

FRED. I'm come to tell something I'm afraid will give you a bad opinion of me. I'm come to tell you and Mrs Garth I can't keep my word. I can't find the money to meet the bill after all. I've only got these fifty pounds towards the hundred and sixty. (*Lays the notes on the table.*)

MRS GARTH (*astonished, looks to* GARTH). What's this?

GARTH (*embarrassed, after a moment*). Oh, I didn't tell you, Susan. I put my name to a bill for Fred. It was for a hundred and sixty pounds. He made sure he could meet it himself.

MRS GARTH. Caleb was one of those rare men who are rigid to themselves and indulgent to others.

(*To* FRED.) I suppose you've asked your father for the money?

FRED. No. But I know it will be of no use – and unless it were, I shouldn't like to mention Mr Garth's name in the matter.

GARTH. It's come at an unfortunate time. I'm rather hard up just now. You see I have to cut out everything like a tailor with short measure. A hundred and ten pounds! What can we do, Susan? I shall want every farthing we have in the bank. The deuce take it!

Pause.

MRS GARTH (*decisively*). I must give you the ninety-two pounds that I've put by for Alfred's school. (*Slight pause*.) And I've no doubt that Mary has twenty pounds saved from her salary by this time.

FRED. Fred's pain beforehand had consisted in the sense that he must seem dishonourable to the Garths.

FAREBROTHER. We are most of us brought up in the notion that the highest motive for not doing wrong is irrespective of those who suffer the wrong.

FRED. But now he suddenly saw himself as a rascal robbing two women of their savings.

MARY. The exercise of the imagination on other people's needs is not common with hopeful young gentlemen...

FRED. I shall certainly pay it all, Mrs Garth – ultimately.

MRS GARTH. Yes, ultimately. But boys can't be apprenticed ultimately; they should be apprenticed at fifteen.

GARTH. I was most in the wrong, Susan. Fred made sure of finding the money. But I'd no business to be fingering bills. I suppose you've looked all round and tried all honest means?

FRED. Yes, I've tried everything – I really have. I should have had a hundred and thirty ready but for a misfortune with a horse I was about to sell. My uncle had given me eighty pounds and I paid away thirty with my old horse in order to get another which I was going to sell for – oh, I wish I and the horse had been at the devil before I'd brought this on you. There's no one else I care so much for – you and Mrs Garth have always been so kind to me. However, it's no use saying that. You'll always think me a rascal now. (*Almost in tears, he hurries from the room*.)

Pause.

MRS GARTH. I'm disappointed in Fred Vincy. I knew he was extravagant, but I didn't think he'd be so mean as to hang his risks on you, who could least afford to lose.

GARTH. I was a fool.

MRS GARTH. That you were. But why should you keep such
things from me? (*Smiling*.) It's just so with your buttons. You
let them burst off without telling me and go out with your
wristband hanging. If only I'd known.

GARTH. You're sadly cut up I know, Susan. I can't abide your
losing the money you've scraped together for Alfred.

MRS GARTH. It's you who'll have to suffer, for you must
teach the boy yourself. You must give up your bad habits.
Some men take to drinking, and you've taken to working
without pay. You must indulge yourself a little less in that.
And you must ride over to Mary and ask the child what
money she has.

GARTH. Poor Mary! (*Slight pause*.) Susan. I'm afraid she may
be fond of Fred.

MRS GARTH. Oh no! She always laughs at him – and he's not
likely to think of her in any other than a brotherly way.

GARTH. Deuce take the bill. These things are a sad interruption
to business.

MRS GARTH. Caleb used the word 'business' with a religious
veneration.

GARTH. He often shook his head on the value, the
indispensable might of that labour, by which the social body
is fed, clothed and housed.

FAREBROTHER. The echoes of the great hammer, the signal
shouts of the workmen –

FRED. – the roar of the furnace, the thunder of the engine –

FEATHERSTONE. – they were a sublime music to him.

LYDGATE. His ambition had been to have as effective a share
as possible in this labour –

FAREBROTHER. – in good practical schemes, accurate work,
and the faithful completion of undertakings –

MARY. – which were peculiarly dignified by him with the name
of 'business'.

GARTH. And though he'd been chiefly his own teacher, he knew more of land, building, and mining than most specialist men in the county.

Scene Twelve

FRED. Meanwhile Fred had ridden over to Stone Court.

MARY. Mary was downstairs in the parlour.

Stone Court downstairs. MARY reading a book. FRED enters slowly.

FRED. Mary. I'm a good-for-nothing blackguard.

MARY (*trying to smile*). I should think one of those epithets would do at a time.

FRED. You'll think I didn't care for you, or your father and mother.

MARY. Tell me what you've done. I'd rather know the truth than imagine it.

FRED. I owed money – a hundred and sixty pounds. I asked your father to put his name to a bill. I thought it wouldn't signify to him. I was sure of paying the bill myself and I've tried as hard as I could. And now I've been so unlucky – a horse has turned out badly – I can only pay fifty pounds. I can't ask my father – he'd not give me a farthing. And my uncle gave me a hundred a little while ago. So what can I do? And now your father has no money to spare, and your mother will have to pay away her ninety-two pounds she's saved, and she says your savings must go too. You see what a –

MARY. Oh, poor Mother, poor Father!

Silence. MARY stares in front of her.

FRED. I wouldn't have hurt you for the world, Mary. (*Slight pause.*) You can never forgive me.

MARY (*passionately*). What does it matter whether I forgive you? Would it make it any better for my mother? To lose the money she's been earning for four years, to send Alfred to Mr Hanmers? Should you think all that pleasant enough if I forgave you?

FRED. Say what you like, Mary. I deserve it.

MARY (*more quietly*). I don't want to say anything. My anger is no use.

FRED. I do care about it... I wanted to ask you – don't you think that Mr Featherstone – if you were to tell him about apprenticing Alfred –

MARY. My family is not fond of begging, Fred. We would rather work for our money. Besides, you say he's lately given you a hundred pounds. He rarely makes presents – he never made presents to us.

FRED. I'm so miserable, Mary – if you knew.

MARY. Selfish people always think their own discomfort is more important than anything.

FRED. It's hardly fair to call me selfish. If you knew what other young men do, you'd think me a good way off the worst.

MARY. People who spend a great deal on themselves without knowing how they shall pay, must be selfish. They're thinking what they can get, not what others might lose.

FRED. Any man may be unfortunate, Mary. There's not a better man than your father, and yet he got into trouble.

MARY. How dare you make any comparison between my father and you. He got into trouble because he was always thinking of the work he was doing for other people and was charging very little. And he's worked hard to make good.

FRED. And you think I shall never try to make good? When you've got power over a man, I think you might try and use it to make him better, but that's what you never do. However, I'm going. I shall never speak to you about anything again. I'm very sorry for all the trouble I've caused – that's all.

MARY. Oh, Fred, how ill you look. Sit down a moment. Don't go yet. Let me tell Uncle you're here. He's been wondering he hasn't seen you for a whole week.

She starts to go. FRED *stands in her way.*

FRED. Say one word, Mary, and I'll do anything. Say you won't give me up altogether.

MARY. As if it were any pleasure to think ill of you. As if it were not very painful to see you idle and frivolous. How can you bear to be so contemptible, when others are working and striving. And with so much good in your disposition, Fred – you might be worth a great deal.

FRED. I'll try to be anything you like, Mary, if you'll say you love me.

MARY. I should be ashamed to say I loved a man who must always be hanging on others, and reckoning on what they'd do for him. What will you be like when you're forty? Like Mr Bowyer, I suppose – just as idle, fat and shabby – hoping somebody will invite you to dinner. Spending your morning learning a tune on the flute.

She is suddenly full of fun. He tries to take her hand, but she slips away towards the door.

You must see Uncle.

FRED. Later, as Fred rode home, he began to be more conscious of being ill than melancholy.

Scene Thirteen

GARTH. Caleb Garth arrived at Stone Court soon after dusk.

Stone Court downstairs.

You see, I've been a bit of a fool again, and put my name to a bill and now –

MARY. I thought you'd come, Father. So I put my four-and-twenty pounds in my pocket. See! (*Takes out the money and puts it in his hand.*)

GARTH. Well, but we only want eighteen – here, put the rest back, child – but how did you know about it?

MARY. Fred told me this morning. He was a good deal distressed.

GARTH. I'm afraid he's not to be trusted, Mary. I should think it a pity for anybody's happiness to be wrapped up in him, and so would your mother.

MARY. And so should I, Father.

GARTH. I don't want to pry, my dear. But I was afraid there might be something between you and Fred and I wanted to caution you. You see, a woman, let her be as good as she may, has got to put up with the life her husband makes for her. Your mother's had to put up with a good deal because of me. Young folks may get fond of each other before they know what life is, and they may think it all holiday if they can only get together, but it soon turns into working day, my dear. However, you've more sense than most – there may be no occasion for me to say this, but a father trembles for his daughter, and you're all by yourself here.

MARY. Don't fear for me, Father. Fred has always been very good to me. He's kind-hearted and affectionate and not false I think with all his self-indulgence. But I'll never engage myself to one who has no independence and goes on loitering away his time on the chance that others will provide for him. You and Mother have taught me too much pride for that.

GARTH. That's right, that's right. Then I'm easy. But it's hard to run away with your earnings, child.

MARY. Ssh, Father! (*Seeing him to the door.*) Take pocketfuls of love to all at home.

Scene Fourteen

FRED. When Fred got home, his mother had to call the doctor –

The Vincys' drawing room. FRED *lying on the sofa.*

Ugh. I feel very ill.

MRS VINCY (*very concerned*). Oh, my poor boy.

FRED. Why is the doctor so slow? I feel much worse.

ROSAMOND (*by the window*). Mamma. There is Mr Lydgate stopping to speak to someone. If I were you I would call him in. They say he cures everyone.

MRS VINCY (*calling*). Mr Lydgate. Please. It's my son. He's coming. Oh, he's here –

As LYDGATE *enters.*

It's Fred. Mr Wrench is our usual doctor, but we saw you there and –

LYDGATE. Let me see.

LYDGATE *examines* FRED *lying on the sofa.* MRS VINCY *shows him a small bottle.*

Mr Wrench sent these drugs?

MRS VINCY. Yes.

LYDGATE (*clearly disapproves*). Mr Wrench, you say. You must go to bed immediately. I think it may be the early stages of Typhoid fever. (*Writes a prescription.*)

MRS VINCY. Oh no. If anything should happen. Why Mr Wrench should neglect my children...

LYDGATE. Mr Wrench may not be to blame. This form of fever is equivocal in its beginnings. Here's a prescription and I will write to Mr Wrench and tell him what I've done.

MRS VINCY. But you must go on attending Fred. I can't have my boy left to anybody who may come or not...

ROSAMOND. So Lydgate was installed as medical attendant on the Vincys.

Scene Fourteen (A)

FRED *almost unconscious*. LYDGATE *in attendance*. VINCY *and* MRS VINCY *standing by*. ROSAMOND *in the background*.

VINCY. It's no joke having fever in the house. Pritchard needn't get up any wine – brandy's the best thing against infection. (*Emphatically.*) I shall drink brandy.

FAREBROTHER. This was not an occasion for firing with blank cartridges.

VINCY. He's an uncommonly unfortunate lad is Fred. He'll need some luck by and by to make up for all this – else who'd have an eldest son.

MRS VINCY. Don't say so, Vincy, if you don't want him taken from you.

VINCY. It'll worret you to death, Lucy, that I can see.

MRS VINCY. He's always been good to me, Mr Lydgate – never had a hard word for his mother.

As LYDGATE *starts to go, she puts her hand on his arm.*

Save my boy.

LYDGATE. I have good hope, Mrs Vincy. I think the critical stage may have passed. Come downstairs with me, and let us talk about his food.

ROSAMOND. Yes, let us go downstairs, Mr Lydgate. (*Follows close behind them.*)

Scene Fourteen (B)

VINCY. Gradually, the visits became more cheerful –

ROSAMOND. – as Fred became simply feeble.

MRS VINCY. So that Mrs Vincy felt as if, after all, the illness had made a festival for her tenderness.

FRED *is sitting up now.* MRS VINCY *is by the bedside.*

There's a message from Mr Featherstone, that you must make haste and get well. Your uncle is very ill himself, says he can't do without you and he misses your visits. (*Pleased.*) There now!

FRED *turns imploringly towards her.*

FRED. But Fred was yearning for some word about Mary.

MRS VINCY (*guessing his thoughts*). If I can only see my boy strong again – and who knows, Master of Stone Court – and you can marry… Mary – or anybody you like then.

MARY. She felt ready for any sacrifice in order to satisfy him.

FRED (*tearfully*). Not if they won't have me, Mother.

MRS VINCY. Oh, take a bit of jelly, my dear.

She feeds him a spoonful.

Scene Fourteen (C)

LYDGATE. So Fred at last recovered –

ROSAMOND. – and Mr Lydgate's services were no longer needed. Until –

ROSAMOND *alone.* LYDGATE *enters.*

LYDGATE. I've come with a message for your father.

ROSAMOND. Oh. Yes. But he's not at home. Pray sit down.

He sits.

LYDGATE. There's a marked change for the worse in your Uncle Featherstone's health. He's not expected to live more than a few days. I thought your family should know. (*Slight pause.*) That's all.

ROSAMOND. Thank you.

Pause. He gets up to go, and she gets up too, dropping her embroidery. They both stoop to pick it up, rise close together. Looking at each other, they are about to kiss, when –

Scene Fifteen

VINCY. So! It won't be long before we hear of Mr Featherstone's 'demise'!

The triumphant confidence of the Mayor –

FRED. – founded on Featherstone's demand that Fred –

MRS VINCY. – and his mother should not leave his side –

MRS WAULE. – was a feeble emotion compared with all that was agitating the old man's other relations…

Stone Court upstairs. The RELATIONS *gather.*

Sister Jane Waule –

SOLOMON. – and brother Solomon – were rich.

MRS WAULE. But knew their brother would never overlook their superior claims.

SOLOMON. They knew his maxim that money was a good egg, and should be laid in a warm nest.

JONAH. But brother Jonah –

MARTHA. – and sister Martha –

TRUMBULL. – and all the other needier exiles held a different view.

The RELATIONS *compete to make* FEATHERSTONE *comfortable in bed.*

There was a general sense that everybody must watch everybody else.

MRS WAULE. And that it would be well for everybody else to reflect that the Almighty was watching too.

FEATHERSTONE. No assiduous beetles for whom the cook prepares boiling water could have been less welcome on a hearth.

MARY, MRS VINCY and FRED are quietly apart, across the room.

MARY. How shall I feed them all?

MRS VINCY. Oh my dear, you must do things handsomely where there's a last illness and a property. Have some stuffed veal always, and a fine cheese in cut. You must expect to keep open house in these last illnesses.

FEATHERSTONE has had enough.

FEATHERSTONE. Back! Downstairs!

The RELATIONS scatter and go. But MRS WAULE and SOLOMON linger.

Back, back, Mrs Waule! Back, Solomon!

MRS WAULE. Oh, brother Peter –

SOLOMON. Brother Peter. It's nothing but right I should speak to you about your shareholdings. The Almighty knows –

FEATHERSTONE. – Then he knows more than I want to! (*Keeps his gold-handled stick ready to strike.*)

SOLOMON. There's things you might repent of, brother, for want of speaking to me. I could sit up with you tonight, and Jane with me, willingly, and you might take your time to –

FEATHERSTONE. Yes, I'll take my time – you needn't offer yours!

MRS WAULE. But you can't take your own time to die in, brother – and when you lie speechless, you may be tired of having strangers about you – and you may think of me and my children – (*Moved to tears.*) Rebecca and Joanna and then there's John…

FEATHERSTONE. No I shan't. Shan't think of any of you. I've made my will. (*Looks pointedly towards FRED.*)

SOLOMON *and* MRS WAULE *turn to face* MRS VINCY *and* FRED.

MRS WAULE. Some people would be ashamed to fill a place belonging by rights to others.

SOLOMON. Oh, sister. You and me are not fine and handsome enough. We must be humble and let smart people push themselves before us.

FRED. Shall my mother and I leave the room, sir, that you may be alone with your family.

FEATHERSTONE (*to* MRS VINCY *and* FRED). Sit down! Stop where you are! Goodbye, Solomon. Goodbye, Mrs Waule. Don't come again.

They start to go, then turn.

SOLOMON. I shall be downstairs, brother, whether or no. I shall do my duty, and it remains to be seen what the Almighty will allow –

MRS WAULE. Yes, in property going out of families. But I pity them who are not such, and I pity their mothers. Goodbye, brother Peter.

They start to go, then turn.

SOLOMON. Remember I'm the eldest after you, brother.

FEATHERSTONE *pulls his wig down over his ears and shuts his eyes.*

But I bid you goodbye.

They finally go.

Scene Sixteen

MARY. Downstairs, in the wainscoted parlour, relatives and
    guests came daily from far or near – and sat at the post of
    duty – waiting for death.

   SOLOMON *and* MRS WAULE *have taken the best seats on
   the sofa.* MARTHA *and* JONAH *go where they can. They
   wait quietly, but follow each other's sporadic conversations
   avidly.*

JONAH. Brother Jonah –

MARTHA. – and Sister Martha were poor.

JONAH. He will surely remember us at last –

MARTHA. – if only because he's done nothing for us till now.

JONAH. Men like to make a surprise of their wills. Ssh –

   MARY *enters, delivers a ham sandwich on a plate to*
   SOLOMON, *then sits with her book. Silence. They all turn
   as* TRUMBULL *enters importantly from upstairs, as if with
   knowledge.*

TRUMBULL. I don't mind if I have a slice of that ham if you'll
    allow me.

MARY. Of course. (*Leaves her book, and goes out.*)

MRS WAULE (*after a moment*). You've seen the old man, Mr
    Trumbull? You're highly favoured.

TRUMBULL. Yes. You see he's relied on me considerably as
    an agent. (*Thoughtfully.*) Mmmm...

SOLOMON. Might anybody ask what their brother has been
    saying?

TRUMBULL. Oh yes. Anybody may ask. Anybody may give
    their remarks an interrogative turn. This is constantly done
    by good speakers.

SOLOMON. I shouldn't be sorry to hear he'd remembered you,
    Mr Trumbull. I never was against the deserving. (*Looks up.*)
    It's the undeserving I'm against.

TRUMBULL. Ah, there it is, you see. It can't be denied that undeserving people have been beneficiaries.

MRS WAULE. Do you mean to say for certain that my brother has left his land away from our family? (*Slight pause.*) It would be flying in the face of the Almighty.

TRUMBULL, *humming casually, wanders over to* MARY's *work table. Opens her book. Is he giving a hint? Reads from the book, muttering 'took place on the Continent', stressing the last syllable.* MARY *returns with a ham sandwich for* TRUMBULL, *who sits to eat.*

TRUMBULL. I take a snack where I can. (*After a moment.*) This ham is better than the ham at Freshitt Hall – and I think I'm a tolerable judge.

He stops MARY *who is about to leave.*

You've an interesting work there. Sir Walter Scott. It commences well. Do you subscribe to our Middlemarch library?

MARY. No. Mr Fred Vincy brought it me. (*Leaves.*)

SOLOMON (*quietly*). I should say my brother has done something for *her* in his will.

MRS WAULE. Though his first wife was a poor match, and this young woman is only her niece. And very proud.

TRUMBULL. A sensible girl though. I've observed her mixing medicine drops. She minds what she's doing. That's a great point in a woman. A man, whose life is of any value, should think of his wife as a nurse. That's what I should do, if I married. (*Has finished his sandwich.*) I wish you good morning, Mrs Waule, Mr Solomon. (*Throws a doubtful look to* JONAH *and* MARTHA.) I trust we shall meet under less melancholy auspices. (*Leaves.*)

SOLOMON. You may depend, Jane, from the way he talks, my brother has left that girl a lumping sum.

MRS WAULE. As if my daughters weren't to be trusted to give drops!

Scene Seventeen

MARY. That night, Mary Garth relieved the watch in Mr Featherstone's room.

Stone Court upstairs. Night. FEATHERSTONE asleep in bed. MARY, with a candle, sits quietly in a chair, watching the glow from the fire. A clock strikes three.

MRS GARTH. The red fire seemed calmly independent of the petty passions, which were daily moving her contempt.

MARY (*smiles to herself*). They're so ridiculous!

Silence.

FEATHERSTONE (*suddenly*). Missy, come here. (*Draws the tin box from under the bedclothes. Unlocks it and takes out another key.*) How many of 'em are in the house?

MARY. You mean of your own relations, sir?

FEATHERSTONE. Mm.

MARY. Mr Jonah Featherstone and young Cranch are sleeping here.

FEATHERSTONE. Oh, ay. They stick, do they? And the rest – they come every day I warrant – Solomon and Jane and all the young 'uns. They come peeping, and counting up?

MARY. Not all of them every day. Mr Solomon and Mrs Waule are here every day, and the others come often.

FEATHERSTONE. More fools they. Harken, Mary. It's three o'clock in the morning and I've got all my faculties. I know all my property, and where the money's put out and everything. And I've made everything ready to change my mind and do as I like at the last. Do you hear, Mary?

MARY. Well, sir?

FEATHERSTONE. Now, you do as I tell you. This is the key to the drawer in my table there.

MARY takes it.

Open it and take out the topmost paper.

She goes slowly to the table.

Last will and testament – big printed.

MARY *stops. He lowers his voice with an air of deep cunning.*

I've made two wills and I'm going to burn the last one.

Slight pause.

Do as I tell you.

MARY (*firmly*). No, sir, I can't do that.

FEATHERSTONE. Not do it? I tell you you must.

MARY. I can't touch your will. I must refuse anything that might lay me open to suspicion.

FEATHERSTONE. I tell you, I'm in my right mind. Shan't I do as I like at the last? Open it, I say.

MARY. No, sir, I will not.

FEATHERSTONE. I tell you there's no time to lose.

MARY. I can't help that, sir. I'll not let the close of your life soil the beginning of mine.

FEATHERSTONE *pauses, staring. Starts to empty his tin box.*

FEATHERSTONE (*hurriedly*). Missy, look here! Take the money – the notes and the gold – look here – take it – you shall have it all – do as I tell you.

He stretches out the money towards her. She retreats.

MARY. I'll not touch your will or your money, sir. Pray don't ask me again. If you do, I must go and call your brother.

FEATHERSTONE *starts to cry.*

(*As gently as she can.*) Pray put up your money, sir. (*Goes back to the fire.*)

FEATHERSTONE (*a new idea*). Call the young chap. Call Fred Vincy.

MARY (*after a moment's thought*). I will call him. If you'll let me call others with him.

FEATHERSTONE. Nobody else, I say. The young chap. I shall do as I like!

MARY. Wait till broad daylight, sir, when everyone is stirring. Or let me call to fetch a lawyer. He can be here very quickly –

FEATHERSTONE. What do I want with the lawyer? Nobody shall know. I shall do as I like! –

MARY. Let me call someone else, sir. Let me, pray –

FEATHERSTONE. You let me alone! (*Slight pause.*) Look here, Missy. Take the money. You'll never have the chance again. It's pretty nigh two hundred. There's more in the drawer – and nobody knows how much there was. Take it and do as I tell you.

MARY. It's of no use, sir. I will not touch your money. I'll do anything else but –

FEATHERSTONE (*in a hoarse rage*). Anything else! Anything else! I want nothing else. You come here – you come here...

MARY *approaches. He tries to raise his gold-handled stick to strike her.*

MARY. Try to compose yourself. Go to sleep. And tomorrow, by daylight, you can do as you like.

He tries to throw the stick at her but impotently. He takes the keys, lays his hand over the money. He quietens. She goes back to her chair, watches the fire. She looks towards him, he seems asleep now. Gradually the room lightens. She goes to the window, pulls aside the curtains to let in the morning light. She goes over to him, is suddenly worried, touches his hand, is shocked. She runs to the bell and rings it energetically.

The sound of the bell merges with a heavier bell tolling.

FEATHERSTONE (*sits up*). Peter Featherstone was buried in Lowick churchyard.

MRS WAULE. He had left directions for a big burying with people bid to it who had difficult journeys and would rather have stayed at home.

SOLOMON. He loved the means of making others feel his power uncomfortably –

MRS WAULE. – though he had not made it clear to himself that his pleasure in the drama was confined to anticipation.

FEATHERSTONE. So far as he had imagined a future life it had been one of gratification inside his coffin.

Scene Eighteen

MRS WAULE (*as she becomes* MRS CADWALLADER). Even the gentry watched the handsome funeral from the upstairs rooms at Lowick Manor.

Lowick Manor upstairs. DOROTHEA, MRS CADWALLADER, SIR JAMES, CELIA, BROOKE *all looking out of the three windows.*

DOROTHEA. One is constantly wondering what sort of lives other people lead and how they take things.

MRS CADWALLADER. Quite right. Your Lowick farmers are as curious as any buffaloes.

SIR JAMES. I'm told the old fellow left a great deal of money, as well as land.

MRS CADWALLADER. Ah, now they're all coming out of church. Dear me, what a wonderfully mixed set. Mr Lydgate, as doctor, I suppose. But there's a good-looking family – (*To* SIR JAMES.) who are they, do you know?

SIR JAMES. I see Vincy, the Mayor of Middlemarch. They're probably his wife and children.

BROOKE. A good fellow is Vincy, a credit to the manufacturing interest.

MRS CADWALLADER. One of your reforming committee, I dare say. And one of those who suck the life out of our wretched hand-loom weavers in Tipton and Freshitt. That's how his family look so fair and sleek. Oh, those purple-faced people are an excellent foil! (*Giggles.*)

BROOKE. It's a solemn thing, though, a funeral. If you take it in that light, you know.

MRS CADWALLADER. But I'm not taking it in that light. It was time that mean old man died, and none of these people are sorry.

DOROTHEA. How piteous. I can't bear to think that anyone should die and leave no love behind.

MRS CADWALLADER. There's a new face in the neighbourhood – queerer than any of them. A sort of frog-face.

CELIA. Where? – Oh yes. A frog-face.

MRS CADWALLADER. What a procession!

The room dissolves into the funeral procession. FEATHERSTONE's bed may suggest the coffin. With SOLOMON and MRS WAULE at the front, the relations form up, two by two.

FEATHERSTONE. When the animals entered the Ark in pairs, one may imagine that allied species made much private remark on each other –

MRS WAULE (*looking behind*). – and were tempted to think that so many other forms feeding on the same store of fodder –

SOLOMON (*looking behind*). – were eminently superfluous, as tending to diminish the rations.

The procession breaks up, as the FAMILY gather to hear the will.

Scene Nineteen

Stone Court downstairs. SOLOMON *and* MRS WAULE,
JONAH *and* MARTHA, TRUMBULL; MARY *and the*
VINCYS *slightly apart. The whispers among them grow
increasingly insistent, as extra chairs are brought, and they take
their places.* STANDISH, *the lawyer, waits by the table.*

SOLOMON. If Fred Vincy should get the land –

MRS WAULE. Dreadful.

SOLOMON. It should surely come to us –

MRS WAULE. Surely.

SOLOMON. Suppose he leaves something to Mary –

MRS WAULE. It wouldn't be much –

SOLOMON. No, it's the land that matters.

JONAH. Trumbull's worth five hundred.

MRS WAULE. Jonah's undeserving.

SOLOMON. We'll surely get more –

JONAH. Solomon's greedy –

MARTHA. It must be equal shares.

MRS WAULE. My younger sister's children ought not to
    expect –

MARTHA. My children should get just as much –

MRS WAULE. – nearly as much as mine –

MARTHA. – just as much as hers –

JONAH. But it's the land that matters –

SOLOMON. If Fred Vincy gets –

JONAH. If Vincy gets the land –

ALL (*together*). Dreadful.

   The lawyer intervenes to restore order.

STANDISH. Ladies and gentlemen. For those who don't know me, my name is Standish, and I'm the lawyer for the deceased. I'm now going upstairs to bring down the will. I'll be back shortly.

Tense silence, broken by the odd remark aimed at the Vincys.

MRS WAULE. Them who've made sure of their good luck may be disappointed yet...

TRUMBULL. Hopes are often delusive...

MRS WAULE. We none of us know what poor Peter might have had on his mind...

MARTHA. If ever I've begged, it's only to God above...

They wait for the lawyer's reappearance, while across the room –

MRS VINCY. Everything's as handsome as could be.

VINCY. I should be all the better pleased if he'd left lots of little legacies, as well as the land to Fred.

FRED *tries to suppress a giggle.*

MARY. Oh, Fred, sshh, change places with me.

FRED *retreats into a corner.*

FRED. Fred was feeling as good natured as possible towards all those people who were less lucky than he. It was particularly easy to laugh.

The lawyer reappears.

STANDISH. Ladies and gentlemen.

He carries two wills. He crosses to the table – 'utter suspense'.

The will I hold in my hand was drawn up by myself and executed by our deceased friend in August 1825. But I find to my surprise there's a subsequent will, hitherto unknown to me, bearing the date March 1st 1828.

MARY. Mary Garth felt the most throbbing suspense. She had virtually determined the production of this second will, which might have momentous effects.

STANDISH. I should read the first will, since such appears to have been the intention of the deceased, but as it is no longer material, I will here content myself with a summary of its contents...

MRS WAULE. Many present felt the contents of this first will might be a guide to the contents of the latest.

STANDISH. Various small sums were allocated to many members of the family, two hundred apiece to Solomon Featherstone and Mrs Jane Waule –

Shocked reaction: 'Only two hundred!'

– a hundred apiece to Jonah Featherstone and Mrs Martha Cranch –

More shock: 'That's all?!'

– a hundred to Mary Garth, and so on... various nephews and nieces –

Some tears.

But the greater part of the money – ten thousand pounds – was bequeathed to Mr Fred Vincy.

Involuntary noises of delight from VINCY *and* MRS VINCY. *It's hard for* FRED *to stop smiling.*

And the rest of the estate, Stone Court and all the land, bequeathed to –

FRED (*stepping forward*). Oh, possibilities!

VINCY *and* MRS VINCY (*standing together*). Oh, expectations!

STANDISH. To Mr Joshua Rigg.

Silence.

SOLOMON. Who?

JONAH. Who is he?

Everyone looks around and behind.

STANDISH. Who is named sole executor and is henceforth to take the name of Featherstone.

TRUMBULL. Most singular.

MRS WAULE. A complete stranger.

MARTHA. Is he the one with the frog-face?

JONAH (*realisation*). He must be a love child!

Shocked silence.

MRS WAULE. Well!

SOLOMON. But there's a second will, the latest.

STANDISH. Indeed. We've not yet heard the final wishes of the deceased.

MARY. Only Mary knew that they had not been the final wishes.

STANDISH. The last will, which I shall read shortly, revokes the first entirely. Stone Court and all the land, stock and furniture are still bequeathed to Joshua Rigg –

Reaction of disbelief and disgust.

– but all the residue in money will now be devoted to the erection of some almshouses for old men – to be called Featherstone's Almshouses, the deceased wishing – so the document declares – to please God Almighty. And now I shall read this final will in detail…

FRED. Fred had not a farthing.

MRS WAULE. Nobody in the room had a farthing.

TRUMBULL. Though Mr Trumbull had the gold-headed cane.

VINCY. The most unaccountable will I ever heard! (*Turns to* STANDISH.) I should say he was not in his right mind!

Some agreement.

STANDISH. Everything's quite regular. A very respectable solicitor drew it up, from Brassing.

Slowly they all begin to disperse, in various stages of shock, anger and grief.

MARTHA (*weeping*). Dear, dear. I must say it's hard…

SOLOMON. It'll do him no good where he's gone, that's my belief.

MRS WAULE. And the trouble I've been at to come here and be sisterly…

JONAH. It's a poor tale…

TRUMBULL. The gold-headed cane is farcical as an acknowledgement to me!

Meanwhile, MRS VINCY *is holding* FRED*'s hand, crying silently.* VINCY *goes to her.*

VINCY (*in an undertone*). Don't make a fool of yourself, my dear, before these people. (*More loudly.*) Order the carriage, I've no time to waste. (*Angrily to* FRED.) And I hope you've made up your mind to go up next term and pass your examination.

He takes his wife away. FRED *is left alone with* MARY.

MARY. Mary was conscious that without meaning it, she had perhaps made a fatal difference to Fred's lot.

Be brave, Fred. I do believe you're better off without the money. What was the good of it to Mr Featherstone?

FRED. That's all very fine. What's a fellow to do – I must go into the Church now. I know that will vex you. Well then, you must tell me what else I can do. And I thought I'd be able to pay your father at once and make everything right. And you've not even a hundred pounds left you. What shall you do now, Mary?

MARY. Take another situation, of course, as soon as I can get one. My father has enough to do to keep the rest of the family without me. Goodbye, Fred. (*Goes.*)

FRED *alone*.

FRED. Twenty-four hours ago, Fred had thought that he should need to do nothing –

MRS VINCY. – that he should hunt in pink, have a first-rate hunter, ride to cover on a fine hack, and be generally respected for doing so –

VINCY. – all this without study, or other inconvenience –

MARY. – and that Mary could no longer have any reason for not marrying him.

FRED. But now –

(*Sinks into a chair*.) It's rather hard lines...

MRS VINCY. He was too utterly depressed.

VINCY *re-enters in a fury, and addresses the audience*.

VINCY. This about Fred, and Parliament going to be dissolved, and machine-breaking everywhere, and an election coming on – we may all be ruined for what I know, the country's in that state. Some say it's the end of the world and be hanged if I don't think it looks like it!

Blackout.

End of Act One.

ACT TWO

Scene Twenty

The Garths' back parlour. After breakfast. GARTH *reads his morning letters at the table,* MRS GARTH *with a pupil's book,* MARY, *with* LETTY *on the sofa, sewing.* BEN *close by.*

BEN. Oh, don't sew, Mary. Play with me.

MARY. No, no, mischief. (*Pricks his hand lightly with the needle.*) I must get this done. It's for Rosamond Vincy – she's to be married next week and she can't be married without this handkerchief.

LETTY. Why can't she?

MARY (*turning the needle towards* LETTY'*s nose*). Because this is one of a dozen, and without it there would only be eleven.

MRS GARTH. Have you made up your mind, my dear?

MARY. I shall go to the school at York. I'm less unfit to teach in a school, than a family. And you see I must teach – there's nothing else to be done.

MRS GARTH. Teaching seems to me the most delightful work in the world. I could understand your objection if you hadn't knowledge enough, or disliked children.

MARY. I like the outside world better. It's very inconvenient.

BEN. It must be stupid to be in a girls' school. They can't throw. No wonder she doesn't like it.

GARTH (*opening a new letter*). What's that Mary doesn't like?

BEN. Being among nincompoop girls.

GARTH. Is it the situation you'd heard of, Mary?

MARY. Yes, Father. The school at York. I've determined to take it. It's quite the best. Thirty-five pounds a year and extra pay for teaching piano.

GARTH. Poor child. I wish she could stay at home with us, Susan.

MRS GARTH. Mary wouldn't be happy without doing her duty.

BEN. Nasty duty.

LETTY. But she's an old brick.

BEN (*beating it out on* MARY*'s arm*). An old brick, an old brick!

GARTH (*reading*). Oh!

MRS GARTH watches as he suddenly laughs joyously.

What do you think, Susan?

She goes behind him as they look at the letter.

It's Sir James Chettham, offering me the management of the family estates at Freshitt, *and* he's been asked by Mr Brooke of Tipton to see whether I'd resume the agency of the Tipton property. Wants to see them under the same management. Wants to see me at the hall twelve o'clock tomorrow. He writes handsomely, doesn't he, Susan. (*Amused.*) Brooke didn't like to ask me himself, I see.

MRS GARTH. Here's an honour to your father, children. He is asked to take a post again that he lost long ago. That shows he did his work well, so they feel the want of him.

BEN. Hooray!

MRS GARTH. Now mind you ask fair pay, Caleb.

GARTH. Oh, yes. It'll come to between four and five hundred the two together. (*Starts up.*) Mary, write and give up that school. Stay and help your mother. I'm as pleased as punch now I've thought of that!

BEN. Hooray! Hooray!

An uproar of celebration. They all hold hands, and the whole family dance round the table with delight.

And Alfred must go off to the engineering – I've made up my mind to that. I shall make Brooke have new agreements with the tenants, and draw up a rotation of crops. It's a fine bit of work, Susan. A man without a family would be glad to do it for nothing.

MRS GARTH (*alarmed*). Mind you don't, though!

GARTH. No, no. But it's a fine thing to come to a man in the nature of business. To put men into the right way with their farming and getting a bit of solid building done – that those who come after will be the better for. I'd sooner have it than a fortune. It's a great gift of God, Susan.

MRS GARTH. That it is, Caleb. (*Glancing out of the window.*) Oh, who's that coming up the orchard? It's the Reverend Mr Farebrother…

FAREBROTHER (*entering, greeting the children*). Good evening. I come as an envoy, Mrs Garth. (*Shaking hands.*) I've something to say to you both on behalf of Fred Vincy.

GARTH. Run along and play, children. Off you go!

They go. FAREBROTHER *sits.* MARY *listens intently.*

We haven't seen the lad for months. I couldn't think what was become of him.

FAREBROTHER. Yesterday he came and poured himself out to me. I'm very glad he did, because I've seen him grow up – I'm so much at home at the Vincys', he's almost like a nephew. However, he's asked me to come and tell you that he's going away, and he's so miserable about his debt to you, that he can't bear to come himself, even to bid you goodbye.

GARTH. Tell him it doesn't signify a farthing. We've had the pinch and have got over it. And now I'm going to be rich as rich –

MRS GARTH. We're going to have enough for Alfred's apprenticeship and keep Mary at home and –

FAREBROTHER. What's the treasure trove?

GARTH. I'm going to be agent for two estates, Freshitt and Tipton. I've got an opportunity again. It's an uncommonly cramping thing, as I've often told Susan, to sit on horseback and look over the hedges at the wrong thing, and not be able to make it right.

FAREBROTHER. I congratulate you heartily, Garth. This is the best sort of news I could have had to carry to Fred.

MRS GARTH. Where's he going?

FAREBROTHER. He's going back to study for his degree. I've advised him to do that. If he'll go and pass, that will be some guarantee that he has energy and will. He's quite at sea, he doesn't know what else to do. I've promised in the meantime to try to reconcile Vincy to his son's adopting some other line of life. I'd do anything to hinder a man from the fatal step of choosing the wrong profession. He quoted what you said, Miss Garth – do you remember?

MARY. I've said so many impertinent things to Fred – we're old playfellows.

FAREBROTHER. You said he'd make one of those ridiculous clergymen who help make the whole clergy ridiculous. That was so cutting, I felt a little cut myself.

GARTH (*laughing*). She gets her tongue from you, Susan.

MARY. It's too bad of Fred to repeat my flippant speeches to you, Mr Farebrother.

FAREBROTHER. But what he cares most about is having offended you, Mrs Garth, he supposes you'll never think well of him again.

MRS GARTH. I have been disappointed in Fred. But I shall be ready to think well of him again when he gives me good reason.

LETTY (*reappearing in the doorway*). Mary...?

MARY. Oh, Letty. Come outside with me.

They go.

GARTH. Oh, we must forgive young people when they're sorry. And there was the very devil in that old man. (*Glancing out of the window.*) Now Mary's gone out, I must tell you a thing. It's only known to Susan and me, and you'll not tell it

again. The old scoundrel wanted Mary to burn his last will
the very night he died – he offered her money. Now, you see,
if Mary had done what he wanted, Fred Vincy would have
had ten thousand pounds by the will before. The old man did
turn to him at the last. That touches poor Mary close – she
was in the right to refuse, but she feels it. I feel with her
somehow, and if I could make amends to the poor lad I
should be glad. Now what's your opinion, sir? Susan doesn't
agree with me – she says – tell them what you say, Susan.

MRS GARTH. It seems to me, a loss which falls on another
because we've done right, is not to lie upon our conscience.

FAREBROTHER *considers*.

GARTH. It's the feeling. The child feels that way, and I feel
with her.

FAREBROTHER. One could hardly say that feeling was
mistaken – though no man ought to make a claim on such
feeling.

GARTH. Well, well. You'll not tell Fred.

FAREBROTHER. Certainly not. (*Stands*.) But I shall carry the
other good news – that you can afford the loss he has caused
you.

They shake hands.

Scene Twenty-One

FAREBROTHER. On leaving, he went to say goodbye to Mary
in the orchard.

The orchard. MARY *is lifting* LETTY *up so she can reach
an apple*.

GARTH. Mary and Letty made a pretty picture in the slanting
light which brought out the brightness of the apples on the
old boughs.

MARY *and* LETTY *notice* FAREBROTHER *and come forward, with the apple*.

MARY. Mary admired the handsome vicar more than any man she had had the opportunity of knowing.

MRS GARTH. She had never heard him say a foolish thing though she knew he did unwise ones.

FRED. Remarkable that the actual imperfections of the vicar's clerical character never seemed to call forth the same scorn which she showed for the predicted imperfections of a clerical Fred Vincy.

MRS GARTH. Will anyone guess towards which of these widely different men Mary had a special tenderness?

FAREBROTHER. Have you any message for your old playfellow, Miss Garth? I'm going straight to see him.

MARY. No. But I'm glad to hear he's going away to work.

FAREBROTHER. And I'm glad to hear you're not going away to work. My mother will be all the happier if you'll come to see her at the vicarage? You'd really be doing a kindness.

MARY. I should like it very much if I may. Everything seems too happy for me all at once. I thought I would always long for home, and losing that grievance makes me feel rather empty. I suppose it served instead of sense to fill up my mind.

LETTY (*to* MARY). May I go with you to see Mr Farebrother?

MARY *and* LETTY *look at* FAREBROTHER, *who kisses* LETTY *affectionately*.

FAREBROTHER *alone*.

FAREBROTHER. As Mr Farebrother walked home, he thought –

Perhaps there's more between Fred and Mary than the regard of old playfellows. (*Slight pause*.) She's a great deal too choice for that crude young gentleman. (*Shrugs*.) I'm jealous! As if I were able to marry! It's as clear as any balance sheet that I'm not.

Scene Twenty-Two

GARTH. When Mr and Mrs Garth were alone in the parlour –

Susan, guess what I'm thinking of…

MRS GARTH (*after a moment*). The rotation of crops?

GARTH. No. I'm thinking I could do a great turn for Fred Vincy. Alfred will be gone soon, and I shall want help, and Fred might come in and act under me and it might be the making of him. What do you think?

MRS GARTH (*decidedly*). I think there is hardly anything his family would object to more.

GARTH. He has sense and quickness enough and likes being on the land.

MRS GARTH. His father and mother wanted him to be a fine gentleman and I think he has the same feeling. They all think us beneath them. And I'm sure Mrs Vincy would say we wanted Fred for Mary.

GARTH. Life's a poor tale if it's to be settled by nonsense of that sort.

MRS GARTH. Yes, but there's a certain pride which is proper, Caleb. And it seems to be fixed that Fred's to go back to college. Will it not be better to wait and see what he'll choose for himself.

GARTH. Ay – well, it may be better to wait. But I'm pretty sure of getting plenty of work for two. Why only yesterday – bless me I don't think I told you. Bulstrode and that Rigg or Rigg-Featherstone were both at me to value Stone Court.

MRS GARTH. Can that man be going to sell the land just left him?

GARTH. Deuce knows – but Bulstrode has long been wanting to get a handsome bit of land under his fingers, that I know. The ins and outs of things are curious. Here's the land they've been all along expecting for Fred, which the old man left to this side-slip of a son that he kept in the dark, and it's getting into Bulstrode's hands. And the old man hated Bulstrode …

Scene Twenty-Three

FAREBROTHER. Meanwhile, Mr Farebrother's fortunes were also about to change.

DOROTHEA. In the spring, after her husband's death, Dorothea Casaubon had the living at Lowick Church to give away –

LYDGATE. – and Mr Lydgate at last saw an opportunity to speak on behalf of his friend.

The library at Lowick Manor.

Farebrother's present living is a poor one and gives him stinted position for himself and his family. His mother, aunt and sister all depend on him. I believe he's never married because of them. I never heard such good preaching. His talk is just as good about all subjects, original, clear…

DOROTHEA. Why has he not done more?

Dorothea was interested in all who had slipped below their own intention.

LYDGATE. That's a hard question. He's very fond of natural history and is hampered in reconciling this with his position. He has no money to spare and that's led him into card-playing. He does play for money and wins a good deal. Yet looking at him as a whole I think he's one of the most blameless men I ever knew. He has neither venom nor doubleness in him.

DOROTHEA. I wonder whether he wishes he could leave off his card-playing.

LYDGATE. I've no doubt.

DOROTHEA. I'm told Mr Tyke is an apostolic man. You supported him for the infirmary.

Slight pause.

LYDGATE. I don't pretend that Farebrother is apostolic. But do hear him preach. I trust to the effect of that…

DOROTHEA. And it was not long before Mr Farebrother was appointed to the living at Lowick.

Scene Twenty-Four

FAREBROTHER. There was joy in the old-fashioned parlour.

FAREBROTHER*'s house*.

So, Mother, we'll be moving to the parsonage at Lowick!

MRS FAREBROTHER. The greatest comfort, Camden, is that you've deserved it.

FAREBROTHER. When a man gets a good situation, Mother, half the deserving must come after.

MRS FAREBROTHER. You must marry now.

FAREBROTHER. With all my heart. But who is in love with me? I'm a seedy old fellow.

MRS FAREBROTHER. You're a handsome man, Camden. Though not so fine a figure as your father. But I wish you'd marry Miss Garth. She'd make us so lively at Lowick.

FAREBROTHER. Very fine! You talk as if young women were tied up to be chosen like poultry at market, as if I had only to ask and everybody would have me.

MRS FAREBROTHER. We don't want everybody, only Miss Garth. But your choice shall be mine. You'll want your whist at home when we go to Lowick.

FAREBROTHER. I shall do without whist now, Mother. I shall have no need.

Scene Twenty-Four (A)

FAREBROTHER (*moving to his study*). The vicar felt as if his share of duties would be simplified.

DOROTHEA. But Duty has a trick of behaving unexpectedly –

GARTH. – like a heavy friend whom we've asked to visit –

LYDGATE. – and who breaks his leg within our gates.

FRED. Hardly a week later, Fred Vincy –

MRS VINCY. – having returned from college with his bachelor's degree –

FRED. – presented himself in Mr Farebrother's study…

FAREBROTHER*'s den. He is packing up his insect display.*

FAREBROTHER. Ah, Fred – I'm packing up my insects –ready to move house.

FRED. I'm ashamed to trouble you, Mr Farebrother, but you're the only friend I can consult.

FAREBROTHER. Sit down, Fred. I'll do anything I can.

FRED. I wanted to tell you – I might go into the Church now. I don't like it but my father has spent a good deal of money – and I can't see anything else to do.

FAREBROTHER. I did talk to your father but made little way with him. What are your other difficulties?

FRED. I don't like divinity and preaching and feeling obliged to look serious. I like riding across country and doing as other men do. My father can't spare me any capital, else I might go into farming. And he's no room for me in his trade. And of course I can't begin to study for law or physic now, when my father wants me to earn something.

FAREBROTHER. Have you any difficulties about doctrines?

FRED. No, I suppose the articles are right. Cleverer fellows than I go in for them entirely. It would be rather ridiculous of me to urge scruples of that sort. And of course if I'm obliged to be a clergyman I shall try to do my duty, though I mayn't like it. Do you think anybody ought to blame me?

FAREBROTHER. For going into the Church? That depends on your conscience, Fred – how far you've seen what your position requires of you. I can only tell you about myself, that I've always been too lax, and have been uneasy in consequence.

FRED. There is another hindrance. (*Slight pause.*) You may guess. There is somebody I'm very fond of. I've loved her since we were children.

FAREBROTHER. Oh. (*Examining a label closely*.) Miss Garth,
  I suppose?

FRED. Yes. I shouldn't mind anything if she'd have me. And I
  know I could be a good fellow then.

FAREBROTHER. And you think she returns the feeling?

FRED. She never will say so. She made me promise not to
  speak to her about it again. And she's set her mind especially
  against my being a clergyman. But I can't give her up. I do
  think she cares about me. I saw Mrs Garth last night and she
  said that Mary was staying at Lowick Rectory?

FAREBROTHER. Yes, she's very kindly helping my mother
  and sister with the move. Do you wish to go there?

FRED. No. I want to ask a great favour of you. Mary would
  listen to what you said – I mean, if you tell her about my
  going into the Church.

Slight pause.

FAREBROTHER. That's rather a delicate task, my dear Fred. I
  shall have to presuppose your attachment to her, and it will
  be asking her to tell me whether she returns it.

FRED. That's what I want. I don't know what to do, unless I
  can get at her feeling.

FAREBROTHER. You mean that you'd be guided by that, as to
  your going into the Church?

FRED. If Mary said she'd never have me, I might as well go
  wrong in one way as another.

FAREBROTHER. That's nonsense, Fred. Men outlive their
  love, but not the consequences of their recklessness.

FRED. Not my sort of love. I've never been without loving
  Mary. If I had to give her up, it would be like beginning to
  live on wooden legs.

FAREBROTHER. Will she not be hurt by my intrusion?

FRED. No. She respects you more than anyone, and she'd not
  put you off with fun as she does me. There's no one else who

could be such a friend to both of us. (*Slight pause*.) And I have worked in order to pass. She ought to believe I would exert myself for her sake.

Silence while FAREBROTHER *considers*.

FAREBROTHER. Very well, my boy. I'll do what you wish.

Now you can help me move this table into the hall...

Scene Twenty-Five

MARY. Mr Farebrother found Mary in the garden at Lowick, gathering roses.

FAREBROTHER. The sun was low and tall trees sent their shadows across the grassy walks.

Lowick Parsonage garden. MARY *stoops, her back to* FAREBROTHER, *admonishing a dog.*

MARY. Off the rosebeds! This is not becoming in a sensible dog. Anybody would think you're a silly young gentleman. Go on, off!

FAREBROTHER. You're unmerciful to young gentlemen, Miss Garth.

MARY *turns, startled*.

MARY. I suppose some of them turn into excellent men.

FAREBROTHER. I'm glad, because I want to interest you in a young gentleman.

MARY (*heart beating*). Not a silly one, I hope.

FAREBROTHER. No, though perhaps wisdom is not his strong point, rather affection and sincerity. You know who I mean?

MARY. It must be Fred Vincy.

FAREBROTHER. He's asked me to consult you about his going into the Church. I hope you won't think I take a liberty –

MARY. On the contrary, Mr Farebrother. Whenever you have anything to say to me, I feel honoured.

FAREBROTHER. But before that, let me just touch on something else. Your father told me what happened on the night of Featherstone's death. But I want you to know that your action made no real difference to Fred's lot. It seems that the burning of the last will would have surely led to a dispute and the first will would not have stood if it had been disputed. So on that score, you may set your mind free. No guilt-offering to Fred is demanded from you there.

MARY. Thank you, Mr Farebrother. For remembering my feelings.

FAREBROTHER. Now. Fred has taken his degree – he's worked his way so far, and now the question is – what is he to do? He's inclined to follow his father's wishes and enter the Church. I confess I see no insuperable objection. I would do my utmost in helping him on. But there is a condition. He's asked me to plead for him. The condition lies entirely in your feeling.

MARY (*moved; then*). Let's walk a little.

FAREBROTHER. To speak plainly, Fred won't take any course, which would lessen the chance that you would consent to be his wife.

MARY. I certainly never will be his wife if he becomes a clergyman.

FAREBROTHER. He wishes me to report exactly what you think.

MARY. I could not love a man who is ridiculous. Fred has sense and knowledge enough to make him respectable if he likes in some good worldly business, but I can never imagine him preaching and exhorting and pronouncing blessings. His being a clergyman would only be for gentility's sake, and I think there is nothing more contemptible.

FAREBROTHER. You are severe –

MARY. He would be a piece of professional affectation.

FAREBROTHER. Then the answer's quite decided. As a
  clergyman he could have no hope?

MARY *shakes her head*.

But if he braved the difficulties of getting his bread in some
  other way – will you give him the support of hope? – may he
  count on winning you?

MARY (*resentfully*). I've already said he ought not to put such
  questions, until he's done something worthy, instead of
  saying that he could do it.

Pause.

FAREBROTHER. I understand that you resist any attempt to
  fetter you, but either your feeling for Fred Vincy excludes
  your entertaining… other attachment, or it does not. Either
  he may count on your remaining single, until he shall have
  earned your hand, or he may in any case be disappointed.
  (*With restrained emotion*.) Pardon me – Mary – but when the
  state of a woman's affections touches the happiness of
  another life – of more lives than one – I think it would be the
  nobler course for her to be perfectly direct and open.

A strange idea flashes across her.

MARY. Mary had never thought that any man could love her
  except Fred.

FRED. Who had espoused her with an umbrella ring when she
  wore socks and little strapped shoes.

MARY. Could she be of importance to handsome, clever Mr
  Farebrother?

Slight pause.

Mr Farebrother, I will tell you. I have too strong a feeling for
  Fred to give him up for – anyone else. I should never be
  quite happy if I thought he was unhappy for the loss of me. It
  has taken such deep root in me – my gratitude to him for
  always loving me best, and minding so much if I hurt
  myself, from the time when we were very little. I can't
  imagine any new feeling coming to make that weaker. I
  should like better than anything to see him worthy of

everyone's respect. But please tell him I will not promise to marry him till then. He is free to choose someone else.

FAREBROTHER (*suppressing his pain*). Then I've fulfilled my commission. (*Shakes her hand.*) With this prospect before him, we shall get Fred into the right niche somehow, and I hope I shall live to join your hands. God bless you.

MARY (*feeling suddenly miserable*). Oh, please stay and let me give you some tea?

FAREBROTHER. No, my dear, no. I must get back.

He had gone through a duty much harder than the renunciation of whist, or even the writing of penitential meditations.

Scene Twenty-Six

VINCY. Now, in Middlemarch that summer, railways were as exciting a topic as the Reform Bill or the horrors of cholera.

MRS WAULE. Women regarded travelling by steam presumptuous and dangerous –

SOLOMON. – and landlords felt that railway companies must pay a very high price for permission to injure mankind.

The open fields. On one side, MRS WAULE *and* SOLOMON. *On the other, two* SURVEYORS *in top hats study a map, and point out features of the landscape.*

MRS WAULE. The cows will cast their calves, brother, if the railway comes across the big pasture –

SOLOMON (*cunning*). The best would be to set somebody on 'em, when they come spying and measuring –

MRS WAULE. Ay, let 'em go cutting in another parish –

SOLOMON. The more spokes we put in their wheel, the more they'll pay us, to let 'em go on.

Some LABOURERS *gather in the corner of the field.*

So Solomon Featherstone sowed suspicion among the labourers in the hay fields, and –

TIM. Nettle-seed needs no digging.

GARTH (*entering*). Now, Caleb was out to measure and value an outlying piece of land for Dorothea – (*Puts down his camp stool.*)

ASSISTANT. – with his assistant and measuring chain –

They start measuring.

HIRAM. – when they encountered a party of labourers attacking some railwaymen.

The LABOURERS *run out aggressively, knocking over* MR GARTH'S ASSISTANT *on the way, and face up to the* SURVEYORS.

GARTH. Caleb ran to the aid of the surveyors – (*Gets between them, facing the* LABOURERS.) and in the fray –

ASSISTANT (*on the ground, clutching his ankle*). – Caleb's assistant was knocked down.

FRED (*entering*). Just then, Fred was coming along the lanes on horseback.

FRED *dismounts and drives the* LABOURERS *back with his whip.*

What do you confounded fools mean?

When they have gone, he and GARTH *turn their attention to the wounded* ASSISTANT.

GARTH. You've strained your ankle…

FRED. You must take my horse and ride home.

They help him to the horse.

I'm glad I happened to be here at the right moment, Mr Garth.

The ASSISTANT *goes.*

GARTH. Ay, ay… But deuce take it, I'm hindered of my day's work. I can't get along without somebody to help me with the measuring chain. However! (*Turns suddenly to* FRED.) What have you got to do today, young fellow?

FRED. Nothing, Mr Garth. I'll help you with pleasure – can I?

Fred had a sense he would be courting Mary when he was helping her father.

GARTH. Well, you mustn't mind stooping and getting hot.

FRED. I don't mind anything.

The LABOURERS *are gathering again.*

Only I want to go first and have a round with those fellows.

GARTH. Nonsense. I shall go and speak to the men myself.

FRED. I shall go with you then.

GARTH. No, stay where you are. I don't want your young blood. (*To the* LABOURERS.) Why, my lads, how's this? You thought those men wanted to do mischief?

LABOURERS. Ay.

GARTH. No such thing! They're looking out to see which way the railroad is to take. The law gives these men leave to come on the land – the owner's nothing to say against it – and if you meddle with them you'll go to Middlemarch jail – and you might be for it now if anybody informed against you.

Silence.

But come, you didn't mean harm. Somebody told you the railroad was a bad thing. It may do a bit of harm here and there, and so does the sun in Heaven. But the railway's a good thing.

TIM. Aw! Good for the big folk to make money out on. I'n seen lots o' things sin' I war a young 'un. The war an' the peace, and the canells, an' oald King George, an' the new King George, an' the new 'un as has got a new ne-ame – an' it's been all aloike to the poor mon. What's the canells been t'him? They'n brought him neyther me-at nor be-acon, nor

wage to lay by. Times ha' got wusser for him sin' I war a
young 'un. An' so it'll be wi' the railroads. They'll on'y leave
the poor mon furder behind. This is the big folks's world, this
is. But yo're for the big folks, Muster Garth, yo are.

GARTH. A labourer in possession of an undeniable truth, which
they know through a hard process of feeling –

TIM. – will let it fall like a giant's club on your neatly carved
argument for a social benefit, which they do *not* feel…

GARTH. If you don't think well of me, Tim, that's neither here
nor there. Things may be bad for the poor man – bad they are
– but I want the lads here not to do what will make things
worse for themselves.

HIRAM. We war on'y for a bit o' foon.

GARTH. Well, promise me not to meddle again, and I'll see
nobody informs against you.

LABOURER. I'n ne'er meddled.

GARTH. Come, I'm as hard at work as any of you today and I
can't spare much time. Say you'll be quiet without the
constable.

HIRAM. Aw, we wooant meddle. 'They may do as they loike
for 'oos.'

GARTH. Good. Let's all go back to work then.

The LABOURERS *go.* FRED *picks up one end of the
measuring chain and they start work.*

FRED. Fred helped Caleb vigorously and his spirits rose. He
heartily enjoyed a good slip in the moist earth under the
hedgerow –

GARTH. – which soiled his perfect summer trousers.

FRED. And when they had finished the day's work –

GARTH *sits on his camp stool.* FRED *stretches on the
ground.*

GARTH. A young fellow needn't be a BA to do this sort of
work, eh, Fred?

FRED. I wish I'd taken to it before I'd thought of being a BA. (*Hesitates*.) Do you think I'm too old to learn your business, Mr Garth?

GARTH (*smiling*). My business is of many sorts, my boy. A good deal can come from experience. But you're young enough to lay a foundation yet.

FRED. Do you think I could do some good at it?

GARTH. That depends. (*From deep conviction*.) You must be sure of two things. You must love your work, and not be always looking over the edge of it, wanting your play to begin. And you must not be ashamed of your work, and think it would be more honourable to you to be doing something else. You must have pride. I wouldn't give tuppence for a man – (*Snaps fingers*.) whether he was the prime minister or the rick-thatcher, if he didn't do well, what he undertook to do.

FRED. I can never feel that, being a clergyman.

GARTH. Then let it alone, my boy, else you'll never be easy. Or if you are easy, you'll be a poor stick.

FRED. That's very nearly what Mary thinks. I think you must know what I feel for Mary, Mr Garth. I hope it doesn't displease you that I've always loved her better than anyone else, and that I shall never love anyone as I love her.

GARTH. That makes things more serious, Fred, if you want to take Mary's happiness into your keeping.

FRED. I know that, Mr Garth. Really, if I could get some other business, I'd work hard. I'd deserve your good opinion. I should like to have to do with outdoor things. I know a good deal about land and cattle already. I used to believe – though you'll think me rather foolish for it – that I should have land of my own. I'm sure knowledge of that sort would come easily to me, especially if I could be under you in any way.

GARTH. Softly, my boy. What have you said to your father?

FRED. Nothing, yet. But I must tell him. I'm only waiting to know what I can do, instead of the Church. I'm very sorry to disappoint him, but how could I know when I was fifteen, what it would be right for me to do now I'm four and twenty. My education was a mistake.

GARTH. But, Fred. Are you sure Mary is fond of you, or would ever have you?

FRED. I asked Mr Farebrother to talk to her because she'd forbidden me, and he says I've every reason to hope, if I can put myself in an honourable position. I dare say you think it unwarrantable in me, Mr Garth, to be troubling you before I've done anything for myself. I've not the least claim – indeed I've already a debt to you which –

GARTH (*with feeling*). Yes, my boy, you have a claim. The young ones have always a claim on the old to help them forward. I was young myself once, and had to do without much help, but help would have been welcome to me. Come to me tomorrow at the office at nine o'clock.

Caleb was absolute.

MRS GARTH. He never chose to be absolute except on someone else's behalf.

Scene Twenty-Seven

GARTH *and* MRS GARTH, *sitting alone in the evening*.

GARTH. It's come round as I thought, Susan. The children are fond of each other. I mean Fred and Mary.

MRS GARTH *lays her work on her knee, looks up sharply*.

The lad would like to be under me, and give his mind to business. And I've determined to take him and make a man of him.

MRS GARTH. Caleb!

GARTH. I shall have trouble with him, but I think I shall carry it through. The lad loves Mary, and a true love for a good woman's a great thing, Susan. It shapes many a rough fellow.

MRS GARTH. Has Mary spoken to you?

GARTH. Not a word. I gave her a warning about Fred once, but his heart is fixed on her, that I can see. It gives me a good opinion of the lad – and we always liked him, Susan.

MRS GARTH. It's a pity for Mary, I think.

GARTH. Why?

MRS GARTH. Because she might have had a man worth twenty Fred Vincys.

GARTH (*surprised*) Ah?

MRS GARTH. I firmly believe Mr Farebrother is attached to her, and meant to make her an offer, but of course now Fred has used him as an envoy, there's an end to that better prospect.

Pause.

GARTH (*now conflicted*). That would have made me very proud and happy, Susan, and I should have been glad for your sake. I've never felt that your belongings have been on a level with you. But you took me though I was a plain man.

MRS GARTH. I took the best and cleverest man I'd ever known.

GARTH. Well, perhaps others thought you might have done better, but it would have been worse for me. And that's what touches me about Fred. The lad's good at bottom if he's put in the right way. And he loves and honours my daughter beyond anything and she's given him a sort of promise according to what he turns out. I say that young man's soul is in my hand, and I'll do the best I can for him, so help me God. It's my duty, Susan.

MRS GARTH (*between affection and vexation*). Few men besides you would think it a duty to add to their anxieties in that way, Caleb.

GARTH. That signifies nothing – what other men would think.

MRS GARTH (*rises and kisses him*). God bless you, Caleb. Our children have a good father. (*But she goes out to cry.*)

She suppressed her opposition. She felt sure her husband's conduct would be misunderstood by the Vincys –

Scene Twenty-Eight

JONAH. – and about Fred she was unhopeful –

SOLOMON. – and with reason.

GARTH*'s office. A desk and chair.*

GARTH. Now, Fred. You'll have some desk work.

FRED *sits at the desk.*

I can't do without help and I want you to understand the accounts, and get the values into your head. So you must buckle to. How are you at writing and arithmetic?

FRED. I'm not afraid of arithmetic, Mr Garth, it always came easily to me. I think you know my writing.

GARTH. Let's see. Copy me a line or two of that valuation, with the figures at the end.

FRED *writes.*

SOLOMON. At that time the opinion existed that it was beneath a gentleman to write legibly –

JONAH. – Fred wrote a script of that kind easy to interpret when you know beforehand what the writer means.

GARTH (*takes the paper*). The deuce! (*Raps it with the back of his hand.*) To think this is a country where a man's education may cost hundreds and hundreds and it turns you out this! I can't put up with this!

FRED. What can I do, Mr Garth?

Fred had a vision of himself liable to be ranked with office clerks.

GARTH. Do? Why, you must learn to form your letters and keep the line. Is there so little business in the world that you must be sending puzzles over the country! It's disgusting!

FRED. I am very sorry.

GARTH. We must make the best of it, Fred. Go at it with a will and sit up at night if the daytime isn't enough. We'll be patient. I can afford to give you eighty pounds for the first year, and more after. But you must let your father know our agreement.

Scene Twenty-Nine

GARTH *becomes* VINCY. *He faces* FRED. MRS VINCY *in the background.*

FRED. So that's what I've done, sir, and I've resolved to work hard at it. And I'm truly sorry I should be the cause of disappointment to you.

VINCY (*bitterly*). So you've made up your mind at last, sir?

FRED. Yes, Father.

VINCY. Very well. I've no more to say. You've thrown away your education, and gone down a step in life, when I'd given you the means of rising, that's all.

FRED. I think I can be quite as much of a gentleman at the work I've undertaken as if I'd been a curate. But I'm grateful to you for wishing to do the best for me.

VINCY. I wash my hands of you. I only hope, when you have a son of your own, he'll make a better return for the pains you spend on him.

FRED. I hope you'll not object to my remaining at home, sir? I shall have a sufficient salary to pay for my board –

VINCY (*disgusted*). Board be hanged! (*Glancing round.*) Of course your mother will want you to stay. But I shall keep no horse for you, you understand; and you'll pay your own tailor. You'll do with a suit or two less, I fancy, when you have to pay for 'em.

FRED. I hope you'll shake hands with me, Father, and forgive me.

VINCY (*hurriedly*). Yes, yes, let's say no more.

They shake hands and FRED *leaves.* MRS VINCY *starts to cry.*

MRS VINCY. Nothing ever cut me so before, Vincy – only his illness.

VINCY. Pooh, pooh. Never mind. We must expect trouble with our children. Don't make it worse.

MRS VINCY (*with a little shake*). Well, I won't.

VINCY. It won't do to make a fuss about one. There's Rosamond as well as Fred, and I can see Lydgate's making a mess of his practice. They'll get no money from me… But it's no use talking. Ring the bell for those lemons you wanted and don't look so dull, Lucy!

Scene Thirty

The Garths' back parlour. MRS VINCY *becomes* MRS GARTH, *knitting or darning, with* FRED.

FRED. I know you think me very undeserving, Mrs Garth. But Mr Garth and Mr Farebrother haven't given me up.

MRS GARTH. A young man would indeed be culpable if he made their sacrifices vain.

FRED. I hope it will not be so with me, Mrs Garth, since I've some encouragement to believe I may win Mary. Mr Garth has told you? You were not surprised, I dare say?

MRS GARTH. That Mary has given you encouragement? Yes, I confess I *was* surprised.

FRED. She never did give me any when I talked to her myself. But when I asked Mr Farebrother to speak for me, she allowed him to tell me there was a hope.

MRS GARTH (*decisively*). You made a great mistake, Fred, in asking Mr Farebrother to speak for you.

FRED (*alarmed*). Did I? Mr Farebrother has always been such a friend of ours. And I knew Mary would listen to him. And he took it on himself quite readily.

MRS GARTH. Yes, young people are usually blind to everything but their own wishes, and seldom imagine how much those wishes cost others.

FRED. I can't conceive how it could be any pain to Mr Farebrother.

MRS GARTH. Precisely. You cannot conceive.

FRED (*moment of realisation*). Do you mean that Farebrother is in love with Mary?

MRS GARTH. And if it were so, Fred, I think you are the last person who ought to be surprised.

FRED. Then you think I'm standing in his way, and in Mary's too?

Slight pause.

MRS GARTH *feels she has said too much.*

Mr Garth seemed pleased Mary should be attached to me. He couldn't have known anything.

MRS GARTH (*backtracking*). I spoke from inference only. I'm not aware that Mary knows anything of the matter.

Scene Thirty-One

FRED. Fred walked on to Lowick Parsonage –

MARY. – where Mary was visiting.

FRED (*to himself*). So if I'd been out of the way, Mary might have made a thoroughly good match… I can't give her up! But I can't help feeling I have a rival.

GARTH. But the fighting must be metaphorical, which was much more difficult to Fred than the muscular.

Lowick Parsonage. FAREBROTHER*'s new study*. MARY *at the desk*. FAREBROTHER *is moving a sofa into position*. FRED *helps, and carries the insect display case which* FAREBROTHER *had wrapped*.

FAREBROTHER. This is my fine new study. I'm still moving in. I saw a stupendous spider this morning! Mary's been writing new labels for me for my insect drawers. Look – she has beautiful handwriting! Put that down there, Fred, for the moment. Now, wait here a minute or two. I'm going to look out an engraving, which Fred can hang for me. I shall be back in a few minutes...

He goes and FRED *and* MARY *are left alone*.

FRED (*after a moment*). It's of no use, whatever I do, Mary. You're sure to marry Farebrother at last.

MARY. What do you mean, Fred?

FRED. You see clearly enough, you see everything.

MARY. I only see that you're behaving very ill, Fred, in speaking so of Mr Farebrother after he's pleaded your cause. How can you have taken up such an idea?

FRED. It's a matter of course. When you're continually seeing a man who beats me in everything, and whom you set up above everybody, I've no chance.

MARY. You're very ungrateful, Fred. I wish I'd never told Mr Farebrother that I cared for you in the least.

FRED. No. I should be the happiest fellow in the world if it were not for this. I told your father everything, and he was very kind. I could go at the work with a will, writing and everything, if it were not for this.

MARY. For this? For what?

FRED. The dreadful certainly that I shall be bowled out by Farebrother.

MARY. Fred?

She tries to catch his eyes, which are sulkily turned away.

You are too delightfully ridiculous. If you were not such a charming simpleton, what a temptation this would be to play the coquette and let you suppose that somebody besides you made love to me.

FRED. Do you really like me best, Mary? (*Tries to take her hand*.)

MARY. I don't like you at all at this moment. (*Retreats, hands behind her*.) I only said that no mortal ever made love to me besides you. And that's no argument that a very wise man never will.

FRED. I wish you'd tell me that you couldn't possibly ever think of him…

MARY (*serious again*). Never dare mention this to me any more, Fred. Don't you see, Mr Farebrother has left us together on purpose that we might speak freely? I'm disappointed you should be blind to his delicate feeling –

FAREBROTHER (*entering*). Here we are. Here's the engraving. I think it needs to go there.

As the men assess the wall, MARY *looks at* FAREBROTHER.

MARY. It was impossible for Mary to help fleeting visions of new dignities with Mr Farebrother and an acknowledged value of which she had often felt the absence.

And then looks at FRED.

But these things with Fred outside them – ? (*Slight pause*.) To have a reason for going home the next day was a relief.

Scene Thirty-Two

VINCY. Months later, there was a New Year's party at the Vincys', to which Mr Farebrother and his mother were invited –

FRED. – and on Fred's insistence, even Mary Garth and the children.

The Vincys' drawing room. MARY, on the sofa, with LETTY on her knee. She is about to tell a story. FRED carries BEN in, on his shoulders.

MARY. Come and hear a story.

FRED sits with BEN on the floor to listen.

Once upon a time…

Across the room, MRS VINCY is with MRS FAREBROTHER and ROSAMOND.

MRS VINCY. You know, Mrs Farebrother, ours is a cheerful house. I'm of a cheerful disposition myself and Mr Vincy always likes something to be going on. And my children are good tempered, thank God.

MRS FAREBROTHER (*to* ROSAMOND). Though I suppose you have to give up a great deal of your husband's society, Mrs Lydgate.

ROSAMOND. Yes. The life of a medical man is very arduous: especially when he is so devoted to his profession as Mr Lydgate is. Excuse me… (*Moves away to stand by the piano.*)

MRS VINCY. It's dreadfully dull for her when there's no company…

Meanwhile MARY comes to the end of her story.

MARY. – 'Rumpelstiltskin!' she cried, and the little man stamped so hard on the floor that his leg went right through, and he could never get it out again!

Applause for the story, as FAREBROTHER comes in.

BEN. Ah, Mr Farebrother. You must hear *Rumpelstiltskin* –

FAREBROTHER *takes* BEN *with him and sits by* MARY.

LETTY. Yes – tell it again, Mary.

FRED. You'll never care any more about my lolloping giant,
Letty –

LETTY. Yes I shall! – tell about him now! (*Starts to go to*
FRED.)

FRED. Oh, I dare say I'm quite cut out. Ask Mr Farebrother.
(*Stands apart a little*.)

MARY (*taking* LETTY *back on her knee*.) Yes, ask Mr
Farebrother to tell you a story. Ask him to tell you about the
ants whose beautiful house was knocked down by a giant,
and he thought they didn't mind because he couldn't hear
them cry…

BEN *and* LETTY. Please!

FAREBROTHER. No, I'm a grave old parson. If I try to draw a
story out of my bag, a sermon comes instead. Shall I preach
you a sermon?

LETTY (*doubtfully*). Ye… es.

FAREBROTHER. Let me see then. Against cakes. How cakes
are bad things, especially if they are sweet and have plums in
them.

The children are not happy. LETTY *goes quickly to* FRED.
BEN *leaves* FAREBROTHER *for* MARY. *He stands*.

I see it will not do to preach on New Year's Day.

Mr Farebrother had discovered of late that Fred had become
jealous of him.

MARY. But that he was not losing his preference for Mary
above all other women.

He goes to talk to ROSAMOND *at the piano. Meanwhile* –

MRS FAREBROTHER (*to* MRS VINCY). A delightful young
person is Miss Garth.

MRS VINCY. Yes. It's a pity she's not better looking.

MRS FAREBROTHER. I like her countenance. We must not always look for beauty when God has seen fit to make an excellent young woman without it.

Mrs Farebrother was still hoping that her son would choose Miss Garth.

Scene Thirty-Three

FRED. Fred had now been working heartily for six months at all outdoor occupations under Mr Garth –

FAREBROTHER. – and had nearly mastered the defects of his handwriting.

FRED. But he had been rewarding his resolution by a little laxity of late, in visiting the billiards room at The Green Dragon...

Instantly, the company are gathered low around the billiards table, cues poised, as if playing intensely. The sound of billiard balls and the noise of the billiards room.

There lurked in him a prophetic sense that evening, that when he began to play, he should also begin to bet –

I shall enjoy some punch-drinking and prepare myself to feel rather seedy in the morning!

LYDGATE. He was shocked by the sight of his brother-in-law Lydgate there, excited and betting, just as he might have done.

LYDGATE *stops betting and stands staring at him.*

FAREBROTHER. And when a message came that Mr Farebrother was below, he went down to the starlit street.

The billiards room dissolves.

Scene Thirty-Three (A)

The street. Night. FRED *comes out, to find* FAREBROTHER *waiting. The raucous background above slowly fades to silence.*

FAREBROTHER. I disturbed you, young gentleman, because I have some pressing business with you.

FRED. Oh?

FAREBROTHER. You've been going to The Green Dragon often lately?

FRED. Oh, a few times.

FAREBROTHER. We're friends. I've listened to you. May I talk a little about myself?

FRED. I'm under the deepest obligation to you, Mr Farebrother.

FAREBROTHER (*moves about in the shadows*). I confess, Fred, I've been tempted to keep silence with you. When somebody said to me: 'Young Vincy's taken to the billiard table again – he won't bear the curb long' – I was tempted to hold my tongue and wait while you went down the ladder again – Betting first, and then –

FRED. I've not made any bets.

FAREBROTHER. Glad to hear it. But I say, my prompting was to look on, while you wore out Garth's patience and lost the best opportunity of your life. You can guess the feeling which raised that temptation in me – I'm sure you know it – I'm sure you know that the satisfaction of your affections, stands in the way of mine.

Slight pause.

FRED. I could not be expected to give her up.

FAREBROTHER. Not when her affections met yours. But relations even of long standing, are liable to change. You might act in a way to loosen the tie. It must be remembered she's only conditionally bound to you – and in that case another man who may flatter himself he has a hold on her regard might succeed in winning her love. (*Emphatically.*) I can easily conceive such a result. There's a companionship of ready sympathy, which might get the advantage.

LYDGATE. It seemed to Fred that Mr Farebrother had a beak and talons instead of a tongue.

MARY. Was there some actual change in Mary's feeling?

FRED. Of course I know it might easily be all up with me if she's beginning to compare – but I thought you were friendly to me.

FAREBROTHER. I've had a strong disposition to be otherwise. (*Comes more into the light.*) I've said to myself if there's a likelihood of that youngster doing himself harm, why interfere? Aren't you worth as much as he is – don't your sixteen years over his in which you've gone rather hungry, give you more right to satisfaction? If there's a chance of his going to the dogs, let him. You take the benefit.

Silence. FRED *shivers.*

LYDGATE. Fred felt this was a threat, not a warning. What next?

FAREBROTHER. But I'm come back to my old intention. I could hardly secure myself in it better than by telling you what's been going on in me. Do you understand? I want you to make the happiness of her life, and your own, and if a warning from me may turn aside any risk – well, I've uttered it.

He holds out his hand, and FRED *goes to shake it.*

FRED. I'll try to be worthy –

FAREBROTHER. I don't believe there's any decline in her preference of you, Fred. Set your heart at rest. If you keep right, other things will keep right.

FRED. I'll try…

FAREBROTHER. That's enough. God bless you.

They turn away from each other and take a few paces.

LYDGATE. Both of them walked about a long while before they went out of the starlight.

FAREBROTHER (*a deep sigh and a shrug*). Oh well…

FRED. It would have been a fine thing for her to marry
Farebrother. But if she loves me best, and I'm a good
husband…?

MARY. To think of the part one woman can play in the life of a
man –

FAREBROTHER. – so that to renounce her may be a
heroism –

FRED. – and to win her may be a discipline.

Scene Thirty-Four

BULSTRODE. Now, Mr Bulstrode the banker had been making
preparations for quitting Middlemarch, and had consulted
Caleb Garth about the letting of his property at Stone Court.

(*At his desk*.) May I trust you to find me a tenant, Mr Garth?
And tell me the yearly sum which would repay you for
managing these affairs?

GARTH. I'll think about it. I'll see how I can make it out.

An alluring idea occurred to Caleb.

The Garths'. GARTH *and* MRS GARTH.

What if Bulstrode would agree to placing Fred Vincy there,
on the understanding I should be responsible for the
management? It would be an excellent schooling for Fred.
Think, Susan! His mind had been running on that place for
years before old Featherstone died. He should hold the place
in a good industrious way after all – by his taking to
business. I never was better pleased with a notion in my life.
And then the children might be married by and by –

MRS GARTH. You'll not give any hint of the plan to Fred, until
you're sure Bulstrode would agree? And as to marriage,
Caleb, we old people need not help to hasten it.

GARTH. Oh, I don't know. Marriage is a taming thing. Fred would want less of my bit and bridle. However, I shall say nothing, till I know the ground I'm treading on.

MRS GARTH. Suppose the whole scheme should turn out to be a castle in the air?

GARTH. Well then, the castle will tumble about nobody's head.

Scene Thirty-Five

GARTH. But shortly after, at Bulstrode's house, the castle tumbled.

BULSTRODE*'s house at The Shrubs*.

I've just come away from Stone Court, Mr Bulstrode.

BULSTRODE. You found nothing wrong there, I hope.

GARTH. Why yes, there is something wrong. A stranger – who is very ill I think. His name is Raffles. And I must request you to put your business into other hands.

BULSTRODE. This is sudden.

GARTH. It is but it is fixed.

Slight pause.

BULSTRODE. You've been led to this by some slanders uttered by that unhappy creature?

GARTH. I can't deny that.

BULSTRODE. You're a conscientious man, Mr Garth, accountable to God. You wouldn't believe a slander.

GARTH. I'm obliged to believe that this Raffles has told me the truth. I can't be happy working with you. I must beg you to seek another agent.

BULSTRODE. Very well. But I must at least know the worst he's told you.

GARTH. What he has said to me will never pass my lips. If you led a harmful life for gain, and kept others out of their rights by deceit, I dare say you repent. You'd like to go back but can't. That must be a bitter thing. It's not for me to make your life harder.

BULSTRODE. But you do – you do make it harder, by turning your back on me.

GARTH. I'm sorry. I don't judge you. But I have that feeling that I can't go on working with you. Everything else is buried. And I wish you good day. (*Starts to leave.*)

BULSTRODE. One moment, Mr Garth. I may trust then that you will not repeat –

GARTH. Why should I have said it if I didn't mean it? And what I say I've no need to swear. I wish you good day.

Scene Thirty-Six

BULSTRODE. But despite Caleb's silence, nothing could prevent Mr Bulstrode hurtling to disgrace and ruin.

LYDGATE. Those closest to the scandal of Raffles' death, were often the last to know.

MRS BULSTRODE. Even the banker's wife –

MRS BULSTRODE *faces the Vincys*.

VINCY. God help you, Harriet – you know all?

MRS BULSTRODE. I know nothing, brother. What is it?

VINCY. Your husband's in disgrace. They say this fellow Raffles was blackmailing him. And then he died in your husband's care and Lydgate was implicated as doctor. People will talk. And nod, and wink. I don't pretend to say what is

the truth. I only wish we'd never heard the name of either
Bulstrode or Lydgate. You'd better have been a Vincy all
your life and so had Rosamond...

ROSAMOND. Even the doctor's wife –

ROSAMOND *faces the Vincys.*

Is there anything the matter, Papa?

MRS VINCY. Oh, my dear – have you heard nothing?

ROSAMOND. Is it about my husband?

MRS VINCY. Oh, my dear, yes. To think of your marrying into
this trouble. Debt was bad enough, but this will be worse.

VINCY. Stay, Lucy. Have you heard nothing about your Uncle
Bulstrode, Rosamond?

ROSAMOND. No, Papa.

VINCY. I'll tell you everything. It's better for you to know, my
dear. Things have gone against Lydgate. I think he must
leave the town.

MRS VINCY. And so must Bulstrode.

Scene Thirty-Seven

BULSTRODE. Bulstrode was withering under the
consciousness that all men knew that he was not the man he
had professed to be.

BULSTRODE*'s house at The Shrubs.*

Tell me anything you'd like me to do, Harriet. I mean with
regard to property. It's my intention not to sell the land I
possess in this neighbourhood, but to give it to you, as a safe
provision. Do you have any wish on such subjects?

Slight pause.

MRS BULSTRODE. I should like to do something for my brother's family, Nicholas. I think we're bound to make some amends to Rosamond and her husband. My brother says Mr Lydgate's practice is almost good for nothing, and they've very little left to settle anywhere with.

BULSTRODE. It's not possible, my dear. Mr Lydgate has rejected any further service from me. He's returned a thousand pounds I lent him. Mrs Casaubon advanced him the sum for that purpose.

MRS BULSTRODE (*crying*). Oh, it's hard…

Slight pause.

BULSTRODE. There is another means, Harriet, by which I might do a service to your brother's family. It would be an advantageous way of managing the land I mean to be yours.

MRS BULSTRODE. Yes?

BULSTRODE. Garth once thought of undertaking the management of Stone Court in order to place your nephew Fred there. The stock was to remain as it is, and they were to pay a certain share of the profits instead of an ordinary rent. That would be a desirable beginning for a young man, in conjunction with his employment under Garth. Would that be a satisfaction to you?

MRS BULSTRODE. Yes, it would. My poor brother is so cast down, I'd try anything in my power to do him some good before we go away.

BULSTRODE. You must make the proposal to Garth yourself, Harriet. I mention this because Garth gave up being my agent. But I think it's not unlikely he'll accept when you propose the thing.

Scene Thirty-Eight

MARY. Mary was in a grassy corner of the orchard, with Letty.

The orchard at the Garths'. MARY swings LETTY about in a circle; laughter and screams. GARTH and MRS GARTH arrive. MRS GARTH takes LETTY and goes.

GARTH. I came to look for you, Mary.

MARY. Father?

She puts her arm within his. They walk.

GARTH. It'll be a sad while before you can be married, Mary.

MARY. Not a sad while, Father – I mean to be merry. I've been single and merry for four and twenty years and more – I suppose it'll not be quite as long again. If you're contented with Fred.

He considers.

Now, Father, you did praise him last Wednesday. You said he had an uncommon notion of stock and a good eye for things.

GARTH. Did I?

MARY. Yes, I put it all down, and the date and everything. You like things neatly booked. And he has a deep respect for you.

GARTH. Ay, ay. You want to coax me into thinking him a fine match.

MARY. No, Father. I don't love him because he's a fine match.

GARTH. What for then?

MARY. Oh dear. Because I've always loved him. I should never like scolding anyone else so well, and that's a point to be thought of in a husband.

GARTH. Your mind is quite settled then, Mary? There's no other wish come into it of late?

MRS FAREBROTHER. He was thinking of Mr Farebrother.

GARTH. Because better late than never...

MARY. My feelings have not changed, Father. I shall be constant to Fred as long as he's constant to me. I don't think either of us could like anyone else better, however much we might admire them. It would be like seeing all the old places altered, and changing the name for everything. We must wait a long while, but Fred knows that.

GARTH. Well, I've got a bit of news. What do you think of Fred going to live at Stone Court and managing the land there?

MARY. How can that ever be, Father?

GARTH. He'd manage it for his Aunt Bulstrode. The poor woman's been to me begging and praying. She wants to do the lad good and it might be a fine thing for him. With saving, he might gradually buy the stock, and he has a turn for farming.

MARY. Oh. It's too good to believe!

GARTH. Ah, but mind you. (*Warns.*) I must take it on my shoulders and be responsible and see after everything. And that will grieve your mother a bit, though she mayn't say so. Fred had need to be careful.

MARY (*her joy checked*). Perhaps it's too much, Father.

GARTH. Nay, nay, work is my delight, child, when it doesn't vex your mother. And then if you and Fred get married, he'll be steady and saving. I wanted to tell you first, because I think you'd like to tell him. After that, I could talk it over with him and we could go into business.

MARY (*putting her hands round his neck*). Oh, you dear, good Father, you're the best man in the world.

GARTH. Nonsense, child, you'll think your husband better.

MARY. Impossible. Husbands are an inferior class of men who require keeping in order!

MRS GARTH (*calling*). Tea's ready!

GARTH *goes back to the house.*

MARY. But Mary saw Fred at the orchard gate.

FRED *carries a hat. He flourishes it with 'playful formality'
as* MARY *approaches.*

What fine clothes you wear, you extravagant youth. You're
not learning economy.

FRED. Now that's too bad, Mary. Just look at the edges of these
coat-cuffs. It's only by dint of good brushing I look
respectable. I'm saving up one suit for a wedding suit.

MARY. You'll look very droll by then. Like a gentleman in an
old fashion-book.

FRED. No, they'll keep two years.

MARY. Don't encourage flattering expectations.

FRED. Why not? One lives on them better than on unflattering
ones.

MARY. I've heard a story of a young gentleman who once
encouraged expectations, and they did him harm.

FRED. Mary, if you've got something discouraging to tell me I
shall bolt. I'm out of spirits. My father's so cut up – home's
not like itself. I can't bear any more bad news.

MARY. Should you call it bad news to be told you were to live
at Stone Court, and manage the farm, and be remarkably
prudent, and save money every year till all the stock and
furniture were your own, and you were a 'distinguished
agricultural character', as Mr Trumbull says – rather stout, I
fear, with the Greek and Latin sadly worn…?

FRED. You don't mean anything except nonsense, Mary?

MARY. That's what my father just told me, and he never talks
nonsense.

FRED. Oh, I could be a tremendously good fellow then, Mary,
and we could be married directly!

MARY. Not so fast, sir. How do you know I wouldn't rather
defer our marriage for some years. That would leave you
time to misbehave, and then if I liked someone better, I
should have an excuse for jilting you.

FRED. Pray, don't joke, Mary. Tell me seriously that all this is true, and that you're happy, because you love me best.

MARY (*in a tone of obedient resignation*). It's all true and I'm happy because I love you best.

Slight pause.

FRED. When we were first engaged, with the umbrella ring, Mary, you used to let me…

They are about to kiss, when –

MRS GARTH (*calling*). Fred and Mary –

BEN. Are you ever coming in?

LETTY. Or may I eat your cake?

The FAMILY *come out, and embrace* FRED *and* MARY. *Wedding bells. The* COMPANY *gather.* FRED *and* MARY *stand before* FAREBROTHER.

FAREBROTHER. I now pronounce you man and wife.

They kiss and then pass down an archway of congratulatory Middlemarchers. At the end they turn. Everyone cheers.

FRED. Marriage is a great beginning.

BULSTRODE. As it was to Adam and Eve –

ROSAMOND. – who kept their honeymoon in Eden, but had their first little one –

MRS BULSTRODE. – among the thorns and thistles of the wilderness…

GARTH. It is still the beginning of the home epic. The gradual conquest –

LYDGATE. – or the irremediable loss –

MRS GARTH. – of that complete union, which makes the advancing years the harvest of sweet memories in common.

Epilogue

DOROTHEA. Fred never became rich, but he remained steady.

FAREBROTHER. He told Mary his happiness was half-owing to Farebrother –

JONAH. – who gave him a strong pull-up at the right moment.

MARY. There were three boys.

BEN. Boys are better than girls, aren't they?

MRS GARTH. They're both naughty, but boys are stronger… and throw better.

BEN (*hitting out at* LETTY). See!

MRS GARTH. But Letty knew her superiority was stronger than any muscles.

MRS GARTH *and* LETTY *nod to each other in agreement, then to the audience.*

JONAH. Fred was sorry for other men, who couldn't have Mary for their wife –

FAREBROTHER. – especially Mr Farebrother.

FRED (*to* MARY). He was ten times worthier than I was.

MARY. To be sure he was. And for that reason could do better without me.

LYDGATE. There is no creature whose inward being is so strong that it is not greatly determined by what lies outside it.

MRS BULSTRODE. And we insignificant people with our daily words and acts are preparing the lives of many others –

FRED. – and that things are not so ill with you and me as they might have been –

MARY. – is half-owing to the number who lived faithfully a hidden life and rest in unvisited tombs.

The play and the trilogy ends with a joyful country dance.
FRED *with* MARY, GARTH *with* MRS GARTH,
BULSTRODE *with* MRS BULSTRODE, LYDGATE *and*
ROSAMOND, *even* DOROTHEA *with* CASAUBON.
FAREBROTHER *joins in too. And the children. They mix
and merge into one company.*

The End.

JEEVES AND WOOSTER IN 'PERFECT NONSENSE'
The Goodale Brothers
Adapted from P.G. Wodehouse

THE JUNGLE BOOK
Stuart Paterson
Adapted from Rudyard Kipling

KENSUKE'S KINGDOM
Stuart Paterson
Adapted from Michael Morpurgo

KES
Lawrence Till
Adapted from Barry Hines

NOUGHTS & CROSSES
Dominic Cooke
Adapted from Malorie Blackman

PERSUASION
Mark Healy
Adapted from Jane Austen

THE RAILWAY CHILDREN
Mike Kenny
Adapted from E. Nesbit

SENSE AND SENSIBILITY
Mark Healy
Adapted from Jane Austen

SWALLOWS AND AMAZONS
Helen Edmundson and Neil Hannon
Adapted from Arthur Ransome

A TALE OF TWO CITIES
Mike Poulton
Adapted from Charles Dickens

TO SIR, WITH LOVE
Ayub Khan-Din
Adapted from E.R. Braithwaite

TREASURE ISLAND
Stuart Paterson
Adapted from Robert Louis Stevenson

WOLF HALL *and* BRING UP THE BODIES
Mike Poulton
Adapted from Hilary Mantel

www.nickhernbooks.co.uk

facebook.com/nickhernbooks

twitter.com/nickhernbooks